SCHOOL CHOICES
IN GREATER PORTLAND

An Informed Guide to
Choosing the Best School for Your
Child in the Portland Area,
Including the Public School
Districts of Beaverton,
Gresham-Barlow, Hillsboro,
Lake Oswego, North Clackamas,
Portland, Riverdale, Tigard-Tualatin,
and West Linn-Wilsonville

by Molly Huffman

TACT

School Choices in Greater Portland
ISBN 0-9639879-6-8

Forewarning

Every effort was made by the author to ensure that the information
presented here was accurate on the date of publication. However, the
subject matter deals with public agencies, independent schools,
nonprofit organizations and businesses. Any of these may change at any
time. Therefore this book is sold as is, and without a warranty of any
kind. Neither the author nor the publisher shall be liable to the
purchaser or any other person or entity with respect to any liability, loss
or damage caused or alleged to be caused directly or indirectly by
information appearing in this publication.

We neither expressly guarantee, warrant or endorse the schools,
businesses and/or subjects to which this guide provides descriptions and
other general information.

Bulk Sales

Copies of this book in case lots are available at discount.
Contact the publisher for more information.

Nan Booth Simpson, Editor

Printed in the United States of America.
Published by:

The **Authors** Communication Team
Post Office Box 25211
Portland, Oregon 97225 U.S.A.
Phone & Facsimile 503/297-0873

Text printed on
recycled paper

4

Chapter Three:
Suburban Public School Districts 99
Beaverton School District 99

Chapter Five:
Portland Area Preschool Programs 213

Chapter Six:
How to Enrich Your Child's Education 227

Index 252

About the Author

Molly Huffman was born in Portland. Her undergraduate degree is from Scripps College in Claremont, California and she holds a Master's Degree in Public Administration from Lewis and Clark College. Molly held an Oregon Teaching License and now holds an Oregon Administrative License. She served as a teacher in the Peace Corps in French West Africa and has lived in Barbados and Morocco. Molly is the Head of Touchstone School in Lake Oswego. As a student, teacher, administrator and parent of students in various public and private schools in the Portland area, she brings a wealth of knowledge and expertise to this work. She is a frequent speaker on schools in Portland and has appeared on AM Northwest.

Dedication

This book is dedicated to my children and yours. They are this state's greatest natural resource.

Acknowledgements

I wish to thank Julie Powell, my friend and co-author of the first edition of this book. I also wish to thank some of the dedicated educators in Portland who made this book possible. Lew Frederick, Director of Public Information at Portland Public Schools has been a great resource for both editions of this book. Betsy Biller, Director of Communications for the Hillsboro School District, and Jim Carlile, who recently retired as Superintendent of the Gresham-Barlow School District were instrumental in adding those two school districts to this addition. I am grateful for the support and skills of my editor, Nan Simpson.

I also want to give readers an update on the I Have a Dream Foundation, which we mentioned in the first edition. If you'll recall, in 1990, three Portland attorneys started the first "Dream Class" in Oregon for 108 fifth graders at Martin Luther King Elementary, a school where 90% of families qualify for free or reduced lunch under federal poverty standards. In some areas, less than half the children in the fifth grade will complete high school. This program is designed to change that with mentoring, tutoring, summer programs and other services. It is not cheap, but it is paying big dividends. One of those students became Jefferson High School student body president and Rose Festival Queen, and was accepted at Stanford. Another graduated from St. Mary's and was accepted at Harvard. Thirty-three are now in college or vocational schools. Congratulations to Pamela Jacklin, Leonard Girard, and

Kenneth Lewis, who made the difference for these students. They have a future and can access the American Dream. The I Have a Dream Foundation-Oregon needs volunteers and contributions. Call them at 503/287-7203 if you can help.

In the spring of 1998, a group of alumni of a New York City public high school pledged $10 million over the next five years in endowment funds. The money will generate up to $800,000 in annual income for the high school. Brooklyn Technical High School will use the funds for computers, tuition assistance for specialized professional staff development and an electron microscope among other things. The principal was quoted in the New York Times, "I feel as if the 4,000 kids here have just won the lottery." Wouldn't it be wonderful if the alumni of Portland area public high schools raised the money to fund such endowments? Think what it could do!

Introduction

School Choices in Greater Portland is designed to help both long-time residents and families new to the Portland area discover educational programs that are a good fit for their children. Parents sometimes agonize over whether to choose public schools or private schools. I hope the information I've compiled on the breadth of educational opportunities in the Portland area, both public and private, will answer those concerns.

The first chapter deals with the broad subject of public education in Oregon, which should be of interest to every taxpayer. There's good news and bad news on this front. At the same time that taxpayers voted for a reduction in property taxes (Measure 5), the state has legislated major school reform. In this chapter is a discussion of the new Certificate of Initial Mastery (CIM) for tenth graders that was awarded beginning in the 1998-99 school year. The legislature now mandates testing for all public school children in grades 3, 5, 8 and 10 called Oregon Assessment Testing (OAT). Testing is a hotly debated issue in education, and I have included a discussion on the pros and cons of standardized testing. In this chapter, I also give criteria for selecting a school and talk about the future of education in Oregon.

Chapter 2 looks at Portland Public Schools, and Chapter 3 covers the suburban districts of Beaverton, Gresham-Barlow, Hillsboro, Lake Oswego, North Clackamas, Riverdale, Tigard-Tualatin and West Linn-Wilsonville. The introductions to each of these districts detail special programs and other ways these districts are attempting to meet the needs of local residents. There are many advantages to neighborhood schools. Children who can walk to school and to their friends' houses feel a sense of community. American parents often select a neighborhood especially for its nearby public school and the community it offers.

Magnet schools, which are open to any child in the district, special needs programs, language immersion programs and prekindergarten programs are listed. The information on individual schools includes admission criteria for getting your child into these programs. I tell you where these schools are, how to contact them, and what they offer. Increasingly schools in the Portland area are accessing the Internet. If the school has a home page on the Internet, the address is listed.

Private schools can also provide a sense of community. Independent and religiously affiliated private schools are listed in Chapter 4. Families often choose a private school because they share similar values with the other families in the school and feel comfortable having their children in these settings. The classes are usually smaller at private schools, and most children benefit from this. For the parents, however, the disadvantages of driving to and from birthday parties all over metropolitan Portland may outweigh the benefits. Information includes tuition, curriculum, athletics, special programs and location. I have given the reader some criteria to consider in selecting a private school and, where possible, covered the admissions process.

Chapter 5 lists programs for preschool through kindergarten. These programs were selected because they have a strong learning component and are not simply daycare facilities. I've addressed what to look for in a preschool program. There is also a quick reference list of private schools that have preschool programs.

Chapter 6 is designed to help parents enrich their children's education, including tips for helping with homework and getting your child to set goals. As athletics and the arts are cut from public school budgets due to the effects of Measure 5, finding these programs outside of the school setting has become more important. I have listed quite a number of enrichment activities available in the community, with the artistically oriented programs in one group and the athletic programs in a second group. There are also some resources for children with special needs and for parents who are home-schooling their children.

As an educator, I do not advocate home schooling. I believe that one of the greatest gifts a teacher can bestow upon a child is the love of learning. Sometime during the K-12 years your child will undoubtedly experience a teacher who is passionate about a subject, whether it is sharks, Shakespeare or Spanish. For this reason I don't favor any program in which a student has the same teacher for more than two grades. Kids have different learning styles, and they need a variety of teaching styles.

We are lucky in this community to have such a good selection of schools and so many dedicated teachers. Your child is likely to enjoy school and grow up to be a fully functioning adult whether or not your choice of schools is perfect. There will be days your child doesn't want to go to school, just as there are days you'd rather not go to work. As a rule of thumb, if the days your child protests outnumber the days he or she is eager to go, it's time to find out why. The child may need a different academic program. Sometimes the problem is behavioral, and your child may need some help with socialization. Make an appointment with your child's teacher and/or counselor and find out why this child is unhappy at school.

Kids also need time to just hang out and be kids. If you are rushing your child from school, to piano, to soccer, to art class - stop. David Elkind wrote a book in 1981 titled The Hurried Child: Growing Up too Fast too Soon, which I recommend if this sounds like your routine. Elkind makes the point that we encourage kids to look like adults, act like adults and achieve like adults. Yet, they need time to grow up emotionally, and that process cannot be hurried except at great cost to the child.

I encourage parents to get involved in the schools they select for their children. Volunteer in the school, serve on committees, and help with fundraisers. Attend Back-to-School Nights and Parent-Teacher conferences. Parents need to become informed-ask questions about the curriculum, find out what the teacher needs and find out how you can contribute. Research demonstrates that children do better in school if their parents get involved in their education.

This book was researched and written during the 1997-'98 and 1998-'99 school year. Let me know how you like your child's school, what information I missed and whether you wish to order another copy of this book for a friend. If I omitted your child's school, please send me information about it. I want to hear from you.

Please direct all correspondence to:

 School Choices
P.O. Box 302
Lake Oswego, OR 97034

Buzzwords

As you read this book, you are going to encounter a lot of acronyms and some educational jargon. Therefore, I've included the following list of "buzzwords."

ACT (American College Testing) — entrance exam, newer than the SAT, now required of high school seniors for admission to some colleges and universities.

ADD (Attention Deficit Disorder) — significant inability to focus on subject matter resulting in poor academic performance.

Basal Reader — reading textbook adopted by a school district for a specific grade level.

Benchmarks — measurements at successive grade levels to determine if the child is building a body of knowledge and the skills necessary to progress to the next level.

Bilingual — speaking two languages. Bilingual education involves classroom instruction in two languages.

Charter Schools — schools created by a private group (often by concerned parents and teachers) that operate with public funding.

CIM (Certificate of Initial Mastery) — recognition that a child has met all standards in English, mathematics, science, history, civics, geography, economics, the arts and a second language set by the Oregon Department of Education.

Climate — the physical, emotional and social environment of a classroom.

Coalition of Essential Schools — a group of schools that follow nine common principles. The Coalition research and information comes from Brown University. The program supports integrated curriculum, personalized teaching, and student-as-worker rather than teacher as deliverer of instructional services. The Coalition has adopted the small schools research and believes teachers should have a maximum of 80 students, which is substantially fewer than many area high school teachers now have.

Constructivist Teaching — a method of teaching that encourages kids to learn on their own and construct meaning from what they are learning.

Cooperative Learning — students of different ability levels who work in small groups to learn how to work together and learn from one another.

Cultural Literacy — having background knowledge of the past and present.

Dyslexia — a specific language disability caused by a dysfunction of the central nervous system. It is characterized by problems with reading, spelling, writing, speaking and/or listening.

ESL (English as a Second Language) — program for students whose native language is not English.

Foundation — nonprofit organization that raises money for individual schools or school districts.

Higher Order Thinking Skills — the ability to analyze and evaluate, not just memorize material.

IEP (Individualized Education Program) — for students who have been identified as eligible for special education programs.

Inclusion — serving special education and/or disabled students in the regular classroom (also called "mainstreaming.")

Interdisciplinary Teams — a team of teachers who teach math, science, language arts and social studies to a specific group of students (usually a middle school group).

Language Immersion — learning a foreign language by being taught all subject matter (math, science, language arts, etc.) in that language.

Learning Disabilities — a variety of syndromes that cause children of average or above average intelligence to achieve significantly below expectations in one or more academic areas and whose test results suggest a neurological basis for this performance. Children with learning disabilities may show an imperfect ability to listen, think, speak, read, write, spell or do mathematical calculations. The term does not include children whose problems are primarily the result of visual, hearing or motor handicaps; of mental retardation; or of economic disadvantage.

Learning Style — specific way a child most readily processes new information (may be by seeing, hearing, touching or doing).

Magnet — programs first introduced to draw white students back into inner city schools; now includes diverse programs for children with special interests or talents. Federal dollars are available for school districts to create these programs. Students from any school in the district can apply for a magnet program.

Manipulatives — such tools as beads or blocks that help a child visualize an abstract mathematical concept.

Montessori — an educational philosophy based on Italian educator Maria Montessori's observations of children's learning styles at different stages of their development. Teachers are trained by the Montessori organization, and Montessori schools use teaching materials purchased from the association. Teachers serve as guides to help young children explore a rich educational environment designed to encourage self-directed learning.

Multiculturalism — an understanding of other cultures and respect for the differences that exist among cultures.

OAT (Oregon Statewide Assessment Testing) — testing mandated by the Oregon legislature for grades 3, 5, 8 and 10.

Outcome-based Education — a system of setting specific, consistent goals and then monitoring and assessing how well students are meeting those goals at different benchmark levels.

Parent-Teacher Conferences — meetings for the purpose of developing and maintaining open communication, examining expectations, evaluating performance, and determining direction for the school year.

PASS (Proficiency-based Admission Standards System) — a new system of admission requirements for Oregon's public universities that will be based on knowledge acquired and skills mastered rather than courses taken and grade-point average maintained. The program will be phased-in, beginning in 2001.

Peer Tutoring — a system of students helping other students learn.

Portfolio — a compilation of the student's best work from several different subject areas; may be on a computer disk or in hard copy as in an artist's portfolio. Selective universities use this method to look beyond a student's test scores and transcript.

Rubric — a scale used by teachers and students to assess the student's work. The scales, which may be designed by either the teacher or the student, describe specific levels of achievement. For example, a first grade writing rubric might include the ability to make capital letters, space letters correctly, use periods at the end of sentences, etc. The indicator for the highest level of achievement would be "using capital letters correctly." A lesser level would be "using capital letters correctly most of the time." Rubrics give students specific skills to master. They help children know what the teacher expects and teach them to edit their own work.

SAT (Scholastic Assessment Test) — traditional exam given to high school seniors seeking college admission.

Special Education — instruction designed to meet the needs of students with disabilities, defined by Oregon as those who suffer mental, physical, emotional, or learning problems. These include mental retardation, hearing impairments, communication disorders, visual impairments, serious emotional disturbances, orthopedic or other health impairments, autism, traumatic brain injury, or specific learning disabilities.

Standardized Testing — objective tests usually given to a wide group of students, frequently used to compare student achievement between schools and states.

TAG (Talented and Gifted) — students for whom many schools have special programs. Students must be identified to be in a TAG program.

Title 1 — federally-funded programs for disadvantaged students.

Whole Language — a philosophy of education that guides and supports students in developing as independent readers, writers and learners.

Chapter One
The State of Education in Oregon Today

The vision we have for our children and their children cannot be realized unless we support and pay for excellence in public education. Our very economic and cultural survival depends on our ability to educate our children as well as (if not better than) other nations are educating their children. Public education is critical to a functioning democracy, and our investment in it may be the best demonstration of our commitment to a pluralistic society.

The Present Situation

Ninety percent of the students in this country are educated in public schools, and the Portland area mirrors this national statistic. It is critical that all taxpayers in Oregon support our public schools not only because they prepare our children for jobs and post-secondary education, but also because public schools prepare them to be good citizens.

The United States is experiencing the largest sustained influx of immigrants in our history. Twenty percent of children in school in this country are immigrants or have parents who are immigrants. Just as earlier waves of immigrants were assimilated into our culture and taught the values of democracy in public schools, schools today teach our children about our government, the values of a representative democracy and how to get along with peoples of different cultures and points of view. Given that thirty-five percent of children under the age of 18 in 1997 represented minority groups (the number is expected to be 45% by the year 2020), these skills are crucial for holding together the social fabric of this country. And, they will assume even greater importance in the global economy of the next century.

The population in Oregon is growing at nearly double the national average. From 1990 to 1997 it grew 13.2% while the national growth rate for the same period was 7.6%. Almost one-quarter of all Oregonians arrived here in this decade! Washington County, the fastest growing county in the Portland metropolitan area, has experienced a 23.6% increase in population. There are 1,246 public schools in Oregon, educating 573,000 students. Just when we need more classrooms, more technology and better-trained teachers, Oregon is facing major problems with school funding.

The news is not all bad, however. College entrance test scores in Oregon are still improving, and Oregon students do well in nationwide comparisons. Oregon ranked first in the nation in SAT (Scholastic Assessment Test) scores in 1997 and 1998 among the twenty-three states where more than 40% of students take the SAT. Fifty-three percent of Oregon seniors took the SAT in 1998 and the average score was 1056 of a possible 1600.

Oregon students also had the highest scores in the nation on the 1997 ACT (American College Testing), a newer entrance exam that is now required by some colleges and universities. Fourteen percent of Oregon graduating seniors took the ACT, compared with a national average of thirty-seven percent of seniors. In 1999, Oregon students tied Washington students for second place in the nation behind Rhode Island. Of course, students who take the more difficult high school classes do better on the ACT. Oregon has some remarkable high school programs, including the International Baccalaureate programs at Lincoln, Tigard and Tualatin High Schools, a Young Scholars program at Wilson and high tech at Benson. There is even a small college prep public high school in the area, Riverdale, which is in its fourth year.

In 1997 the statewide math scores went up in third, fifth and tenth grade. Eighth grade scores stayed the same. Reading scores increased in third, fifth and eighth grades, and stayed the same in tenth grade. While that is certainly good news, a third of our students failed to reach state standards in both reading and math. Eighth graders in Oregon did very well on the National Assessment of Educational Progress in science in 1998, but not very well in math. When the scores were compared with students in 40 countries, only students in Singapore scored significantly higher than our eighth graders in science. In math, however, students from Austria, Belgium, The Czech Republic, France, Hong Kong, Hungary, Japan, Korea, Singapore, Slovak Republic, Slovenia and Switzerland beat our kids.

The Department of Education will rate Oregon schools beginning next year. Schools will be rated exceptional, strong, satisfactory, low or unacceptable. The details have yet to be finalized, but schools are expected to receive scores based on students' performance and behavior, class size and teacher experience.

The most heartening news is that Oregon has set high goals for the future. In 1991, seeking to raise academic standards and increase student performance, the Oregon legislature passed "The Oregon Educational Act for the 21st Century," also known as House Bill 3565. It was revised by the 1995 Oregon Legislature in HB 2991. The newer bill defines the purpose of the public school system as "fostering academic learning and achievement." Unfortunately perhaps, it de-emphasizes the role of schools in work force development and the prevention of social problems, which were given more emphasis in the original bill. Oregon Public Education Network's Web site (www.open.k12.or.us) provides up-to-date information on school reform issues.

Where the Problems Lie

Oregon schools face many of the same problems that beset schools throughout the United States. What our public schools will need to meet ambitious goals include adequate funding, plus the ability to make decisions about hiring and spending at the individual school level, the discretion to try new programs, and the time to modify them, if need be.

Funding

Oregon must find a better way to fund schools. Property owners who do not have children in public school systems resist supporting schools. In 1990 Oregon passed Measure 5, which limited the tax rate for governments to $10 per assessed $1,000 and the rate for schools to $5 per $1000. That rate was to be phased in over five years. The state has made up some of the funding gap with lottery money and other revenue. However, the percentage of the state budget devoted to K-12 education has fallen from 56.4% in 1991-93 to 52.8% in 1997-99. The legislature allocated $4.811 billion for the current biennium. This is $550 million short of the $5.1 billion that the members of the Coalition for School Funding Now! believe is essential to keep services at current levels and provide minimal funding to help students meet the higher standards that were mandated, but not funded, by the legislature.

Because the state is now responsible for 70% of school funding, it has begun tracking how the money is spent. The legislature approved a $2.9 million Database Initiative Project to collect consistent, detailed information from 16 pilot school districts over two years. Data on expenditures, educational practices and achievement results will help the state identity what it costs to educate a child in Oregon. The 16 districts chosen included Portland and represented urban and rural, large and small, and demographically diverse districts. KPMG Peat Marwick was awarded a $1.2 million contract to help build the database and to put it on the Internet.

The legislature got a report on the database, now called the Quality Education Model, in March of 1999. It has been estimated that a quality education that restores funding for art, music and drama and would ensure that 90% of high school students meet state standards will cost $5.65 billion in this biennium. This is $1 billion more than the legislature authorized. The cost of financing proposed improvements in the early grades only would cost $4.95 billion. These include a class size limit of twenty, full-day kindergarten, music, PE, art and computer instruction and second language instruction in all schools.

Bond measures are not affected by Measure 5's $5 limit, and Portland passed a $197 million school bond in November of 1995. The City of Portland provided $3.2 million to public schools in the city in 1997; $2.5 of that went to Portland Public Schools. Additionally, Multnomah County voters approved a one-year increase in the business income tax in March of 1998. The extra half-percent will generate $12.3 million for county public schools, with $9,362,070 going to Portland Public Schools. The stipulation is that funds must be spent on teachers, and districts will submit a list of the teaching jobs they will save. Those districts that are not facing layoffs must spend the tax proceeds on additional teachers or on instructional materials.

In addition to basic funding shortfalls, there have been inequalities in per-student funding from the state to school districts in the metropolitan area. For example, in 1996-97 Portland students were allocated $4,655 each, Tigard-Tualatin received $4,506 and Beaverton, $4,216. While these may not seem like big differences, the Beaverton District would have enjoyed an additional $17.7 million in 1995-'96 if it received the same funding per student as Portland. As the state tries to equalize school spending, Portland has actually had to cut more than other districts because urban districts are more expensive to run.

Compounding the funding problem is an enormous influx of students who do not speak English. Some of the Portland public schools have enrollments of up to 30% non-native speaking students. It costs more money per student to educate immigrant children than non-immigrant children. So far, the school system seems to be doing a good job with a problem of crisis proportions in this time of budgetary cutbacks. Portland has a "newcomer" program that helps such students and transfers them to the nearest local school with an English as a Second Language (ESL) program as soon as possible. The Beaverton District also has a large English as a Second Language program.

The $64,000 question is what will we have left five years from now? We cannot afford any more cuts — too many kids are disaffected, discouraged and dropping out. They are walking into classrooms where there are not enough chairs, desks and textbooks let alone access to computers. The message they get is that their education is not a priority for us.

The Oregon legislature, in a boom economy, passed a school budget that will result in larger high school class sizes in many districts statewide, from Medford to Portland. Given what we know about high schools and high school students, can we afford not to adequately fund our schools? As former Superintendent Jack Bierwirth said in his farewell address at the City Club of Portland, "a school system that is slightly better than Detroit's isn't a great source of solace."

The state's funding problems extend even beyond K-12, which is the scope of this book. It's interesting to note, however, that Oregon has disinvested in higher education at the same time that college tuition at state institutions is skyrocketing. In ever-higher numbers, students who graduate from Oregon high schools are electing to go out of state for higher education. The cost of an education at a small private liberal arts college is now not much more than at the large state universities. Kids at the top are leaving Oregon or choosing private colleges.

We are the stewards of a public school system in need of help. Many Oregonians worked very hard to make these schools as good as they are. Our children depend on us to make sure we give them as good an education as our parents gave us!

Class Size

Class sizes have grown in all public school districts in the Portland area since the first edition of this book in 1996. According to the National Center for Education Statistics, Oregon's average expenditure per pupil has increased only 0.93% in the last five years. The national average is up 9.13% while the ten states with similar student populations have increased their per-pupil spending by 12.12%.

Investing in reducing class size may have a greater impact on student achievement than investing in other areas. A study done by the John F. Kennedy School of Government at Harvard of 2.4 million elementary school students in 900 Texas school districts showed that reducing class size by as few as three students improved school climate and student achievement.

As one would expect, it is the students from the lowest socioeconomic levels that benefit most from smaller class sizes. These children are often not ready for first grade, have low skill-levels and may not be native English speakers. However, all students, preschool through high school, can benefit significantly from small classes. Students learn more with more teacher attention, and parents of students in smaller classes say their children are happier.

School Size

A substantial amount of research has also been done on school size. Given a choice, a small school (250-350 students) is a better environment than a large one. Research shows that students are more successful in smaller schools where the teachers know the students well.

Students in small high schools consistently score higher in math, reading, history and science. High school teachers who see 150+ students per week simply cannot grade the papers and exams necessary to teach critical thinking skills. Research has shown that students in small schools feel a greater involvement in the school community and attendance is better; discipline problems, vandalism and drop out rates are lower.

Why Do Students Do Better in Small Schools?

(Reprinted with the permission of Kathleen Cotton)

Kathleen Cotton's comprehensive review of the research for the Northwest Regional Educational Laboratory, *School Size, School Climate, and Student Performance*, published in 1996, is available from Northwest Regional Educational Labs in *Close-Up* Number 20, 1996. You can visit their Web site (www. nwrel.org). The research article makes the following points:

Everyone's participation is needed to populate the school's offices, teams, clubs, and so forth, so a far smaller percentage of students is overlooked or alienated.

Adults and students in the school know and care about one another to a greater degree than is possible in large schools.

Small schools have a higher rate of parent involvement.

Students and staff generally have a stronger sense of personal efficacy in small schools.

Students in small schools take more responsibility for their own learning: their learning activities are more often individualized, experiential, and relevant to the world outside of school; classes are generally smaller; and scheduling is much more flexible.

Small schools more often use instructional strategies associated with higher student performance — team teaching, integrated curriculum, multi-age grouping (especially for elementary children), cooperative learning, and performance assessments.

Students at Risk

At the same time that our state's college-bound students are achieving well, Oregon has experienced a drop in the number of high school students who are graduating, down from 89% to 75% since the national goal for 90% graduation was set in 1990. No longer can students who drop out expect to find good jobs waiting in the timber or fishing industries. The era of well-paying jobs for people with limited skills is over. Intel is now Oregon's largest manufacturing employer. All of our students need to be educated to a level not required in the past. The alternatives for students who drop out of high school are especially dismal: low paying jobs, inability to support a family and all the problems that accompany poverty.

Twenty to twenty-five percent of children in this country are raised in poverty. In the richest country in the world, this is a public policy failure that goes largely unnoticed. Studies published in the journal *Pediatrics* in January of 1998 showed that habitually hungry children from low-income families are seven times more likely to misbehave in class, fight, be enrolled in special education or have psychological problems. Other chronic problems associated with low wages include increased drug and alcohol use, welfare and a growing prison population.

As taxpayers, we will pay for education or we will pay for the social programs to alleviate the problems created by low skills and low-paying jobs. Good preschool programs are, among other things, much less expensive than prisons. In 1989 the nation's governors collectively set as their first educational goal that all children would start school ready to learn. While public school kindergarten has become widely available, fewer than 50% of children from families with annual incomes of less than $40K attend preschool.

Research on Head Start and other preschool programs shows that children who have had the benefit of these early childhood education programs do better in school and lead more productive lives. A new study by the David and Lucille Packard Foundation, based on 25 years of research, determined that "children who attended early childhood programs are less likely to drop out of school and to commit crimes, and they do better in math and science than their peers."

The Carnegie Foundation issued a report in September of 1996 about children ages 3 to 10 called "Years of Promise: A Comprehensive Learning Strategy for America's Children." The report says too many three to five-year-olds are in sub-standard early childhood programs where teacher turnover is high and pay is low. As many as one-third of American students entering kindergarten need extra help to keep up with their peers.

The Carnegie Council on Adolescent Development estimates that each year of high school education reduces by 35% the probability a student will be dependent on welfare as an adult. One year's class of high school dropouts in this country, over their lifetimes, costs taxpayers $260 billion in lost earnings and taxes.

School-to-Work Programs

While the United States has the largest number of university graduates of any country in the world, what we do not have is a good school-to-work educational system. An American Federation of Teachers study concluded that the 75% of American students who do not go on to college lag behind students in France, Germany and Scotland. The study looked at these European school systems and found that they do a better job of giving average achievers a solid academic background. Many European systems also have good apprenticeship programs. It should come as no surprise that American manufacturers are lamenting the lack of skilled workers available to operate increasingly high-tech machinery.

The study also noted that half of all high school graduates have not found steady jobs by the time they are 30. "Instead they spend their young adulthood laboring in low-skill, dead-end jobs with little opportunity for training or career advancement. The harsh truth is that the United States currently has the worst school-to-work system in the industrialized world."

The Sunday, January 7, 1996 business section of *The Oregonian* published two articles about school-to-work programs here and abroad. The features noted that Oregon is a pioneer in this area. Yet despite having received $9 million in federal money, only 5,000 of Oregon's 70,000 high school juniors and seniors are getting meaningful work experience while in high school.

The high-value-added industries, such as computers, biotechnology, microelectronics, and telecommunications, pay the highest wages and offer the standard of living American workers have come to expect. (For Oregon, these are also the kinds of industries that help preserve our environment.) High-tech industries have lobbied to increase the number of highly skilled foreign workers allowed H-1B visas to work in the United States because there is a shortage of computer programmers, systems analysts and engineers.

Senators Kennedy and Feinstein introduced a bill to allow an increase from the current ceiling of 65,000 to 90,000 over the next three years, but called for improving our educational system so that American students can meet this demand in the future. European and Asian countries are doing a better job of educating kids, particularly in science and math. We need to be sure that Oregon is educating our kids for jobs in the high-tech industry. The rapidly changing economy of the next century will require workers who are flexible, adaptable and able to problem-solve and think critically. These are the very skills our American schools have not been proficient at teaching. We've delivered information and taught kids to parrot it back to us.

Places We Are Making Progress

We're seeing some hopeful signs. Taking cues from private schools, public school districts are looking for new sources of funding, and individual schools are demanding higher levels of parental involvement, from aggressive fundraising to classroom support. Schools are also becoming more inventive: restructuring old programs, looking at new ways of doing things and evaluating the results. Oregon schools are beginning to look at new ways of teaching kids the kinds of skills they will need in the workforce of the 21st century. Parents are organizing to do something about school funding. Portland has an Active Parents Network, which is a politically active group of parents who are making class size an issue. You can read all about it on the Portland Public School home page (www. pps.k12.or.us).

A Push for Smaller Classes

Legislation was introduced in Salem to limit class size statewide to 20 for kindergarten through third grade, 25 in grades four and five, and an average of 27 in middle and high school. California has already reduced class sizes to 20 or fewer students in kindergarten through third grade and 18 other states are following suit. Research shows that school districts with smaller classes have better school climates and higher student achievement.

Smaller classes require more teachers and more classrooms, and that brings us back to funding problems. Governor Kitzhaber believes that new revenues should support higher levels of achievement (i.e. additional funding for schools must be connected to increased performance.) He is less interested in adding a fixed percentage to a district's current budget for inflation and growth than in adjusting funding to reflect "what it takes to get the kid over the bar." It appears from the Quality Education Model that his budget of $4.55 billion for the biennium is just that, the state's current budget adjusted for inflation and new enrollments. We now know what it will take to get students "over the bar" — $5.6 billion. The governor helped get the school reform bill through the 1991 legislature. Hopefully, he will provide the leadership to find the funds necessary to meet those standards.

School Foundations

Many schools and school districts are starting foundations to ease the program cuts resulting from Measure 5. Parents, grandparents and members of the community can make tax-deductible donations to the school district's foundation. That money can be used to provide for programs and materials that have been cut under Measure 5. While this won't make up for the fact that we need a better system of funding public education in this state, it will help alleviate some of the short-term problems caused by lack of funding.

Business/ School Partnerships

Another bright spot in the local picture is that our public schools are actively seeking meaningful relationships with the business community. The old style partnership was one in which the business donated a computer or some library books to the school. In return, the company basketball team practiced two nights a week in the school gym and student art hung in the company cafeteria. Educators have come to understand that our youth need a greater sense of purpose to their education and more solid ties to the community.

The African saying, "It takes a whole village to raise a child" has been restated often in the past several years. There can be little doubt that today's children are isolated from the life of their communities. Fewer of us go to church, participate in communal activities or have large extended families. This makes it difficult for young people to see diverse models of how adults live and work and to hear what adults think about and value. Schools have sought to use local businesses as resources to help to fill this gap.

New, more effective partnerships have emerged in some of our local schools. For example, Paragon Cable gave the Portland Public Schools a $250,000 grant to create a distance learning network at three Portland high schools. Kevin Kidd, the General Manager said, "It is no longer acceptable to watch the educational system from a distance and wonder whether or not the School Board will be able to handle the multiple pressures placed upon it by the needs of the students and the reality of budgetary concerns." He challenged individuals and businesses to help the schools in any way they can. Intel gave 550 computers to the new Century High School in Hillsboro, and its employees volunteer in district schools.

Given a chance to work with members of the community, students take on the role of apprentices, much like the system that was commonly used to train young people before the industrial revolution. This type of learning draws people together around a common task. Not only does the student learn from a master, but also the adolescent's need to belong to a group can be fulfilled by group-learning about biotechnology, or Internet or recycling. School/ business partnerships can be the motivating force for some teens to stay in school. Young people tie their educational experience to work life by being involved in opportunities like "Take Your Child to Work Day." Knowing what jobs are offered in the community and seeing what local people do for a living helps them understand how education expands their choices as adults. Putting learning in context makes it meaningful.

Parental Involvement

Just as many independent schools require parents to give a fixed number of volunteer hours per year to the school, public schools are beginning to ask parents for more of their time. Children do better in school when parents get involved. Research clearly shows a correlation between parental involvement and higher grades and test scores. Attendance and behavior are also better when parents help with homework, talk to the teachers and visit the classroom. Parents who are able to volunteer in their child's school are rewarded with a better understanding of their child's world. They also gain some insight into the job that the school is doing.

Parent Teacher Associations make an enormous difference in the environment of a school because their activities create a feeling of community. The PTA can help display students' work throughout the school and organize and run after school classes in art, music, foreign languages and dance. Portland area schools have parades, potluck dinners, story time for little ones and their parents, ski swaps, bike swaps, field days and fun runs. Such links between the school and the community give children a sense of belonging to a culture and a value system.

There are other ways in which our public schools might do well to emulate private schools. Adam Urbanski, a vice-president of the American Federation of Teachers, addressed this subject in an article in *Education Week*, January 31, 1996. He proposed that parents be able to choose the public school they feel would best serve their child and that parents have more say in the running of their schools. He believes that each school needs the independence to choose its own staff and set its own (higher) standards.

"Give the chosen school the authority to require that parents and students who select that school sign a compact outlining mutual obligations vis-à-vis behavior codes, academic performance standards, parental involvement, teacher and school commitments. Parents and students would have to adhere to this compact in order to continue in that school — or shop around for a better match." Urbanski concludes, "Let schools not chosen by parents and students diminish in size. The vacated space could be filled by satellites of more effective schools or by other newly developed schools."

What Every Parent Should Expect from a Public School

Native Oregonians have traditionally chosen public schools for their children and until recently there were relatively few independent schools in the area. Many old Portland families still prefer to send their children to public schools for all the right reasons. Knowing that their children will live and work with people of many backgrounds, they appreciate the diversity that a public school offers.

What should you look for in a public school? Schools that are participatory, where parents, teachers and administrators share in the decision-making process offer a better learning environment. They also teach students about the process of decision-making in a democracy.

Technology is also a critical issue to consider in your child's curriculum. As computer terminals make available unprecedented volumes of information, students need the skills to sort, evaluate and use the data. They'll need critical thinking skills to determine what is relevant and reliable. And because technology is advancing so rapidly, citizens of the 21st century will need to become lifelong learners. Portland's November 1995 bond measure promised to put four computers in every classroom. Beaverton, Gresham-Barlow and Tigard have also recently passed bond measures to update the technology in their schools.

Questions Parents Should Ask

Does the school have a site council to promote parent involvement in the planning processes?

What kinds of decision-making authority does the site council have?

Is there a strong Parent Teacher Association?

Does the principal hire the teachers or are they assigned to the school by a central administrative office?

What kind of input will you, as the parent, have in decisions about which teachers your child will have?

Is the curriculum presented as a body of knowledge to be memorized or as a process of inquiry?

Does your child's school have a computer literacy program?

Will your child be able to work on a computer during his or her school day?

Is the technology up-to-date?

If Your Child is Entering Kindergarten

Look for a program that nurtures each child's social, emotional, physical and intellectual development. It should be staffed by teachers who love children. The classrooms should be light and airy, with colorful bulletin boards and lots of kids' work on display. Both the space and the learning materials should foster curiosity. Because young children learn primarily through play and exploration, the classrooms should be designed to promote a wide range of activities. At this age, children need to work on large and small motor skills. An outdoor playground with age-appropriate play equipment is very important. (For more details on what to expect of a kindergarten environment, see page 213.) If your child will be riding a school bus for the first time, an award-winning video "*Operation School Bus Safety*" is available free of charge at Blockbuster Video stores. (The six-minute video was produced by National PTA and a company that makes school buses.)

At the Elementary School Level

It is in elementary school that your child will build his or her foundation in "the three Rs." Pay attention to how the curriculum is taught. Programs that cover large quantities of facts and emphasize lecturing and textbook learning may work for students who are articulate and have good memory skills. However, most children thrive on programs that emphasize learning concepts rather than facts. Learning-by-doing allows them to acquire lifelong learning skills. Children are not empty bottles on an assembly line waiting to be filled with facts!

There are three styles of teaching. In the traditional approach, the teacher delivers instruction using strategies such as lecturing and memorization. Students are expected to be able to repeat back what they have learned at test time. Students perceive that there is one correct answer, the answer the teacher wants, and they will try to oblige by providing it. Creativity and questioning suffer. A second method has the teacher using different strategies, but still directing student learning. One might see cooperative learning, interdisciplinary thematic units, and work designed to fit different students learning styles. This is what most elementary classrooms use today. Students are more likely to make connections and there is room for some creativity.

A third model, using brain-based research, has the teacher and student learning together, as a collaborative effort. Teachers in these classrooms use many strategies and an ongoing challenge, question and analysis mode. They create real-life, complex experiences that help kids learn new ideas. This kind of teaching works very well with technology and offers kids the opportunity to learn higher order thinking skills, to make connections and to be creative. It also teaches them to be self-motivated and take responsibility as well as credit for their own learning. Unfortunately, few teachers are trained this way and staff development dollars in Oregon are few.

Al Shanker, former President of the American Federation of Teachers, once observed that if you froze a doctor, a steelworker and a teacher in 1900, and brought them back today, only the teacher could hit the ground running. Classroom teaching has changed that little. No educational system can teach children everything there is to learn, so it's important to teach them *how* to learn. An inquiry-based approach allows students to ask the question "How do we know?" The more students participate in active learning experiences, the more likely they are to grasp the concepts. Ask whether the science programs are designed to develop thinking and problem-solving skills.

Find out if the math programs use "manipulatives" — geometric shapes, measuring devices and counters — to practice addition, subtraction, fractions and geometry. Does the program teach kids how to use a calculator? While they certainly need to memorize the multiplication tables, children should also be learning to use calculators from third grade up. Does your school take advantage of the wonderful math software programs now available? Students should be encouraged to view mathematical concepts as essential in our highly technological world. Some schools will send accelerated students to the local middle or high school for advanced math classes. Find out if your child is eligible.

Interdisciplinary units, which are very common in elementary schools today, combine core subjects in thematic units. For example, a unit on volcanoes would involve math, writing, reading, geography and science. Students are taught to use critical thinking skills in a variety of ways, through written and oral expression, art and media, scientific and mathematical research. This approach makes learning more relevant and interesting, and it helps tie the classroom to the real world. Is your child's school incorporating this type of teaching technique?

Language arts programs should emphasize writing and the writing process. Are the students keeping a daily journal? Are they writing stories, autobiographies, and research papers? Are they publishing them on the computer? Most primary classrooms use both phonics and whole language to teach reading. Reading is the most important thing your child will learn in grade school and many are not learning it well.

The congressionally mandated National Assessment of Educational Progress shows that 44% of our kids in elementary and high school read below the "basic" level. Thirty-two percent of fourth graders whose parents both had college degrees did not meet the basic level and neither did 72% of black students in this country. Teachers should use whatever works for a child; usually it will be a combination of methods.

Look for literature-based reading programs. If basal readers are used, they should be supplemented with a wide range of children's literature. Teachers should provide a sampling of authors, so children are introduced to various styles of writing. Parents should supplement the school's reading program at home. Encourage your children to read. Help them get to know their public library. For birthdays, buy books and gift certificates at a bookstore. Parents need to set aside family reading time, model that you read for pleasure and to get information. Read to your kids and listen to them read to you.

Art and music have been cut from the public schools as the budgets tightened. There are 15% fewer music teachers in Oregon today than there were in 1992. Oregon has 133 elementary art teachers for 751 elementary schools. The new research on the brain and how and when we learn indicates that art and music are important in the curriculum. We know that music in early childhood programs improves spatial learning. The College Board found that studying music significantly improved student's SAT scores. Students with experience performing music scored an average of 52 points higher on the verbal section and 37 points higher on the math section of the SAT than students without this experience. Students of music appreciation scored an average of 62 points higher on the verbal and 42 points higher on the math.

Higher test scores are also correlated to the study of art. Students who took art for all four years of high school scored an average of 48 points higher in verbal and 36 points higher in math than students who did not take art in high school. Oregon students will have to meet standards in the arts, and to do that we will have to get the arts back into the schools. There is no question that an appreciation of the arts will improve the quality of a child's life.

The teacher-student ratio is also an important factor to consider. A teacher who is stretching to work with 25 to 30 students and has one or two "special needs" students in the class does not have much time to give the average child individual attention. When budget cuts mean increasing the number of students in the classroom, it is the students who seem to be doing "just fine" who get less from the teacher. An article in the October 27, 1997 issue of *Time*, "What Makes a Good School?" notes, "While there is no ideal number of students per class, studies show that small classes work best — especially for reading and math in the early primary grades. They are expensive, however, requiring an expanded teaching staff and more classroom space per student." As noted earlier, prisons are also expensive and not just financially, as the citizens of Wilsonville will tell you.

Emotional intelligence, or the ability to use interpersonal and intra-personal skills, is also an important part of elementary education. Daniel Goleman has written a best seller on the subject, *Emotional Intelligence: Why It Can Matter More Than IQ*. Kids are having more emotional problems, everything from anti-social behavior to suicide. His findings include the fact that boys who are very impulsive and always getting into trouble in the second grade are six to eight times more likely than other kids to commit crimes and be violent in their teens. Sixth grade girls who confuse feelings of anxiety and anger, boredom and hunger are the ones most likely to develop eating disorders in adolescence. Children need to learn interpersonal skills and how to handle their own emotions.

Parents are working longer hours and there are more dual career families. Kids have less experience with caring adults modeling healthy emotional responses. Many kids are spending more time alone at home in front of the TV or the computer and less time playing down the street with other kids. Knowledge is power and this research will help you evaluate how your student is doing emotionally. Emotional intelligence can be learned and some schools are teaching kids empathy, how to calm themselves when they are anxious, and techniques for conflict resolution.

The Middle School Years

Research shows that many parents cease to show an interest in their students school life at the middle school level. This has grave consequences. Let your child know you value education and expect that he or she will do well. Ask your student to show you his work, explain things to you. Talk about what she is reading. Be interested, but not critical. Make homework a priority, turn off the TV, and unplug the phone and the stereo. Provide your student with information on what adults do, talk about your job, hobbies etc. and have them talk to relatives and to family friends.

Middle school is the age when kids become passionate about causes — the environment, the homeless, etc. Capitalize on this to help them formulate their value systems. This is the best time to begin to talk to your child about public policy issues. Ask: "What makes Oregon different from other states? In what ways are we stewards of our natural resources? Talk about our beach access laws, salmon recovery and the bottle bill. Ask: "Why doesn't Oregon invest in education the way the State of Washington does?" Perhaps your middle school student could write his/her State senator on that issue.

Middle schools that provide a community atmosphere of respect and trust offer the best environments for students. It is a difficult time for adolescents, given their hormonal imbalances and accompanying mood swings. Anyone who has parented through this period will attest to the challenges. Kids in middle school are learning from their peers how to communicate and how to be socially sexualized. They are also learning what kinds of behaviors are morally acceptable. It is a rather brutal acculturation process and one not many adults would want to repeat. Kids need peer relationships to learn these things. It is difficult for many adults to watch their children go through this painful process. Schools need to recognize these adolescent issues and work to help students cope with the stresses of growing up in our culture.

In March 1998 two Arkansas middle school boys, ages 11 and 13, shot and killed the girls who had broken up with one of them. Then the tragedy at Thurston High School brought this problem home to Oregonians. Adolescents need help coping with the stresses of becoming adults and growing up too fast, which the culture and the media encourage them to do. As the study on teens on page 34 shows, guns have no place in the home. Talk to your kids about the public policy issues of gun control and violence.

On a more positive note, many middle schools are focusing on the school-within-a-school concept, which allows teachers to work with smaller groups of students and helps create a sense of community. Middle schools are developing several ways to foster a small-school atmosphere. There are teams of teachers who teach the core subjects to the same group of students for the two or three years they are at middle school. Or students might be divided into teams and stay with that team throughout the school year. In some middle schools each group has a geographical area within the building, which creates a small school feeling.

Both middle and high schools are moving to block schedules. The traditional fifty-minute period has students dashing all over the building. Block schedules of three or four periods a day give students and teachers more time together. This brings a more personal feeling to the learning environment. Teachers can get to know their students and their learning styles better. They can provide more frequent feedback. Block schedules also provide an opportunity for individual and group projects.

Several private schools are adding the middle years, offering parents an alternative to the large public middle schools. The French American International School, Portland Jewish Academy and Touchstone School will all have preschool through grade eight programs in the near future.

Multnomah Education Service District runs a wonderful program called "Outdoor School." Students in sixth grade spend a week at one of the camps on the Sandy River learning about ecology and the natural resources of this state. High school students from the Portland area serve as camp counselors. Portland middle school students attend, and many private schools in the area choose to participate on a pay-for-service basis.

High School

Students do best in small high schools, where teachers know them well and they have a community of friends. A conference on Restructuring the American High School was held in Portland in June of 1997. The high school of the future is going to be smaller. The large factory model high schools so common in our area will be divided up into manageable units, with two or three small academies in one large building. Jefferson High School was the first public school in Portland to follow that model, which has been used successfully in other cities.

Ted Sizer, who has done a great deal of research on the American high school in conjunction with Coalition of Essential Schools, describes effective schools as "orderly environments where there are adults who care." High schools must be staffed by people who are moved by and can move adolescents. To move them, one must know them. In our large factory-model high schools, teachers are specialists. Most are trained to deliver one aspect of the curriculum: biology, calculus or Western Civ. They have far too many students per week to know any students well.

Unless a student is part of a small group (the academic all stars, the jocks or one of the daily discipline problems) he or she becomes anonymous in a large school. Drop out rates, dissatisfaction and acting-out increase as students are unable to connect in their learning communities. Five out of every 100 high school students dropped out in 1996. Students in families with incomes in the lowest 20% are five times more likely to drop out than kids whose families have incomes in the top 20%. There is a growing belief that the structure of the American high school must change to become effective.

There is great variety in the special high school programs available in the Portland metropolitan area. Which one might best fit your student will depend on what your child's strengths are and what he/ she wants to do. Portland Public Schools offers several magnet high school programs that give students curriculum choices outside of their neighborhood schools. Beaverton, Lake Oswego and Tigard-Tualatin also offer some school choices at the high school level. Riverdale offers a small college prep high school using Ted Sizer's research.

If you have more than one child, the same high school will not necessarily be the best fit for each of them. Districts have different enrollment policies for students seeking to change high schools. The Oregon State Athletic Association also has rules to prevent student athletes from being recruited by other than their local high school. Usually, however, a student may switch high schools within a district if both the sending and receiving principals approve. Inter-district transfers are more problematic, some districts allow them and others don't.

Sleep research done at John Hopkins University shows that teenager's biological clocks are set later than those of the rest of us. Nevertheless, most school districts start high school first, often with kids getting on the buses as early as 7:00am so that the same buses can pick up the younger students later. Early classes can be wasted time for many teens. They are unable to readjust their internal time clocks to go to bed earlier. Students who had to be at school by 9:30am instead of 7:30am did significantly better academically and got more sleep. Two schools that I know of in the Portland area have read this research and are using it — West Sylvan Middle School and West Linn High School. A friend of mine here in Portland went through Wilson High School when the school had a double shift of students. She had the late shift, which she credits for her academic performance. This is one of those "no-brainers" for those of us who have parented teenagers.

A new $25 million federally funded longitudinal study of teenagers published in the Journal of American Medicine last year concluded that feeling loved, understood and paid attention to by parents helps teens avoid high risk behaviors and this holds true whether it is a single or two parent household. High school students whose parents are involved in their lives and who have a good relationship with at least one teacher are less likely to use drugs, alcohol or engage in destructive behaviors. Specifically, what the study told us is that an emotional bond with a parent is six times more important than the amount of time teens spend with their parents. And, the presence of parents at home at key times — in the morning, after school, at dinner and at bedtime does make teens less likely to use alcohol, tobacco and marijuana.

Over 90,000 students in grades 7 through 12 were interviewed for this study and more information is expected to be forthcoming — the information reinforces what we already know. Family is crucial. Parents need to be aware that depression affects teenagers. Statistics from the Oregon Health Division show that teens here are 50% more likely to commit suicide than the national average. An average of 40 children between the ages of 10 and 19 kill themselves in Oregon every year. Between the ages of 15 and 24 the number goes up to 75. Childhood depression is the number one mental health risk factor for suicide. If you suspect that your teen is depressed, seek professional help.

What Can Parents Do?

Set high academic expectations for their teen.

Be as accessible as possible.

Send a clear message to avoid alcohol, drugs and sex.

Lock up alcohol.

Get rid of guns in the house. The presence of a gun at home increases the likelihood that a teen will think about or attempt suicide or get involved in violent behavior. This holds true even if the gun is not easily accessible.

Discourage outside jobs. Teens who work 20 hours a week or more, regardless of the family's economic status, are more likely to use alcohol and drugs, smoke, engage in early sex and report emotional distress. Why this is so is not clear.

What Every Parent Should Expect from the Teacher

Three traits every parent has the right to demand are competency, rapport and fair-mindedness! Talk to the teacher, visit the class and observe, if possible. Ask to volunteer in the classroom or for a PTA-sponsored event. You, as the parent, can usually tell what kind of rapport the teacher has with his/ her students. Some public schools have specific times when tours are available. Others are difficult to get into until your child has enrolled in the school.

More Questions Parents Should Ask

Does the school list the academic credentials of its teachers?

Are they teaching in the area in which they were trained and staying current in their fields?

Does the school have a written policy on continuing education? Is it funded?

Does your child's teacher attend workshops, take classes, participate in site councils, and school committees?

Does your child's school encourage these things by paying for substitute teachers to allow the faculty to participate in meetings and workshops?

Does the teacher truly like children?

A Fair Deal for Your Daughter

Nine out of ten women work for pay at some time, yet girls are still told they will have a choice as to whether or not they will work for pay. Women are nine times as likely as men to be single parents. Most women still work in traditional female occupations, yet we know that women who choose non-traditional careers can expect lifetime earnings that are 150% of those of women in traditional female careers.

Developmentally, girls start off in the lead. In preschool, they score higher on IQ tests than boys. They tend to talk, read, and count earlier, and they get better grades in elementary school. Yet by fifth grade, in public schools, far more gifted boys than girls are identified. Between fifth and ninth grades, girls begin to lose interest in competing in the classroom.

The American Association of University Women released a study in 1992 called "How Schools Shortchange Girls." The findings are important for parents of girls in middle and high school. The study found that boys are five times more likely than girls to receive teachers' attention and twelve times more likely to speak up in class. Only one-seventh of all textbook illustrations of children depict girls. Boys are called on more frequently. They are likely to be praised for academics and intellect and to be criticized for behavior. The message is: "You are smart; get to work." Girls are praised in school for their clothing, behavior and obedience. They are often criticized for being inadequate intellectually. The message is: "Nice try, but you are just not good at this." Girls have great difficulty keeping their confidence and self esteem when these are the kinds of messages they are getting.

Encourage your daughters to take math and science courses, even if they are difficult. In seventh and eighth grade, girls will make the decisions that will determine the math and science course work available to them in high school. Stress the importance of these classes, and praise a B or C as you would an A in an easier class. Developing spatial reasoning and analytical skills is important, as are the problem-solving and independent thinking skills they will acquire in math and science.

Ask your daughter's teachers what math, science or computer programs are available for her to use. Do girls have equal access to computers? When I asked this question at my daughter's school several years ago, the answer was that computer room passes were given on a first-come, first-served basis. A group of boys who arrived early at school every morning before the buses were being given all of the passes for the computer room. The same boys had the use of the computer room before school and at lunchtime every day.

Girls are more likely than boys to stop taking math after algebra and geometry. Parents may have to push ninth and tenth graders to stick with it. Often in our public schools, there are many more boys in the advanced math and science classes, and this can make it difficult for girls to speak out and ask questions. Boys tend to express frustration by acting out; girls "act in" and become silent and withdrawn. Push girls to speak up, be heard, take risks and challenge themselves. Talk to your daughter's math and science teachers; make sure they know what her strengths and weaknesses are. There are many very good math and science enrichment classes and summer camps. Check the OMSI, Saturday Academy and University of Oregon listings in Chapter Six. Another great resource for parents is Mount Holyoke College's Web site, "Expect the Best from a Girl. That's What You'll Get" (www.academic.org). The information comes from the Women's College Coalition.

Parents can make a difference. Research shows parents have greater influence on their daughter's choices than either their peers or the media. Praise girls' skills and ideas rather than appearance and behavior. Push in math. Women who take more than two college level math courses often make as much money as men. Share what you know about gender issues with your daughter's middle and high school math and science teachers. Many teachers (especially males) are unaware of the research on girls. Teach your children to question the stereotypes of men and women they see on TV and in magazines. Encourage both boys and girls to explore non-traditional areas of interest.

Kathy Masarie, a Portland pediatrician, has founded a group called "Full Esteem Ahead" that seeks to encourage and preserve healthy self-esteem in teens and particularly girls, as they go through adolescence. The group offers events for parents and teens and a newsletter with valuable information on educational resources in our community. Coming of age ceremonies, which many cultures use to mark the transition from child to adult, are one area of interest addressed in the newsletters. A subscription to the newsletter, *Wings*, is available for $10 from Wings, 663 S.W. Beaverton-Hillsdale Highway #214, Portland, OR 97225. (Telephone 503/296-6748 or FAX 503/297-8742).

Something Every Girl's Parents Should Know

A second AAUW study called "Hostile Hallways" outlines the sexual harassment girls experience in middle and high schools. About 70% of our daughters are experiencing sexual harassment at school and 50% experience unwanted sexual touching in the classrooms and hallways of their school. The AAUW study found the harassment to be much more graphic and mean-spirited than the kind of teasing we remember from junior high. Girls are going into puberty earlier than they did even ten years ago. This may be due to the hormones in beef and chicken and it may be due to other causes, but it is a fact. Just as their bodies are changing and seem somewhat out of control, they continually get the message that there is only one road to success and it is not accomplishment, but beauty.

Teenage girls in our culture are told by the media that the ideal body type to achieve is the long-legged, lean look of young girls before puberty sets in. High fashion models have become thinner over the past decades and now weigh twenty-three percent less than the average woman. The result is a million women with eating disorders and 150,000 deaths annually from anorexia and bulimia. Girls who go to school starving themselves have no energy to pursue their studies. Yet, girls are continually pressured to be thin to be considered pretty.

Another point in favor of small schools is that they are easier environments for adolescent girls. K-8 schools are also good choices because girls are less likely to be the victim of thoughtless remarks from the boys they've known since kindergarten. Adolescent girls are at great risk in today's American culture. There are many reasons. Children see sex in movies and on TV. They see violence and sex intertwined. Domestic violence, date rape, and unwanted sexual advances happen to these girls or to someone they know. Parents of boys should demand that their sons treat women with respect, beginning at home with their mother and sisters.

Often girls are reluctant to report sexual harassment, and often the perpetrator goes unpunished. This gives girls the message that the world is not a safe place for women. It is difficult, if not impossible, to be an adolescent girl in this culture and have a wholesome attitude about oneself and one's sexuality. Parents of all girls in this age group should read *Reviving Ophelia: Saving the Selves of Adolescent Girls* and *Failing at Fairness: How America's Schools Cheat Girls*. Middle and high school teachers and counselors should also read these two books.

You Are Your Child's Best Advocate

No one is going to advocate for your child but you. Read this book and any information available about the options that are possible for your children. Ask public and private schools for their printed materials. You can learn a great deal about the school by reading its publications. The way in which the information is worded will tell you a lot about the values of the school.

A word of caution here... Some children need to be gently pushed to achieve their best. Others respond poorly to pressure. There is a fine line between expecting too much or too little, and as a parent you must choose a school situation that you believe will best serve your child.

What Every Parent Should Know About Standardized Testing

Oregon law mandates that public school students be tested annually in grades 3, 5, 8 and 10. The Oregon Statewide Assessment Test (OAT) is given to all students in the public school system in these grades. In this edition, scores are given for 1995, 1997 and in some cases 1998. In 1995, grades 3, 5, 8 and 11 were tested. The test has been moved from 11th grade to 10th grade now that Oregon is moving toward the Certificate of Initial Mastery. Updated scores for Portland area schools can be found on-line (www.oregonlive.com). The Department of Education also has a Web site (www.ode.state.or.us) that lists the percentages of students meeting, exceeding and failing to meet state standards at all public schools in Oregon. Oregon Public Education Network's Web site (www.open.k12.or.us) offers sample test papers written by students and scored using the state standards.

A socioeconomic ranking for the school population that accompanies the OAT scores reveals where the school falls in relation to schools ranked. (1 is the lowest score; in 1997 the top score was 750 for grade five, 355 for grade eight and 254 for grade 10, based upon the number of schools that were ranked at that grade level.) The Socioeconomic Rank is determined by student attendance rates, changes in residency, parent income and parent education levels. Private schools can choose to participate in the OAT, but they are not ranked socioeconomically.

This book provides OAT scores in reading and math and high school SAT scores because it is information most parents will want to have. Whether or not it helps you decide which program is best for your child is another matter. The SAT was "recentered" in 1996 to better reflect averages. Scores before 1996 that have not been recentered do not offer an accurate comparison to 1997 scores. Some of the schools whose SAT scores we used in 1995 were recentered, but others were not. We have listed the SAT scores for 1995, 1996, 1997, 1998 and in some cases 1999 to give you the best picture we have of how an individual high school's students did on the SAT. Here are the average scores nationwide.

	Verbal				Math			
	1999	*1998*	*1997*	*1996*	*1999*	*1998*	*1997*	*1996*
Oregon	525	528	525	523	528	528	524	521
National	505	505	505	505	511	512	511	508

Standardized test scores show how the students at an individual school performed, on average, in relation to the statewide averages or nationwide averages, depending on the test. What is more important to parents is how their own children are performing!

What Testing Reveals

Three types of comparison can be made for each school: improvement or decline within the school itself over time, ranking against all other schools statewide, and a comparison of the school with demographically similar schools (hence the socioeconomic rankings). Three levels of performance, Basic (partial mastery of a subject), Proficient and Advanced, also allow schools to see what proportion of their students have achieved the various levels of subject mastery.

The state's purpose in assessing students is to provide information for policy decisions and to help districts and individual schools conduct self-evaluations. In 1995, for example, one-third of Oregon's students in grades 3, 5, 8, and 11 scored in the Advanced level of reading performance. The 1995 OAT scores also revealed that while average mathematics scores remained the same as the previous year, there was a 2% increase in the number of 11th grade students in the Advanced category. In science, the results could be judged discouraging; 34% of 11th graders fell into the Basic (lowest) level, and only 16% reached the Advanced level.

A University of Chicago research study of testing results over a thirty-year period from the 1960s to the 1990s showed that more boys than girls perform at the highest levels in math and science. Boys scored higher than girls (by about three to one) in the top ten percent for math and science; in the top one percent, boys outranked girls by seven to one. The West Linn-Wilsonville District reported in 1994 that their high school girls scored 467 in math on the SAT and the boys scored 546. In 1995, girls scored 494 and boys scored 559.

More boys than girls are at the bottom of the scale in reading and writing. Fewer boys than girls scored in the top ten percent in reading skills. There are some good books out on gender differences in learning and teaching. *Failing at Fairness: How America's School Cheat Girls* by Myra and David Sadker is a book all parents of girls should read. Kathleen Odean, a children's librarian, has published *Great Books for Boys: More Than 600 Books for Boys 2 to 14*. She believes that we send boys the message that reading is not as important as other activities. Parents can make a difference, according to Odean, by modeling reading, reading to their sons and understanding that boys like to read alone in their rooms. Let them!

Generally, higher test scores correlate to higher socioeconomic status. Lincoln High School, where only 4% of students qualify for free school lunches had a combined math/verbal score of 1186 in 1997. Jefferson, where 60% of the kids qualify, had a combined score of 834. The gap between these schools appears to be widening; in 1996, Lincoln students scored 1178 and Jefferson, 867.

There are many reasons why socioeconomic factors matter. The ability to afford good early childhood education is one. However, children who grow up in homes where parents read to their offspring, discuss current events with them, and take them to the library often are children who perform better in the classroom. The skills of a lifelong learner can be successfully modeled by any parent.

There is a substantial amount of research showing that children live up to the expectations we have of them. Children in classrooms where the teacher expects them to perform well tend to do so. Girls who are expected to do well in science and math do better than girls who are not expected to understand science and math. Expect your child to succeed, to choose to go to college, or to develop his or her talents. This does not mean that a child who is gifted in music will necessarily bloom in the program with the highest SAT scores. It does mean that the fit between the school and the child should include nurturing those things at which the child excels.

The Future for Education in Oregon

"The Oregon Educational Act for the 21st Century" passed in 1991, requires the development of "rigorous academic content standards." In seeking to foster academic achievement, school reform mandates changes in curriculum, outcomes and assessment. The ability to think will be essential for citizens of the 21st century. Students will need to learn how to make decisions and solve problems. They must be capable of self-directed research and able to effectively collaborate and communicate with others.

Higher Standards

Education is changing in this state. By setting goals and then finding specific methods of teaching these skills, the Oregon Department of Education hopes to build a framework upon which children can progress to a point of mastery in several fields. The Department's plans are innovative and bold.

Benchmarks are being designed to make sure that students are proficient in certain areas at the end of a specific number of years of schooling. In the field of earth science, for example, a 3rd grade student should be able to describe how the parts of an organism help it survive. By 5th grade the child would be expected to describe the functions of the major human organ systems. At the 8th grade-level, the child would describe the structure of an organism in terms of organ systems, organs, tissues and cells. By the 10th grade the student would be able to describe, explain and compare the structure and function of cells in organisms.

A Certificate of Initial Mastery (CIM), which should be obtained by the end of the 10th grade, and a proposed Certificate of Advanced Mastery (CAM) will be the outward acknowledgments of performance assessments. Once a student has obtained the Certificate of Initial

Mastery, he or she can choose to enter a college prep program or select programs designed to make the transition to the work world.

Controversy surrounding the program centers on this choice. Opponents contend that it amounts to tracking. Students who select the transition-to-work programs might lack the academic skills they may need later if they decide to go back into post-secondary education. Proponents believe that the program will bring us in line with the European systems, offering apprenticeships, and a better school-to-work transition.

The first group of students to receive the Certificate of Initial Mastery were 10th graders in 1998-99. Only one in four 10th graders met the standards for the certificate. School administrators and teachers are worried about how many students can meet the tough standards. In addition to the test score requirements, students must obtain passing scores for 8 work samples.

Students who do not earn the CIM and the CAM can still get a high school diploma. State School Superintendent Stan Bunn and many other educators in Oregon are reluctant to lower the standards.

The purpose of the standards is to raise the bar, and lowering the standards defeats the purpose. A compromise was worked out in February of 1998 when the Board of Education voted to postpone for two years some of the requirements for the CIM. The work samples in reading writing and math will now be phased in over a two-year period. Eight work samples will be required in 1998-99; twelve in 1999-2000, and students will be responsible for the full sixteen work samples in 2000-2001. Students will still need to meet the test score requirements.

Tenth graders need to score 239 out of a possible 300 on the Oregon Assessment Tests in reading and 239 in math on a 60 question multiple choice test. Two-thirds of 10th graders did not meet state standards on the 98-99 multiple choice math test. There is also a 45 minute open-ended math problem with four assessment areas: conceptual understanding, processes and strategies, demonstrating the steps to solution, and reviewing the reasonableness of results. In the area of writing, students must score 4 out of 6 in each of four categories: ideas and content, organization, sentence fluency and spelling, and grammar and punctuation. Students will have three 45-minute sessions to produce the writing sample.

How the Reforms May Work

The Portland School District has raised its exit standards to meet the State System of Higher Education's admissions standards. By the year 2001, the District will expect all graduates of Portland Public High Schools to be qualified to go on to higher education if they so choose. An editorial in *The Oregonian* recently posed the question, "Why is that good for the 60% who won't go on to college?" Former Portland Superintendent Jack Bierwirth argued that a "greater expectations" approach would well-serve kids in vocational or professional programs because today's high-skill, high-pay jobs require higher qualifications.

"And it will leave the higher-ed option open to them." Whatever the ultimate policy decision, parents can expect that their children will be pushed harder in the next few years as the proficiency standards go into effect.

The End of "Social Promotion"

The practice of moving students to the next grade level regardless of their academic achievement has become a hotly debated public policy issue in the last year. Several states have passed laws requiring schools to end social promotion.

The problem is that retention and promotion are two ends of the spectrum. A student who is not learning needs a rich learning environment, well-trained teachers and extra help. Policy-makers want the easy answer. Studies have shown that retention does not work. Summer school, after-school programs and early intervention are costly, but effective. *The Harvard Education Letter*, Jan/Feb 1999, outlines the research that has been done on retention versus social promotion and addresses the public policy issues. Portland Superintendent Ben Canada announced that he will ask the District to ban social promotion beginning in 1999-2000. He estimates that the cost of special summer school programs and other interventions for students who are not promoted will be about $1 million annually.

Lengthened School Year

School reform also seeks to increase the length of the school year. If we believe that schools need to be improved and that our students are coming up short in comparison with their European and Asian counterparts, how can we justify closing all of our educational facilities for two to three months a year? The problem with one, long summer break is that teachers spend a lot of time in the fall reviewing the previous year's work because many students have not retained what they learned the previous year. In American school districts where year-round school has been tried, students and teachers seem to do better with six to seven week cycles of learning then a break of a week or two. Concentration and retention are higher. There is less fatigue. Additionally, the long summer break no longer serves our needs as a society. Working parents find it difficult to meet childcare needs for a three-month period. In cities where several short breaks have been tried, the schools have developed programs to fill the need for childcare. Some Oregon schools and school districts are looking at a more year-round schedule.

Decentralized Decision Making

Another aspect of reform is school management, in particular, decentralizing decision making authority. Site-based management would allow the individual school to make decisions about hiring and firing personnel, and how money will be spent, among other things. The great advantage of site-based management is that a school can more effectively meet the needs of the students in it's neighborhood if the school can make it's own decisions. Currently, many central administrative offices do the hiring and make policies for all schools in the district. Schools work better when those most affected by the decisions make those decisions themselves.

Children in one neighborhood may need, and parents may want, a longer school day, a second language program or teachers who are bilingual. A Salem elementary school has decided to require students to wear uniforms. Some communities have even discussed giving up Friday night football to fund Internet-linked computer labs. These kinds of decisions need to be made school-by-school, not district-by-district. Oregon's school improvement laws are turning the decision-making processes over to local schools. Many schools currently have site councils consisting of parents, staff and community members to help make decisions affecting the school.

Increased Discipline

There has been much discussion in recent years as whether or not schools should teach values. And if so, what values should be taught? Oregon has a 1929 statute that requires public schools to teach citizenship, courtesy, honesty and respect. Communities are encouraged to identify the civic values they want to emphasize and to make these a part of the school's curriculum. The legislature has put some teeth into the ability of school administrators to discipline students. Students can have their driver's license revoked for a number of anti-social behaviors, including bringing weapons to school, damaging school property or harming other students or school staff. Students can also be expelled for up to a year for obscene language or other unacceptable behavior.

Five hundred forty students were expelled from Oregon public schools in the 1997-98 school year for bringing weapons to school. These include 57 handguns, 10 shotguns or rifles, 69 other guns and 404 knives and other weapons. An additional 504 students were expelled for violent behavior. State law requires a one-year expulsion from school for a student who takes a weapon to school. The shootings at Thurston High School in Springfield will cause some policy changes in how we handle students who bring weapons to school and how we handle troubled kids. Bills before the current legislature would require the detention of a student for a minimum of 24 hours if he/she brings a gun to school. Another bill would require districts to offer counseling and alternative programs to students expelled for taking a weapon to school. The American Association of School Administrators recently issued a report, "Preparing Students for the 21st Century." Along with academic knowledge, the report calls for restoring the basic ethical principles that Horace Mann espoused in the 19th century when he championed the cause of public education. In addition to listing behaviors that students will need to exhibit if they are to be successful, the report emphasizes that interpersonal skills and such traits as adaptability and flexibility will be essential. The 74-page report is available for $11.95 plus shipping and handling.
To order, telephone 301/ 617-7802.

Preparing Students for the 21st Century

According to the American Association of School Administrators, some of the Behaviors Necessary for Success in the 21st Century are:

Honesty and integrity.   Practice of the "golden rule."

Respect for the value of effort.

Understanding of the work ethic.   Self-discipline.

Understanding and respect for those not like you.

Ability to work with others as a team member.

Responsibility for one's own actions.   Respect for authority.

Commitment to family life, personal life and community.

Pride in U.S. citizenship.

Knowledge of individual responsibilities in a democracy.

Willingness to resolve disagreements in a civil way.

Excitement about life.   Goals for lifelong learning.

Charter Schools

The legislature is also considering charter schools, which would operate with public money but have autonomy from many district and state regulations. These schools would give the charter school applicants (a group of parents, teachers or both) authority over the school's schedule, curriculum, budget and, in some cases, even over teacher hiring. But the contract would also hold them responsible for results. In most cases, governments require charter school students to perform at or above average on academic tests. If students can't meet that standard, the school is closed.

Where charter schools have been tried, they usually serve special populations, such as dropouts or students in danger of failing. Some have a special emphasis on science or arts or traditional basic skills. Most offer an alternative to traditional, mainstream schools. The idea is appealing because it offers teachers and parents more choice and control over children's education without forcing them to leave the public system. "They are more politically palatable than voucher plans, which would allow parents to spend public money in private schools," says Tim Zayac, a researcher at the Center for Education Reform in Washington DC, a nonprofit policy agency that tracks charter schools.

Critics maintain that charter schools would benefit only a small number of children and drain money from sponsoring districts. Some also fear they can become elitist. "But so far, 12 percent serve students in danger of failing, and 40 percent serve minority students. Many are dominated by children from the bottom half of the academic ladder," Zayac says.

The Oregon Senate passed a charter school bill in 1999 that the governor has said he would veto. Moneys for a charter school come from the budget of the school district granting the charter. Governor Kitzhaber fears that funding charter schools would drain school districts already short of funds. If charter schools can offer students a better education because they are able to circumvent the rules and regulations that our current public schools must deal with, would it not make more sense to eliminate the red tape for all public schools. The debate then gets into issues of whether teachers must be licensed and the role of the teacher's union. A teaching certificate does not guarantee competency. Whether the union adds to the professional status of teachers or detracts from it is also a question.

Great Expectations

There's no doubt that education is on the minds of both parents and policy makers today. The Carnegie Foundation's 1996 report, "Years of Promise: A Comprehensive Learning Strategy for America's Children," offers concrete ideas for improving education in America. (Copies of the report are available for $10 from the Carnegie Corp., PO Box 753, Waldorf, MD 20604.) Its basic recommendations are:

Promote children's learning in families and communities. All families should have access to parent education. And early childhood teachers should involve parents in their programs. Communities also should expand and improve out-of-school programs.

Expand high-quality early-learning opportunities. High-quality public and private early care and education programs should be expanded and supported by national, state, and local funding.

Create effective elementary schools and school systems. States should set standards for what students should know and be able to do in all subject areas by the end of 4th grade, and schools should monitor students' progress toward those goals. Staff development also is critical to student success.

Promote high-quality children's television and access to other electronic media. The Children's Television Act should be enforced, ensuring that communities have a variety of quality children's educational programming.

Link the key learning institutions into a comprehensive, coordinated education system. Leaders should develop strategic plans to address the educational needs of children.

Oregon has been a leader in school reform. Other districts are following the Portland School District's decision to make its exit standards match the State System of Higher Education's admission standards. This should be a major factor in improving the quality of education in the state. Research demonstrates that greater expectations of students result in better performance. Oregon's students could have an edge in both the job market and college admissions. Just as Oregon has become a model for the nation in its land use planning, the state can lead the way in new approaches to education — if the political will and public support are there.

Chapter Two
Portland Public School District

2

Portland is the largest public school district in the Northwest. PPS educates 56,000 children in ninety-four schools. Seattle, which is a larger city, has only 43,000 students enrolled in its public schools because families there have tended to flee to the suburbs in search of better schools. Portland has always had a very good school system, and it attracts students from across the socioeconomic spectrum. It was better before Measure 5 cut school funding, but it is still a system with many options, several exceptionally fine schools and many excellent programs.

Portland Public Schools

I was able to report in the 1996 edition of this book that the district had dealt with Measure 5 cuts by eliminating support services rather than classroom teachers. Unfortunately, that is no longer the case. Class sizes have gone up, and 11% of the teaching staff has been cut along with 17% of non-teaching staff. Spending per student has fallen 8% when adjusted for inflation. The average age of district school buildings is fifty-seven years, but building maintenance has been cut by 30%. The school population dropped in 1998 for the first time in many years. Private school enrollments are up.

A business tax increase of one-half percent approved by Multnomah County voters in March of 1998 generated $9,362,070 for Portland Public Schools. However, the district faces a $30 million shortfall in 1998-'99. The city will contribute $7.4 million and the county will be asked to help make up the shortfall. The District has considered closing as many as 10 schools and sending those student populations into neighboring schools. Given what we know about student achievement and small schools, this is a less than optimal solution to the budget crunch. The school board is also considering selling "surplus" real estate to the city for parks.

Portland's new Superintendent, Ben Canada, announced some innovative changes in an address to The City Club of Portland in January of 1999. He plans to end the practice of "social promotion." Students who are not promoted will need special summer programs and other services to help them catch up. Dr. Canada estimates that this will cost the district $1million annually. He also announced that he will require administrators to substitute teach one day a month. (I do this at my school as do many private school administrators. It enables us to get to know the students and their learning styles and to appreciate the concerns a teacher may have.)

Portland is piloting an innovative program to reward principals for increasing student performance. The superintendent feels that if principals are to be held accountable for student outcomes, they ought to be able to select their staff rather than taking the teachers assigned to the school by the central office. He has established a task force to study this proposal. Finally, Dr. Canada is offering schools the opportunity to reconfigure the grades the school offers to better fit the needs of the community. For example, if space is available in an elementary school and parents want a K-6 or K-8 program, the community will have this option. This is particularly good news for parents of middle school students because Portland's large middle schools can be very difficult for many preadolescent students to navigate.

Programs That Work

Portland Public Schools deserves high marks for efforts to make its schools fit the communities they serve. Portland has used cultural diversity to the students' advantage. There are language immersion programs at Richmond and Ainsworth and early foreign language learning programs at Beach, Bridlemile and Chapman. A Chinese immersion program was added at Woodstock in September of 1998 for kindergarten and first grade, and Atkinson has a K-1 two-way Spanish/English immersion program in which mixed groups of native Spanish and native English speakers receive 2½ days of instruction per week in each language.

The district would like to offer full-day kindergarten at all of the schools. Currently, most schools offer half-day kindergarten. Those that have full-day programs (Atkinson, Ainsworth, Bridger, Bridlemile, Chapman and Richmond) charge parents between $120 and $180 a month for the extra half-day. Financial aid is available for families who cannot afford to pay. However, the schools can only run these programs if there are enough paying parents to cover the costs. For most parents, the extra cost is much less than day-care and a much better option for their children. Eight schools in North or Northeast Portland also have Early Childhood Education Centers, which are funded with desegregation funds.

The system is experimenting with many innovative programs, and the school board has a policy of considering proposals from parents, teachers and the community for alternative educational concepts. Superintendent Canada has asked the school board to support establishing charter schools within PPS. There are "school-within-a-school" programs at all levels to help children who need smaller classes and more time with the teacher. The District has special programs for students who have dropped out of high school or are in danger of doing so. The International Learning Program, a joint venture with SOAR (Sponsors Organized to Assist Refugees), provides a high school program with English instruction and tutoring to help students who do not speak English and have not succeeded in the regular high school programs. PPS runs Moshi Moshi, an interactive Japanese language distance learning program for elementary students. Lessons are broadcast on Channel 53 (Paragon and TCI) on Tuesdays, Wednesdays and Thursdays. Level One is live from 10:30 to 11:00 a.m. and Level Two is from 9:00 to 9:30 a.m.

In an attempt to create a more personal environment, block scheduling and multi-age classrooms are replacing the traditional seven-period day in several middle schools. The Northeast Community School is one of three small new alternative schools in the district. The school has now moved to the Sabin site. Boise-Eliot Early Childhood Education Center in North Portland offers full-day kindergarten, and last fall it added the middle school grades in a program for fifty students called "The Boise-Eliot School of Thought." A new Environmental Middle School shares space with Abernethy Elementary.

Sunnyside Elementary School is a magnet for students who wish to learn sign language. Seven Portland schools (Ball, Clarendon, Sitton, Whitaker, Hayhurst, George and Portsmouth) have adopted a program called "Accelerated Schools" that has been used successfully in San Francisco. The philosophy is that each child is gifted at something. The staff determines each child's special gift. They then work with that student and his/ her family to support the child's talents.

Portland Public Schools also has an exceptional magnet high school program. Any student in the District may apply to attend a magnet program. There is an International Studies/ International Baccalaureate Program at Lincoln. Students who pass IB exams during their senior year can get college credits at University of Oregon and other institutions of higher learning. Schools adopting the International Baccalaureate program must be accredited by the IB organization. The IB trains teachers, and qualified instructors from other IB schools assess students. An IB program opened at Cleveland in the fall of 1999. Other innovative magnet programs include business management and marketing at Cleveland and professional/ technical studies at Benson.

Most of the Portland High Schools have significant school-business partnerships. Wacker Siltronic Corporation built a million dollar "clean room" in the basement of Benson to train students to work on electronic circuitry and crystals, and the company is funding a teaching position in chemistry. Paragon Cable committed $250,000 to create a shared learning network linking three high school classrooms. Jefferson, Grant and Madison will have simultaneous, two-way video and audio links to facilitate distance learning. Legacy Health Systems, Oregon Health Sciences University, and other organizations are working with Jefferson High School in the new biotech magnet program. The District received a large federal grant for this program.

Portland high school science teachers and their students will work with Oregon State University researchers and undergraduate and graduate students in a program called Science Connection. This is a pilot program bringing research from OSU into the classrooms in Portland. Cleveland science teacher and meteor expert Dick Pugh will lecture at OSU. Terri Lomax, OSU associate professor of botany and plant pathology kicked off the program by bringing her research on mutant tomatoes to science classes at Jefferson in February of 1998. Thirty OSU researchers have signed on to date and the district would like to expand the program into the middle schools.

Grant High School offers Einstein's Universe, a class for seniors that Portland State University offers as Freshman Inquiry Class. The PSU professors work with Grant teachers. Seniors at Grant who take the class can get credit at PSU. One hundred twenty kids took the class in 1997-'98. They received high school English, science and history credits for this challenging two period class. Funding came from a Pew Trust grant.

Many PPS schools have home pages on the Internet (www.pps.k12.or.us). A live, interactive cable television program called "Homework Helpline" offers assistance and general information to students and their families. Broadcast from Vancouver on Channel 30, Tuesdays through Thursdays, from 6:30 to 8:00 p.m., the program allows students to call-in with questions (360/896-4357).

Portland Parks and Recreation runs a program called "Community School" in many of the Portland Public Schools, offering after-school classes and sports programs, including swimming. Indoor pools are housed at Buckman and the Metropolitan Learning Center. Outdoor pools are located at Creston, Grant, Peninsula and Wilson. (Portland Parks and Recreation is listed on page 241; call for a current brochure.)

What Programs are Planned?

Recognizing that there will be fewer opportunities for people with low skills, the Portland Public School District is working to make its programs more challenging. The District announced in 1995 that it would align its graduation standards to meet the new admission requirements for Oregon colleges and universities. These are much higher standards than are currently in place at the high school level and among the highest in the nation. Portland and the state's higher education system received a $1.6 million grant from the Pew Trust to train teachers and restructure Portland's curriculum to fit the new standards.

Furthermore, the District is implementing these standards for all students, not just the college-bound. While the District will expect all students to meet the high standards, they will not expect all students to meet them in the same amount of time. One student may take two months to get through algebra, another may need two years. The State System of Higher Education is currently working with the twelve Portland high schools. Curriculum will be evaluated at each grade level to determine what students will need to know.

Plans call for significant changes in math and science. General math classes, personal finance and pre-algebra classes will be moved down from the high school level to the middle school curriculum. Algebra will be the lowest-level math offered in high school for credit. Science standards will likewise be much higher than they are now. All future Portland high school graduates will have read a broad selection of classical, contemporary and multicultural literature and should be able to communicate in a second language.

The Northwest Association of Schools and Colleges accredits Portland schools. On the following pages, I have listed all of the Portland high schools. I've also listed the middle and elementary schools with special programs or students that perform exceptionally well. Information is also included on magnet programs. The magnet programs are open to all students in the Portland District who meet certain criteria. The Public Information Office (503/916-3304) has information available on the Portland Public Schools Web site (www.pps.k12.or.us). The e-mail address is pubinfo@pps.k12.or.us.

We have listed the OAT scores for PPS. Portland students do not actually take the OAT; they take tests called "Portland Levels." The state accepts these scores as equivalent to the OATs in each of the grades. The district has 30 years of data using the Portland Levels, so it chose not to switch when the state began mandating standardized testing several years ago. Up until 1998, the Portland Levels were calibrated to be at the same level as the OAT. In 1998, they were found to be a little more difficult, thus the scores for some Portland schools may be slightly lower than the scores would have been had students taken the state test.

The state is now going to adopt the "levels" idea and give students in the same grade different tests. Easy, average and hard tests will be available for each grade level. If the teacher is not sure at which level the child should be tested, there will be a 15-minute locator test to determine the level. The theory is that this type of testing will give teachers a more accurate picture of what a student has actually learned in a year. This is particularly true for students well below or well-above average. More information about these changes in the Oregon Assessment Tests will be included in the next edition.

Portland High Schools

Benson High School

546 N.E. 12th Avenue
Portland, OR 97232
℃ **503/916-5100**
FAX 503/916-2690
Grades: 9 through 12
Enrollment: 1,455
Faculty: 80
Founded: 1908

Benson functions only as a Professional/ Technical/ Medical-Dental magnet school. Admission is by application and an essay on why the student wishes to attend. Students must have average or above-average grades and attendance, and they must provide teacher recommendations. During their first two years, Benson students take academic and professional/technical courses. They choose a major area of study at the end of their sophomore year. As juniors and seniors, students spend between two and four periods each day working in their major area. At the senior level, much of the math and English curriculum is integrated with the professional/technical program so students can apply math and English skills to their area of interest. Students who opt for the Health Occupations program apply as eighth graders and go into the four-year program as freshmen. The program serves students interested in such health careers as Certified Nursing Assistant, dental assistant and emergency care. Benson students are involved in active, hands-on learning. When they graduate from high school, students are prepared to enter the workforce and to continue their education.

Benson offers communications technology, including the KBPS radio station, construction technology, manufacturing engineering technology, electric/ electronics engineering technology and industrial mechanics technology. KBPS broadcasts school closures on snow days in eight languages. The drafting technology area includes sketching and blueprint reading, CAD-CAM, and architectural and engineering drafting.

A school-to-work program is in place, and students receive real job experience. Benson has business partnerships with Sequent Computers and Portland Development Commission. Wacker Siltronic built a million-dollar "clean room" in the basement to train students on electronic circuitry and crystals. Every other year architecture students design a house, and construction students build and sell it. The school has offers to buy the next three houses the students build.

SAT Scores 1997:	Verbal: 512	Math: 548
1996:	486	522
1995:	499	526

Number of students taking the test in 1997: 162

OAT Scores 1997 (10th Grade):	Reading: 234	Math: 235
1997 Statewide Average:	236	233
1995 (11th Grade):	235	235
1995 Statewide Average:	235	232

Socioeconomic Rank: 182 of 233 possible

Cleveland High School

3400 S.E. 26th Avenue
Portland, OR 97202
© 503/916-5120
FAX 503/916-5135

Grades: 9 through 12
Enrollment: 1232
Faculty: 89
Founded: 1915
Middle Schools: Hosford and Sellwood

Cleveland established a magnet program in business management and marketing in 1978, offering specialized courses in retailing and business. Magnet students run the Shopping Mall, a group of on-campus student stores. Work experience is gained in unpaid off-campus internships and paid cooperative work experiences. An International Baccalaureate magnet program came on-line in September 1999. The Oregon Department of Fish and Wildlife and the U.S. Forest Service operate a cooperative program at Cleveland that provides field studies and hands-on science activities for students. A student chapter of Northwest Steelheaders teaches fisheries management. The science program includes advanced study classes in chemistry, biology, physics, anatomy and physiology as well as off-campus learning experiences.

Cleveland serves an ethnically and socioeconomically diverse student body. Its foreign language program includes four years of Japanese, plus Spanish, French and German. East Asian studies and a humanities program are also strong in the curriculum. Students who complete advanced placement courses can enroll in the Reed College "Young Scholars" program or Portland State University's "Challenge" program. The school has a joint-venture vocal music program with Hosford Middle School and good visual and performing arts departments. The athletic program is strong. Cleveland boasts a state championship dance team.

The PTA is active; parents volunteer for school activities, and they are developing a foundation to support activities cut by Measure 5.

SAT Scores 1997:	Verbal: 499	Math: 499
1996:	501	510
1995:	509	515
Number taking test 1997: 95		
OAT Scores 1997 (10th Grade):	Reading: 235	Math: 232
1997 Statewide Average:	236	233
1995 (11th Grade):	230	231
1995 Statewide Average:	235	232
Socioeconomic Rank: 183 of 254 possible		

Franklin High School
5405 S.E. Woodward
Portland, OR 97206
✆ **503/916-5140**
FAX 503/916-5780
Grades: 9 through 12
Enrollment: 1564
Faculty: 89
Founded: 1914
Middle Schools: Kellogg and Mt. Tabor

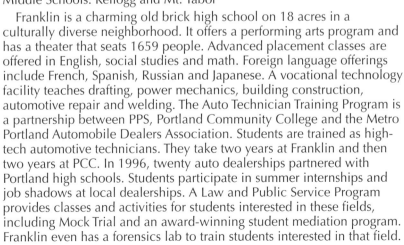

Franklin is a charming old brick high school on 18 acres in a culturally diverse neighborhood. It offers a performing arts program and has a theater that seats 1659 people. Advanced placement classes are offered in English, social studies and math. Foreign language offerings include French, Spanish, Russian and Japanese. A vocational technology facility teaches drafting, power mechanics, building construction, automotive repair and welding. The Auto Technician Training Program is a partnership between PPS, Portland Community College and the Metro Portland Automobile Dealers Association. Students are trained as high-tech automotive technicians. They take two years at Franklin and then two years at PCC. In 1996, twenty auto dealerships partnered with Portland high schools. Students participate in summer internships and job shadows at local dealerships. A Law and Public Service Program provides classes and activities for students interested in these fields, including Mock Trial and an award-winning student mediation program. Franklin even has a forensics lab to train students interested in that field.

A preschool program is available for children of students. There is a large parent volunteer group that helps with athletics, library and counseling. The football field features a grandstand that seats almost 3,000.

SAT Scores 1997:	Verbal: 482	Math: 522
1996:	491	515
1995	477	493
Number taking the test 1997: 99		
OAT Scores 1997 (10th Grade):	Reading: 233	Math: 230
1997 Statewide Average:	236	233
1995 (11th Grade):	233	232
1995 Statewide Average:	235	232
Socioeconomic Rank: 75 of 254 possible		

Grant High School

2245 N.E. 36th
Portland, OR 97212
✆ **503/916-5160**
FAX 503/916-5673
Grades: 9 through 12
Enrollment: 1767
Faculty: 150
Founded: 1924

Middle Schools: Beaumont and Fernwood

Grant High School stands on a lovely site in northeast Portland. You may have seen the building and some of Grant's talented students featured in the film, "Mr. Holland's Opus." The school has an award-winning performing arts department and a reputation for great musicals held in an auditorium that seats almost 1700 people. This neighborhood high school also boasts a heated outdoor pool and tennis courts, and it shares Grant Park with Hollyrood Primary School. With its diverse student body, the school encourages cross-cultural communication and subscribes to the philosophy that "all students can learn and excel."

The school maintains a strong college prep program. The Institute for Science and Math, which includes technology, has received commendations for working toward the national standards. The Grant Educational Alliance helps students find mentors and employment. Students can plan their education with business partners like Bonneville Power, ATT Wireless (formerly Cellular One), US West and the US Forest Service.

Grant parents are very active in the school, logging over 30,000 volunteer hours each year. Athletics are important, and Grant is a frequent title contender. The Library Media Center has on-line information systems. English as a Second Language and other special education services are available, as well as the Multnomah County Teen Health Clinic for primary health care. Night school is held at Grant and Benson.

SAT Scores 1997:	Verbal: 515	Math: 506
1996:	541	543
1995:	512	510
Number taking the test in 1997: 210		
OAT Scores 1997 (10th Grade):	Reading: 235	Math: 233
1997 Statewide Average:	236	233
1995 (11th Grade):	236	234
1995 Statewide Average:	235	232
Socioeconomic Rank: 223 of 254 possible		

Jefferson High School

5210 North Kerby Street
Portland, OR 97217
✆ **503/916-5180**
FAX 503/916-5191
Grades: 9 through 12
Enrollment: 788
Faculty: 84
Founded: 1909
Middle Schools: Ockley Green and Tubman

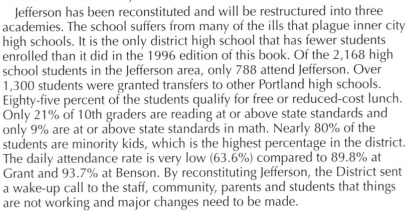

Jefferson has been reconstituted and will be restructured into three academies. The school suffers from many of the ills that plague inner city high schools. It is the only district high school that has fewer students enrolled than it did in the 1996 edition of this book. Of the 2,168 high school students in the Jefferson area, only 788 attend Jefferson. Over 1,300 students were granted transfers to other Portland high schools. Eighty-five percent of the students qualify for free or reduced-cost lunch. Only 21% of 10th graders are reading at or above state standards and only 9% are at or above state standards in math. Nearly 80% of the students are minority kids, which is the highest percentage in the district. The daily attendance rate is very low (63.6%) compared to 89.8% at Grant and 93.7% at Benson. By reconstituting Jefferson, the District sent a wake-up call to the staff, community, parents and students that things are not working and major changes need to be made.

This is a high school that educated generations of immigrant children since opening in 1909 and educated them well. Jefferson has many gifted alumni, and it housed an exceptional performing arts program with a national reputation for excellence. As gang violence increased in the neighborhood in the late 80's along with the perception that the academic program was second-rate, neighborhood students chose Grant, Wilson or Benson. Two out of three students in the Jefferson attendance area attend other high schools. Budget cuts gutted the once stellar performing arts magnet.

Jefferson will have to overcome several problems. The students coming in from the feeder (middle) schools have very low test scores; more that 80% of the eighth graders failed to meet state standards in reading. Parent involvement is low, attendance is low, the drop out rate is high and discipline problems are on the rise. Jefferson started the 98-99 school year with 400 freshman. Over half of those students left during the course of the year. It is going to take more than a committed staff to turn Jeff around. It will take a committed neighborhood. Other inner city schools have done it. Jefferson has an honorable history of great athletic teams (125 state championships), the nationally renowned Jefferson Dancers, an award winning literary journal and a large number of local alumni who are justly proud of their years at Jefferson.

The freshman academy prepares ninth graders for high school with strong classes in math, reading, language arts and science. Then students choose one of two academies for tenth through twelfth grades. One academy offers arts and communication and a health sciences/biotech program. The other offers business and financial services and applied technology. Each academy has no more than 350 students. Teachers will have smaller groups of students, so they should be able to get to know them well. Jefferson is the first PPS high school to implement the research on small high schools.

SAT Scores 1997:	Verbal: 411	Math: 423
1995:	445	441
Number taking test 1997: 75		
OAT Scores 1997 (10th Grade):	Reading: 228	Math: 225
1997 Statewide Average:	236	233
1995 (11th Grade):	232	227
1995 Statewide Average:	235	232
Socioeconomic Rank: 26 of 254 possible		

Lincoln High School

1600 S.W. Salmon
Portland, OR 97205
✆ **503/916-5200**
FAX 503/916-5767

Grades: 9 through 12
Enrollment: 1338
Faculty: 60
Founded: 1869
Middle Schools: West Sylvan

Having celebrated its 125th anniversary on April 29, 1995, Lincoln High School claims distinction as the oldest public high school west of the Rockies. Lincoln houses the International Studies Center (ISC) and

Advanced Foreign Languages magnet program for the Portland Public Schools. Lincoln offers the International Baccalaureate curriculum in the International Studies program, which is an internationally recognized college prep curriculum. Students in the International Studies program are required to volunteer at international organizations in Portland. ISC staff facilitates student exchange programs and off-campus learning opportunities.

Nearly half of Lincoln students are in the International Studies magnet program, and the school produces the highest average SAT scores in the district. Arabic, Italian and Swahili are among the foreign languages offered. Students who have gone through the Spanish immersion programs at Ainsworth and West Sylvan complete their studies here. The school offers many extracurricular programs, including Model United Nations and the Constitutional Debate Team, which has twice won national championships. Lincoln has a fine sports program; the Cardinals are frequent title contenders.

Lincoln has been successful in involving parents as volunteers at the school through the PTA, the Booster Club and the site council. Family and community members help with campus monitoring, work in the library and classrooms, tutor, and chaperone field trips.

SAT Scores 1997:	Verbal: 597	Math: 589
1996:	595	583
1995	585	572
Number taking the test 1997: 238		
OAT Scores 1997 (10th Grade):	Reading: 244	Math: 240
1997 Statewide Average:	236	233
1995 (11th Grade):	Reading: 238	Math: 238
1995 Statewide Average:	235	232
Socioeconomic Rank: 253 of 254 possible		

Madison High School
2735 N.E. 82nd
Portland, OR 97220
✆ **503/916-5220**
FAX 503/916-5220, ext. 431
Grades: 9 through 12
Enrollment: 1243
Faculty: 90
Founded: 1957
Middle Schools: Gregory Heights and Whitaker

Madison and adjoining Glenhaven Park occupy one of the largest pieces of property in the district. The 34-acre site holds tennis courts, a lighted football field, and 4,000-seat grandstand. The spacious gym seats 1,800 in the bleachers, and the auditorium holds 1,300. Because Madison has an elevator, all parts of the building are wheelchair accessible.

Madison has a new business partnership program with the Agribusiness Council of Oregon and Oregon State University College of Agricultural Sciences that is designed to give students information about careers in agriculture. Core courses, such as math and science, utilize agricultural topics to convey the subject matter. There is a "school within a school" alternative program for kids having difficulties. The Teen Health Center provides medical care for students, and the school provides special services for teen parents.

SAT Scores 1997:	Verbal: 459	Math: 476
1996:	490	476
1995	401	466
Number taking the test 1997: 79		
OAT Scores 1997 (10th Grade):	Reading: 233	Math: 230
1997 Statewide Average:	236	233
1995 (11th Grade):	232	229
1995 Statewide Average:	235	232
Socioeconomic Rank: 52 of 254 possible		

Marshall High School
905 S.E. 91st
Portland, OR 97266
© **503/916-5240**
FAX 503/916-5246
Grades: 9 through 12
Enrollment: 1277
Faculty: 125
Founded: 1960
Middle Schools: Binnsmead and Lane

Marshall High School boasts the Technology Learning Center Academy. Students here have developed multi-media information kiosks on the Columbia River Gorge for Skamania Lodge, on the Trailblazers for the Oregon History Center's Blazermania exhibit and on Native American music, art, bead work and coyote stories for the Tamustalik Cultural Institute near Pendleton. Marshall has business partnerships with Intel, Portland Trailblazers, Fred Meyer, Bonneville Power and Skamania Lodge. The school is actively working to develop school-to-work transition programs. *The Verdict*, the student newspaper, has won national and state awards.

This high school has identified its mission as a "high-touch, high-tech, high-performance school for the 21st Century." Students have credit-card-sized laser cards that hold their portfolios, which include thousands of pages of data, homework and completed projects. Marshall is moving towards a school-within-a-school model to provide students with a more personal learning environment. An alternative program called Marshall Alternative School House (MASH) is available for students having trouble in the traditional program. It features smaller class sizes and computer learning programs.

SAT Scores 1997:	Verbal: 448	Math: 494
1996:	444	482
1995	419	484
Number taking the test 1997: 60		
OAT Scores 1997 (10th Grade):	Reading: 231	Math: 231
1997 Statewide Average:	236	233
1995 (11th Grade):	229	227
1995 Statewide Average:	235	232
Socioeconomic Rank: 22 of 254 possible		

2

Metropolitan Learning Center High School
2033 N.W. Glisan
Portland, OR 97209
℃ **503/916-5737**
FAX 503/916-5740
Grades: 9 through 12
Enrollment: 162
Faculty: 6
Founded: 1968

Metropolitan Learning Center was founded in the Couch School for students who wanted to assess and plan their own education. Now an alternative school (K-12), the program has long-since taken over the whole building. Cross-grade classrooms prevail throughout the school, which promotes a non-competitive atmosphere with no letter grades. The high school students and teachers work together to develop a program that meets each individual student's needs and abilities. Students are expected to make personal choices about their educational needs and take responsibility for their own education. Here, you find more flexibility than in traditional programs. Classes are held from 8:45 to 5:30 to accommodate varied schedules and a teenager's biorhythms.

The program offers many opportunities for off-campus learning. A student might take half of the day at MLC and the other half at another Portland area high school, for example. There are also placements with

Portland area colleges, OMSI, the Portland Art Museum and other programs. MLC believes in volunteer community service for its high school students. This magnet program is super for some kids. It's difficult to get into; admission is by application and interview.

SAT Scores 1997:	Verbal: 551	Math: 483
1996:	563	463
1995	495	457
Number of students taking the test in 1997: 14		
OAT Scores 1997 (10th Grade): Reading: 244	Math: 235	
1997 Statewide Average:	236	233
1995 (11th Grade):	236	230
1995 Statewide Average:	235	232
Socioeconomic Rank: 241 of 254 possible		

Roosevelt High School

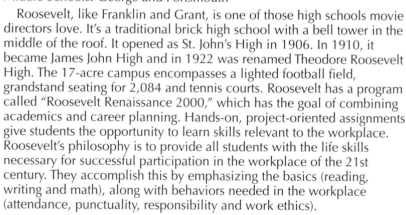

6941 North Central
Portland, OR 97203
✆ **503/916-5260**
FAX 503/916-5663
Grades: 9 through 12
Enrollment: 1205
Faculty: 59
Founded: 1906
Middle Schools: George and Portsmouth

Roosevelt, like Franklin and Grant, is one of those high schools movie directors love. It's a traditional brick high school with a bell tower in the middle of the roof. It opened as St. John's High in 1906. In 1910, it became James John High and in 1922 was renamed Theodore Roosevelt High. The 17-acre campus encompasses a lighted football field, grandstand seating for 2,084 and tennis courts. Roosevelt has a program called "Roosevelt Renaissance 2000," which has the goal of combining academics and career planning. Hands-on, project-oriented assignments give students the opportunity to learn skills relevant to the workplace. Roosevelt's philosophy is to provide all students with the life skills necessary for successful participation in the workplace of the 21st century. They accomplish this by emphasizing the basics (reading, writing and math), along with behaviors needed in the workplace (attendance, punctuality, responsibility and work ethics).

Students can choose a career pathway in business and management, health services, manufacturing technology and engineering, natural sciences and resources, human services, trade and tourism or arts and communications. A "Job Shadow" program provides at least one opportunity for all freshmen to explore a career. Sophomores "shadow" workers in two different career paths. Internships and more structured work experiences involving almost 100 businesses follow in the junior and senior year. Roosevelt is a national model for this kind of school-to-work education.

The school meets student health needs through a Teen Health Clinic. Twenty-seven trained student mediators facilitate disagreements between students and between students and staff. Programs are on line for Drug and Alcohol Counseling and Anger Management counseling. Roosevelt also has a Teen Parent Program. Community involvement is furthered with business and community members serving in the school as mentors and as advisers to both students and teachers.

SAT Scores 1997:	Verbal: 470	Math: 471
1996:	468	484
1995:	401	461
Number of students taking the test in 1997: 59		
OAT Scores 1997 (10th Grade):	Reading: 231	Math: 230
1997 Statewide Average:	236	233
1995 (11th Grade):	233	231
1995 Statewide Average:	235	232
Socioeconomic Rank: 28 of 254 possible		

Vocational Village High School
8020 N.E. Tillamook
Portland, OR 97213
ⓒ **503/916-5747**
Grades: Ages 16-21
Enrollment: 240
Faculty: 23
Founded: 1968

This is a program for students who have not been successful in traditional high school programs. Learning is individualized, self-paced and ungraded. Students can earn a GED, a regular high school diploma or receive certificates of competency in certain vocations. Vocational Village has an open enrollment policy. Students can leave the school and return to complete their competencies until they are 21.

Nine vocations are offered: Child Care, Food Service, Graphic Design and Production, Home Repair Training, Health Occupations, Marketing, Manufacturing Technology, Mechanical Technology, and Office Systems. Each student chooses one focus. Students needing jobs are provided with on-site employment help. There are on-site counseling services, including programs for drug and alcohol problems. A Teen Parent Program, Conflict Managers/ Peer Helper Program and English as a Second Language Program are also available on-site. Students have access to Madison High School's Teen Health Clinic.

Students who apply for this program go through an intake process with their family. The school seeks to support the student's family with information, guidance and other resources. Staff members advocate for students who are living on their own.

OAT Scores 1997 (10th Grade):	Reading: 229	Math: 225
1997 Statewide Average:	236	233
1995 (11th Grade):	Reading: 231	Math: 228
1995 Statewide Average:	235	232
Socioeconomic Rank: 3 of 254 possible		

Wilson High School

1151 S.W. Vermont Street
Portland, OR 97219
© **503/916-5280**
FAX 503/916-2705
Grades: 9 through 12
Enrollment: 1503
Faculty: 120
Founded: 1956
Middle Schools: Robert Gray and Jackson

Wilson is located in southwest Portland on a 20-acre campus next to Rieke Elementary School. The surrounding community values education, and the PTA and Booster Club actively support the school with funds and volunteers. The school offers approximately two hundred courses including a broad range of electives. Wilson has a strong honors program and a culture of academic excellence. Over the last ten years, 86% of graduates have gone on to college. Students do well on the SAT and the ACT. Music and drama performances are encouraged and supported by the community. Five times since 1973 the school newspaper has won the national Pacemaker Award, which is given annually to the five best high school newspapers in the nation. Wilson also has an excellent athletics program and is a frequent contender for state titles. An outdoor pool on campus is used for physical education.

The only problem with Wilson is its size. It's a three-story high school with fifteen hundred students. All classes are big, particularly freshman math and English classes. It takes a very talented teacher to convey algebra to 40 kids (with some sitting on the floor because there are not enough desks). Wilson has tried block schedules, mod schedules and regular 50-minute period schedules. Students who must go from the second floor at one end of the building to a class on the first floor in another end do so at a run. What might work best is dividing the building into smaller academies, as Jefferson is doing. A conference on Restructuring the American High School was held at Wilson in the summer of 1997. Hopefully, the administration at Wilson will use some of the findings of this conference to mitigate the problems the size creates. Students are involved in Model United Nations, Outdoor School and sports. Many Wilson students are going to do well anywhere, but some kids feel anonymous and have a hard time staying engaged. It is difficult to build a sense of community in a school this big.

SAT Scores 1997:	Verbal: 548	Math: 546
1996:	528	535
1995	474	537
Number of students taking the test in 1997: 210		
OAT Scores 1997 (10th Grade):	Reading: 242	Math: 237
1997 Statewide Average:	236	233
1995 (11th Grade):	237	236
1995 Statewide Average:	235	232
Socioeconomic Rank: 247 of 254 possible		

Portland Middle Schools with Special Programs

Beaumont Middle School

4043 N.E. Fremont
Portland, OR 97212
✆ 503/916-5610
FAX 503/916-2609

Grades: 6 through 8
Enrollment: 720
Faculty: 55
Founded: 1914
Cluster: Grant

A neighborhood middle school, Beaumont offers French and Spanish classes for students in grades seven and eight. Jefferson High School dance teachers offer classes here in African dance and tap. Beaumont has a weather station in the 8th grade science room that allows students to see the earth via a student-built satellite dish hook-up. Electives include marine biology and television production through Jefferson's TV Services. The music program features strings, band, chorus and a volunteer jazz band.

Students from Beaumont and Grant High School are involved in a U.S. West Communication project, producing a magazine about the company's products and services. Students work on all aspects of the publication from interviewing and research on the Internet to desktop publishing and even deal with financial aspects of the magazine.

OAT Scores 1998 (8th Grade):	Reading: 232	Math: 232
1998 Statewide Average:	231	231
1995 (8th Grade):	230	237
1995 Statewide Average:	228	230
Socioeconomic Rank: 313of 355 possible		

Da Vinci Arts Middle School

2508 N.E. Everett
Portland, OR 97232
℃ 503/916-5356
FAX 503/916-2721

Grades: 6 through 8
Enrollment: 300
Faculty: 12
Founded: 1996
Cluster: Magnet

This arts-infused middle school program offers dance, drama, art, photography, film and video, textiles, cartooning, strings, band and chorus in a small school setting. The academic program includes language arts, science, math and social studies. Students are placed in multi-age groupings. Emphasis is on problem solving, the application and integration of knowledge and higher-order thinking skills. The program seeks to capitalize on middle school students' needs for self-expression by integrating arts into the curriculum and offering specialized arts instruction.

After-school sports are offered by Portland Parks, and transportation is available to Jefferson for advanced study in dance and music. Created in 1996 to be the middle school link between Buckman Elementary Arts Magnet School and the Jefferson High School Performing and Visual Arts Program, da Vinci is located in the old Monroe High School. Now that Jefferson is reconstituting into three academies, there is some uncertainty about how the programs will be linked in the future. PASA (Portland Advocates for Student Arts), an organization committed to putting the arts back into the public schools, is raising $2 million to refurbish the portion of the building da Vinci uses.

As a magnet program, da Vinci is open to all students in the Portland School District with an interest in the arts. Admission is by application and recommendations are required from the applicant's current school. Decisions are based on grades, attendance, attitude and behavior. Each family is expected to contribute 20 volunteer hours per year in support of the school. Prospective parents are asked to fill out a form showing what they are willing to do as part of their child's admissions process. Options range from scrounging arts materials to grant writing. Transportation to the school is the responsibility of the student's family and is not provided by the district. This is a great new program. If it fits your child's interests, check it out.

OAT Scores 1998 (8th Grade):	Reading: 238	Math: 236
1998 Statewide Average:	231	231
1997 N/A new program		
Socioeconomic Rank: N/A		

Environmental Middle School at Abernethy

2121 S.E. Orange Street
Portland, OR 97214
✆ **503/916-6490**

Grades: 6 through 8
Enrollment: 180
Faculty: 6
Founded:1997
Cluster: Cleveland

This is a special program that draws students from all over Portland. Admission is by application. Students spend several days each week learning outdoors. Students work on gardening and restoration projects in the city's green spaces and parks. Community service is part of the program as is learning from their relationship with the natural environment. EMS offers a small school environment with mixed-age groups. The curriculum includes an appreciation for Native American culture and its relationship to the environment.

OAT Scores 1998 8th Grade):	Reading: 236	Math: 238
1998 Statewide Average:	231	231
1997 (8th Grade):	233	239
1997 Statewide Average:	231	231
Socioeconomic Rank: 333 of 355 possible		

Fernwood Middle School

1915 N.E. 33rd
Portland, OR 97212
✆ **503/916-6480**

Grades: 6 through 8
Enrollment: 654
Faculty: 32
Founded: 1887
Cluster: Grant

In addition to the normal middle school electives, Fernwood offers Spanish, French, health occupations, computers, film study, orchestra, band and choral. Two hundred students participate in the music program, and ninety are involved in the vocal group, "No! Kidding!" Participants in the school's music program are given the opportunity to travel and perform. Advanced math is offered at each grade level, with algebra available in eighth grade.

Students keep the same advisor for the three years at Fernwood, and that advisor serves as an advocate for the student. Conflict resolution is handled through peer mediators and a conflict-manager program. The Portland Park Bureau runs an after-school sports program.

OAT Scores 1998 (8th Grade):	Reading: 235	Math: 239
1998 Statewide Average:	231	231
1995 (8th Grade):	230	239
1995 Statewide Average:	228	230
Socioeconomic Rank: 316 of 355 possible		

Health Sciences Biotechnology Magnet at Harriet Tubman Middle School

2231 North Flint
Portland, OR 97227
℃ **503/916-5630**

Grades: 6 through 8
Enrollment: 518
Faculty: 45
Founded: 1995
Cluster: Jefferson

Tubman is one of three schools participating in the Health Sciences/-Biotechnology Magnet Program, which is modeled on the "school-as-laboratory" format. It seeks to engage students in the work of scientists in a laboratory setting as well as field studies. Partners in the program are Legacy Health Systems, OHSU and Providence Health System. Volunteers from Legacy visit classrooms and provide individual tutoring. Students visit Emanuel Hospital to see health care professionals at work. Elective courses, including zoology, marine biology, biotechnology, Science Technology Applied Research (S.T.A.R.) Lab and Spanish are available for all students to take. After school classes include science, math and technology.

OAT Scores 1998 (8th Grade):	Reading: 225	Math: 224
1998 Statewide Average	231	231
1997 (8th Grade)	222	219
1997 Statewide Average:	231	231
Socioeconomic Rank: 40 of 355 possible		

Jackson Middle School

10625 S.W. 35th
Portland, OR 97219
℃ **503/916-5680**

Grades: 6 through 8
Enrollment: 740
Faculty: 50
Founded: 1966
Cluster: Wilson

In another life, Jackson was a high school. Its 39-acre campus offers great athletic facilities, including an all weather track, tennis courts and a gym that seats 1,180 in the bleachers. The school has an extensive Community School program; its brochure is sent out citywide. Students have an advisory group that meets daily to give each child a sense of belonging and personal support. Jackson is sufficiently large to allow each grade level its own geographical area in the building, which creates a kind of school-within-a-school. Jackson's philosophy is one of supporting the emotional growth of preadolescents and promoting a positive self-image, personal and social responsibility, cooperative behavior and good decision-making skills.

All Jackson students take Spanish and physical education on an every-other-day schedule. Other electives include vocal, instrumental music, and integrated arts (visual, dramatic and communication arts). Nearly half the student body participates in either choir or band.

OAT Scores 1998 (8th Grade):	Reading: 236	Math: 241
1998 Statewide Average:	231	231
1995 (8th Grade):	235	246
1995 Statewide Average:	228	230
Socioeconomic Rank: 342 of 355 possible		

Metropolitan Learning Center Middle School

2033 N.W. Glisan   Grades: 7 through 8
Portland, OR 97209   Enrollment: 88
℡ **503/916-5737**   Faculty: 3.5
FAX 503/916-5740   Founded: 1968
                              Cluster: Magnet Alternative School

The seventh and eighth grade teaching team at MLC focuses on social responsibility, group dynamics, interpersonal skills and cooperative learning in a student-centered learning environment where students take responsibility for their own education. The school practices cross-age grouping to allow all students to nurture and to be nurtured. Middle school students spend mornings rotating through language arts, math and social studies. Afternoon classes offer a wide range of electives. Scholars in the Public Schools (SIPS) bring professionals into the classrooms to teach electives, give workshops, and help with special projects. Field trips are an integral part of the MLC experience. Admission is by application and interview. It is not easy to get in, and my advice is to think ahead and start early if this program sounds right for your child.

OAT Scores 1997 (8th Grade):	Reading: 234	Math: 243
1997 Statewide Average:	231	231
1995 (8th Grade):	238	249
1995 Statewide Average:	228	230
Socioeconomic Rank: 346 of 355 possible		

Mt. Tabor Middle School

5800 S.E. Ash
Portland, OR 97215
© **503/916-5646**

Grades: 6 through 8
Enrollment: 664
Faculty: 34
Founded: 1910
Cluster: Franklin

In September 1995, the first group of graduates of the Japanese immersion program at Richmond Elementary School arrived at Mt. Tabor. This school will become a magnet for Japanese Immersion and will offer both Japanese and Spanish as foreign language electives. It has a large English as a Second Language program, as well. Mt. Tabor's student body focuses on respecting diversity.

The band and marching band are strong here. Cedar Lodge, a school-within-a-school program, involves 120 students, 40 from each grade level. Mt. Tabor also supports community service activities for its students, who volunteer in their communities and raise money to purchase wetlands. The school has Peer Helpers, Peer Tutors and a wellness program that promotes lifelong health practices. There's a lot of parent support, including input into instructional activities planning. Portland Community Schools offers a variety of classes for kids and adults on the Mt. Tabor campus.

OAT Scores 1997 (8th Grade):	Reading: 231	Math: 239
1997 Statewide Average:	231	231
1995 (8th Grade):	229	239
1995 Statewide Average:	228	230
Socioeconomic Rank: 314 of 355 possible		

Northeast Community School

4013 NE 18th
Portland, OR 97227
© **503/916-6335**

Grades: 5 through 8
Enrollment: 60
Faculty: 8
Founded:1996
Cluster: Grant

This is a small school in which teachers, students and families work with the community to provide a rich, nurturing environment for learning. Goals include development of self-esteem; ability to think deeply, critically and creatively; appreciation and understanding of diversity fostered through experience. NCS is located in the Sabin Elementary School.

OAT Scores 1998 (8th Grade):	Reading: 228	Math: 231
1998 Statewide Average	231	231
1997 (8th Grade)	234	236
1997 Statewide Average:	231	231
Socioeconomic Rank: 318 of 355 possible		

Robert Gray Middle School

5505 S.W. 23rd
Portland, OR 97201
℃ 503/916-5676

Grades: 6 through 8
Enrollment: 540
Faculty: 25
Founded: 1953
Cluster: Wilson

Robert Gray is a small, academically strong middle school tucked into a woodsy setting just off the Beaverton-Hillsdale Highway on a 13-acre site with an adjoining park. Curriculum options include a two-hour, integrated language arts and social studies block class called "Humanities." Students are required to take one term of Spanish annually. Robert Gray has an ESL program for thirty students from 20 countries. A Peer Helper program is in place for conflict resolution. Peer Tutoring and tutoring through Neighborhood House, Inc. are readily available. The school has a high number of TAG students.

Electives include band, choir, home economics, technology (computers), drama, and study skills. The school has an activity bus for students participating in after-school sports or classes. Sports programs are administered through the Portland Parks Department.

OAT Scores 1997 (8th Grade):	Reading: 233	Math: 247
1997 Statewide Average:	231	231
1995 (8th Grade):	231	245
1995 Statewide Average:	228	230
Socioeconomic Rank: 328 of 355 possible		

Sellwood Middle School

8300 S.E. 15th
Portland, OR 97202
℃ 503/916-5656
FAX 503/916-6530

Grades: 6 through 8
Enrollment: 550
Faculty: 24
Founded: 1884
Cluster: Cleveland

Sellwood has two teaching teams. The largest is a grade-level team called "Ohana," which means "family" in Hawaiian. At the 6th grade level, students are with one teacher all day except for two exploratory classes. In 7th and 8th grade, students have a three-period language arts/ social studies block, a math class, science class, and health class in addition to two electives. This team offers advanced math classes. Portfolios and ongoing assessment are used and letter grades are given on report cards.

The second team is the multi-age team with 6th, 7th and 8th grade students in each class. Students in these five classrooms remain with the same teacher for three years. One teacher teaches all content areas, with the exception of the two electives. Students use goal setting and portfolio-assessment to guide their learning. No grades are given on report cards. Students present their portfolios and expert projects at several points throughout the year.

Sellwood has an outstanding exploratory program including an award-winning band and an art program that focuses on community service through art. All students also have access to technology. Sellwood's philosophy of creating smaller communities within the school helps students get to know their teachers better and feel more a part of the school.

OAT Scores 1998 (8th Grade):	Reading: 234	Math: 236
1998 Statewide Average:	231	231
1995 (8th Grade):	229	239
1995 Statewide Average:	228	230
Socioeconomic Rank: 305 of 355 possible		

West Sylvan Middle School

8111 S.W. West Slope Drive
Portland, OR 97225
℃ 503/916-5690

Grades: 6 through 8
Enrollment: 890
Faculty: 60
Founded: 1893
Cluster: Lincoln

West Sylvan is a very good middle school with a very involved parent body. The school population, however, exceeds the number of students it was built to serve when it opened in 1954, so it is crowded. West Sylvan was the District's magnet school for the Spanish immersion program. However, due to budget cuts, social studies is no longer taught in Spanish. The immersion students have one period a day in Spanish language arts.

Interdisciplinary teams teach language arts, social studies, math, science and some electives. New science labs promote hands-on learning. Math teacher Dick Brannon has won a national award. The school offers a wide range of electives in academic fields, visual and performing arts and technology. Students use computers for research and word processing. An after-school program that offers chess, sports, theater, foreign language and other classes runs on Tuesdays, Wednesdays and Thursdays. A special activity bus takes students home after the program.

OAT Scores 1998 (8th Grade):	Reading: 239	Math: 243
1998 Statewide Average:	231	231
1995 (8th Grade)	239	250
1995 Statewide Average:	228	230
Socioeconomic Rank: 350 of 355 possible		

WinterHaven

3830 S.E. 14th
Portland, OR 97202
© 503/916-6200

Grades: 1 through 8
Enrollment: 130
Faculty: 5
Founded:1996
Cluster: Magnet

WinterHaven emphasizes the development of intellect, character and creativity with a focus on math, science and technology. Special interest classes and community service are an integral part of the program. See the listing on page 84 under elementary schools.

OAT Scores 1998 (8th Grade):	Reading: 243	Math: 247
1998 Statewide Average	231	231
1997 (8th Grade)	N/A (new program)	
Socioeconomic Rank: not ranked at 8th grade. (ranked 749 of 750 possible at 5th grade		

Other Portland Middle School OAT Scores (1997 and 1998)

Binnsmead

OAT Scores 1998 (8th Grade):	Reading: 224	Math: 225
1998 Statewide Average	231	231
1997 (8th Grade)	226	226
1997 Statewide Average:	231	231
Socioeconomic Rank: 44 of 355 possible		

George

OAT Scores 1998 (8th Grade):	Reading: 223	Math: 221
1998 Statewide Average	231	231
1997 (8th Grade)	223	220
1997 Statewide Average:	231	231
Socioeconomic Rank: 13 of 355 possible		

Gregory Heights

OAT Scores 1998 (8th Grade):	Reading: 227	Math: 233
1998 Statewide Average	231	231
1997 (8th Grade)	229	233
1997 Statewide Average:	231	231
Socioeconomic Rank: 136 of 355 possible		

Hosford

OAT Scores 1998 (8th Grade):	Reading: 229	Math: 232
1998 Statewide Average	231	231
1997 (8th Grade)	230	231
1997 Statewide Average:	231	231
Socioeconomic Rank: 106 of 355 possible		

Kellogg

OAT Scores 1998 (8th Grade):	Reading: 226	Math: 228
1998 Statewide Average	231	231
1997 (8th Grade)	226	228
1997 Statewide Average:	231	231
Socioeconomic Rank: 66 of 355 possible		

Lane

OAT Scores 1998 (8th Grade):	Reading: 222	Math: 222
1998 Statewide Average	231	231
1997 (8th Grade)	226	225
1997 Statewide Average:	231	231

Socioeconomic Rank: 30 of 355 possible

Ockley Green

OAT Scores 1998 (8th Grade):	Reading: 224	Math: 223
1998 Statewide Average	231	231
1997 (8th Grade)	224	222
1997 Statewide Average:	231	231

Socioeconomic Rank: 93 of 355 possible

Portsmouth

OAT Scores 1998 (8th Grade):	Reading: 225	Math: 221
1998 Statewide Average	231	231
1997 (8th Grade)	225	220
1997 Statewide Average:	231	231

Socioeconomic Rank: 36 of 355 possible

Whitaker

OAT Scores 1998 (8th Grade):	Reading: 221	Math: 222
1998 Statewide Average	231	231
1997 (8th Grade)	222	221
1997 Statewide Average:	231	231

Socioeconomic Rank: 25 of 355 possible

Portland Elementary Schools with Special Programs

Ainsworth Elementary School

2425 S.W. Vista Avenue
Portland, OR 97201
© **503/916-6288**
FAX 503/916-6546

Grades: K through 5
Enrollment: 530
Faculty: 22
Founded: 1885
Cluster: Lincoln, West Sylvan Middle School

Ainsworth houses the District's first language immersion program, which was founded in 1986. Three hundred and eight students here get half-day of instruction in Spanish and half-day in English. Kindergarten is a full-day program for these students. Students who are not in the Spanish immersion program also have access to full-day kindergarten, but on a fee-for-service basis, which is currently about $120 a month. In the regular school program, students have Spanish class three times a week. The library has a large collection of Spanish materials.

While the Spanish program is open to all residents of Portland, thirty percent of openings are reserved for Ainsworth-area children, twenty percent for Hispanic children and fifty percent from the remainder of the Portland School District. A lottery is held in the spring to determine admission. Siblings of children already enrolled in the program are given preference. Over 200 applicants compete for 54 kindergarten spots.

Ainsworth offers after-school care, PTA-sponsored language classes, OMSI classes and other activities, including athletic programs organized by the community and Parks Bureau.

Alameda Elementary School

2732 N.E. Fremont
Portland, OR 97212
© **503/916-6036**

Grades: K through 5
Enrollment: 696
Faculty: 31
Founded: 1914
Cluster: Grant, Beaumont Middle School

An attractive yellow and white building, Alameda is one of the largest elementary schools in the District. It won a national award for academic achievement several years ago, and parents are very involved in the school. A program called PEACH (Parents for Enrichment, Achievement, and Challenge) provides extra support for enrichment activities. The school is currently involved in a community playground project. Parents volunteer in the school and serve on the advisory committee.

The school offers family nights in math and science. DARE (Drug Awareness Resistance Education) is a part of the fifth grade curriculum. Third graders study the city of Portland in social studies class and get help from a program called Architects-in-the-Schools. Currently Alameda does not offer after-school care, but after-school programs include Scouts, chess, foreign language classes and Portland Community Schools.

Atkinson Elementary School

5800 S.E. Division
Portland, OR 97206
℘ 503/916-6333

Grades: K through 5
Enrollment: 535
Faculty: 21
Founded: 1868
Cluster: Franklin

Atkinson shares adjoining park space with Franklin High School. The school offers a Spanish/English Two Way Immersion in Grades K and 1 only. Mixed groups of native English- and native Spanish-speaking students receive 2½ days of instruction in English and 2½ days in Spanish in mixed-age K/1 classes to build proficiency in both languages through age-appropriate, real-world experiences.

Beach Elementary School

1710 North Humboldt Street
Portland, OR 97217
℘ 503/916-6236

Grades: Pre-K through 5
Enrollment: 722
Faculty: 38
Founded: 1920
Cluster: Jefferson, Ockley Green
Middle School

Beach is an Early Childhood Education Center with a pre-kindergarten program. The school has a philosophy of early intervention and prevention, and Beach is working to help students succeed. Medical, social, and nutritional needs, as well as family problems, are managed through interagency cooperation under a program called Caring Community. Beach was one of 180 schools nationwide to win the 1991 National Elementary School Recognition sponsored by the United States Department of Education.

A two-way Spanish/ English bilingual program was introduced in 1994-95 in mixed age kindergarten/ first grade classes. Beach has a large Hispanic population, and the program, which will add a grade level each year, is getting a lot of positive feedback. Beach also has the largest English as a Second Language population in the Portland Public Schools. The school teaches pluralism, diversity and the role each individual plays in the success of the whole. This is a good example of a neighborhood school playing to its strengths.

Boise-Eliot Early Childhood Education Center

620 North Fremont Street
Portland, OR 97227
© 503/916-6171

Grades: Pre-K through 8
Enrollment: 696
Faculty: 85
Founded: 1876
Cluster: Jefferson

Boise-Eliot is a voluntarily integrated school with a diverse student body, a devoted group of parents, and a very low staff-turnover rate. Parents and volunteers put in over 8,000 hours annually at the school. The school offers half-day pre-kindergarten and all-day kindergarten programs in addition to before- and after-school care. Boise-Eliot introduces foreign language and cultural studies in pre-kindergarten through fifth grade. The program expanded in the fall of 1995 to include the middle school grades. The Jeanette Crawley Scholarship Fund provides funds for alumni to continue their education at public universities and technical programs in Oregon.

Multi-age classrooms and teachers who stay with the same class for two or more years are both available at Boise-Eliot. Artist residencies provide all children with hands-on art experience. The school is available for "Family Evenings" for computers, gym and academic work. Parenting classes and a grandparent support group are also offered.

Students must register for this program. Neighborhood children are admitted first. Second preference is given to students from feeder schools: Astor, Clarendon, George, Glencoe, Hollyrood, James John, Kenton, Peninsula, Richmond, Sitton and portions of Laurelhurst. Students outside this area are admitted last and are currently being wait-listed.

Bridlemile Elementary School

4300 S.W. 47th Drive
Portland, OR 97221
© 503/916-3614
FAX 503/916 2613

Grades: K through 5
Enrollment: 460
Faculty: 35
Founded: 1958
Cluster: Lincoln, West Sylvan
Middle School

The school and parents have high expectations for students here. They've identified the school's mission as one of empowering students to become self-directed, lifelong learners and contributing members of the community. Bridlemile has a high percentage of students in the Talented and Gifted program. Band and strings are offered for fourth and fifth graders. Junior Great Books, Odyssey of the Mind, the Bridlemile Writers Conference and writers-in-residence are some of the special programs. In 1998-'99, Bridlemile began a full-day kindergarten program. Parents must pay tuition for the extra half-day.

Before- and after-school care is provided by the Vermont Hills Family Life Center. After-school programs include Campfire, Scouts, Goldenball basketball, soccer, Little League, language classes, etc. An active parent body volunteers in the school and raises funds.

Buckman Elementary School

320 S.E. 16th
Portland, OR 97214
© **503/916-6230**

Grades: K through 5
Enrollment: 525
Faculty: 27
Founded: 1887
Cluster: Cleveland, Hosford
        Middle School

Buckman is the magnet arts elementary program for the District. All students at Buckman participate in the arts program; art is integrated into the curriculum and the staff includes full-time teachers for dance, drama, visual arts and music.

Thirty percent of Buckman students are from racial or ethnic minority families; more than sixteen languages are spoken. The school uses a variety of programs to meet its students' needs. There's an English as a Second Language program, a Reading Recovery Program, and mixed-age classrooms. Buckman is one of five Portland elementary schools in Project SAIL (Science and Integrated Language), that uses hands-on science activities to improve the child's command of English. Internet-access is part of this program, which is designed for students in grades 3 through 5.

Buckman has won a number of awards for its ESL and arts programs; both the teaching and the administrative staff have been recognized as outstanding. Buckman is one of those PPS programs that began with someone's dream of making a difference for kids. Former Principal Candace Beck had read the research on bringing a strong arts program into the elementary level to motivate kids and help reach all types of learners. She convinced the district to fund an arts magnet program at Buckman. Enrollment went up and test scores are up and the parents I talked to love the school. Actively involved parents put in over 10,000 volunteer hours annually and raised over $40,000 in 1997. Macintosh computers are in use in all of the classrooms. Buckman was the first PPS elementary school to be connected to Internet. (http://buckman.pps.k12.or.us/buckman.html) The facility also has an indoor pool where students learn to swim as part of their physical education classes. Students who do not live in the Buckman neighborhood must apply for admission. Plan ahead and apply for kindergarten where the greatest number of openings occurs.

Chapman Elementary School

1445 N.W. 26th
Portland, OR 97210
© 503/916-6295

Grades: K through 5
Enrollment: 547
Faculty: 26
Founded: 1891
Cluster: Lincoln, West Sylvan
Middle School

Chapman has an all-day kindergarten, which uses the "Write to Read" program. Writing is further supported in the school's Chapman Publishing House and an in-house postal system called "Bear Mail." The Oregon Elementary School Principals Association recognized Chapman in 1997 for the Chapman-Good Samaritan Hospital Business-School Partnership. Chapman won a National Elementary School Recognition Award sponsored by the United States Department of Education in 1989-90 and an Oregon Education Pioneer Award in 1992-93 for a program called "Circle of Friends," which is designed to build school/community spirit.

The parent body is active. Chapman had one of the first parent-funded educational foundations. There is a site council, an advisory committee, and an active PTA. Before- and after-school care is provided by Friendly Chaps. Portland Community School programs are also available.

Duniway Elementary School

7700 S.E. Reed College Place
Portland, OR 97202
© 503/916-6343

Grades: K through 5
Enrollment: 446
Faculty: 23
Founded: 1877
Cluster: Cleveland, Sellwood
Middle School

Duniway is a lovely brick building designed by architect George Jones to look like the original Reed College buildings. The school has a computer lab and a technology plan to prepare students for the future, as well as a strong music program and marching band. It also offers after-school foreign language classes in Japanese, French, German and Spanish. Facilities include two gyms and a wonderful auditorium.

The school's philosophy is one of high expectations for all children. Peer tutoring and a buddy system are available to help build friendship and nurturing skills. An active PTA sponsors such fundraisers as the Holiday Tour of Homes and Show of Hands, a professional artists show. Duniway has before- and after-school care.

Edwards Elementary School

1715 S.E. 32nd Place
Portland, OR 97214
© **503/916-6204**

Grades: K through 5
Enrollment: 228
Faculty: 10
Founded: 1961
Cluster: Cleveland/ Franklin, Hosford/
Mt.Tabor Middle Schools

Edwards is one of two Portland Public schools currently on a year-around schedule, with five breaks during the school year, and six weeks off in the summer. Edwards is a small school by district standards, and this makes for a nice sense of community. Before- and after-school care is provided, and Spanish classes are available before school.

Edwards participates in the Artist-in-Residence program, bringing professional artists to the school two or three times a year. There are multi-age classes for grades one and two and for grades four and five. Classrooms are equipped with computers. The Talented and Gifted program is strong. Parents are involved in the site council, school advisory committee and PTA. Family math nights, science and math fairs, school carnival and a parent-run reading/tutoring program all bring parents into the school.

Hollyrood Elementary School

3560 N.E. Hollyrood Court
Portland, OR 97212
© **503/916-6766**

Grades: K through 3
Enrollment: 197
Faculty: 10
Founded: 1959
Cluster: Grant, Fernwood
Middle School

This is a small neighborhood school that only goes up through the third grade. The kindergarten is half-day; primary grades are mixed-age or traditional classrooms. Students here traditionally do well on standardized testing. The school embraces Howard Gardiner's "Seven Intelligences" philosophy of learning. Hollyrood is a demonstration site for 21st Century Schools with a Math-Science-Technology focus. A hands-on math program called "Structures" is in place. Hollyrood participates with Grant High School and Fernwood Middle School in a mentor-tutoring program that brings middle and high school students on campus to work with primary students.

After-school activities include Hands-on-Science, chess and foreign language classes. There is before- and after-school care through Northeast Day Care. Parents are active in the PTA, advisory committee and site council. They also coordinate a number of school events and work with students in the year-round ecoscience gardening project. This school asks for 100% parent involvement.

Irvington Early Childhood Education Center

1320 N.E. Brazee
Portland, OR 97212
© 503/916-6185

Grades: Pre-K through 5
Enrollment: 576
Faculty: 25
Founded: 1905
Cluster: Grant, Fernwood
Middle School

Irvington has a diverse student population (some students are bused from feeder schools) and the school values multicultural education. Its mission states that Irvington will "model an understanding and appreciation of cultural diversity, open-mindedness, and will embrace life long learning." It offers both a half-day pre-kindergarten and a full-day kindergarten program. Before- and after-school care is provided by Irvington Extended Day. There are multi-age as well as traditional classrooms in kindergarten through grade four. Kindergarten, first and second grades are paired with classrooms of older children to help create a sense of community. Teachers will often stay with the same group of children for more than one year.

The school boasts a science lab and a science club. Tumbling and jump rope teams, math and computer clubs, and a homework club are among the popular extra activities. Irvington believes in early literacy skills and participates in Reading is Fundamental (RIF), which provides free books to students during the year. The pre-kindergarten Read-Aloud Library lends a book a day to each child in the program.

Parental involvement is encouraged, and family nights for math and science are among the special programs. Irvington offers free child care for infants and preschoolers while parents are volunteering in the school. The child-development specialist also offers parenting classes. Parents are active in the PTA, site council and advisory committee raise funds for field trips and volunteer in the school.

Metropolitan Learning Center Elementary School

2033 N.W. Glisan
Portland, OR 97209
© 503/916-5737
FAX 503/916-5740

Grades: K through 6
Enrollment: 159
Faculty: 7.5
Founded: 1968
Cluster: Magnet Alternative School

Some children thrive in the non-competitive, cross-grade alternative program at Metropolitan Learning Center. It is difficult to get into because the demand is high. Kindergarten is a half-day morning program. The curriculum is organized by teams, K through 3 and 4 through 6. Mornings are spent on the core academic curriculum and afternoons on electives.

Field trips billed as "extensions of the classroom into the urban community" are an integral part of the MLC experience. "Scholars in the Public Schools" brings professionals into the school to hold workshops, conduct special projects and teach electives.

Parents are actively involved; MLC has a site council, advisory council and PTA. Before- and after-school care is available through NW Community Childcare. Community Schools runs a program here, and MLC has one of two indoor swimming pools in the District.

Richmond Elementary School

2276 S.E. 41st Avenue
Portland, OR 97214
✆ 503/916-6220

Grades: K through 5
Enrollment: 521
Faculty: 27
Founded: 1908
Cluster: Franklin/ Cleveland, Hosford/ Mt. Tabor Middle Schools

Richmond houses the magnet Japanese immersion program for Portland Public Schools, and three hundred of Richmond's students are enrolled in the program. The first class of 43 students graduated in 1994-'95 and went on to Mt. Tabor Middle School. Students in the immersion program attend a full-day kindergarten. Half of each day in grades 1-5 is taught in Japanese and half in English. Parents in the immersion program have given hundreds of volunteer hours to Richmond; it had the second highest number of volunteer hours of any school in the district in 1992-'93. They raised enough money to send this first graduating class on a two-week trip to Japan in the summer of 1995. The Oyanokai Japanese Magnet Parent Group, PTA, advisory committee and site council are all very active.

A Piaget All-Day Kindergarten Program is also housed at Richmond. The program emphasizes hands-on activities to solve problems in science and social studies. Richmond uses a thematic approach to the curriculum and the writing as a process method. A cross-age tutoring program offers students at different grade levels the opportunity to work together to build skills. Multi-age classrooms, multicultural education and portfolio assessment are all part of the program.

The YMCA provides before- and after-school care. After-school programs include hands-on science, computer classes, Japanese, calligraphy, a YMCA sports program, strings and band.

Sunnyside Elementary School

3421 S.E. Salmon Street
Portland, OR 97214
© 503/916-6226

Grades: K through 5
Enrollment: 331
Faculty: 20
Founded: 1891
Cluster: Franklin, Mt. Tabor
Middle School

Sunnyside is the first school in the country to teach all students American Sign Language. The neighborhood is culturally diverse, with children from many ethnic backgrounds. There are three "School-within-a-School" programs. The Deaf Regional Program and the Portland Family Cooperative School are housed here. The school also has a Vietnamese Bilingual Program for both Vietnamese and non-Vietnamese students. Students in this program have a mixed-age bilingual program for one third of their day and regular classes for the remainder. Admission to these programs is by application. The English as a Second Language program offers students a chance to learn in their native language as well as English. Native literacy classes are available in Vietnamese, Russian, Spanish and Cambodian.

Working with families, students and support staff, the school has a philosophy of early intervention and nurturing the whole child. The curriculum offers whole language, hands-on experiential learning, cooperative learning, and child-centered learning. Artist-in-Residence programs, DARE (Drug Abuse Resistance Education) and In-School Scouting are available. A strings program is offered to fourth and fifth graders.

Sunnyside provides before- and after-school care. Parents participate in the PTA, site council, and local advisory board. Adult literacy classes are offered, and there are also parent groups for the special programs. Parents of students in the Vietnamese Bilingual Program and the Family Cooperative Program provide direct support to the teachers in implementing the curriculum.

WinterHaven

3830 S.E. 14th
Portland, OR 97202
© 503/916-6200

Grades: K through 8
Enrollment: 130
Faculty: 5
Founded: 1996
Cluster: Magnet

Located in the Brooklyn School, WinterHaven is one of the few K-8 programs left in the district. Its curriculum emphasizes math, science and technology. Students work in mixed age groupings, and the teachers use an integrated cross-disciplinary approach to learning. Students are encouraged to develop their intellect, character and creativity. WinterHaven offers special interest classes and expects all students to perform community service.

This is a new program that has posted some very impressive test scores and the second highest socioeconomic rating in the state — 749 out of 750. K-8 schools offer kids a better sense of community, especially in the difficult middle years. WinterHaven began as a K-8 program, however, due to lack of space kindergarten was cut. If your student is interested in math and science, this is a school to visit.

Woodstock Elementary School

5601 S.E. 50th
Portland, OR 97202
© **503/916-6380**

Grades: K-5
Enrollment:354
Faculty: 40
Founded: 1891
Cluster: Franklin

The district's new Mandarin Chinese Immersion program opened at Woodstock in the fall of 1998. Twenty-two kindergarten and first grade students enrolled. Students receive half of their instruction in Mandarin Chinese and half in English, enabling them to use their second language in work and play. Kindergarten is a full day program for students in the immersion program.

Portland Elementary Schools OAT Scores (1995 and 1997)

1995 Statewide Average:			**1997 Statewide Average:**		
	Reading	Math		Reading	Math
Third Grade	203	201	Third Grade	209	204
Fifth Grade	216	214	Fifth Grade	218	217

Abernethy

Enrollment: 202

1995 Third Grade	193	194	1997 Third Grade	204	205
1995 Fifth Grade	217	226	1997 Fifth Grade	219	223

Socioeconomic Rank: 474 of 750 possible

Ainsworth

Enrollment: 530

1995 Third Grade	210	213	1997 Third Grade	212	215
1995 Fifth Grade	225	236	1997 Fifth Grade	223	231

Socioeconomic Rank: 706 of 750 possible

Alameda

Enrollment: 696

1995 Third Grade	209	210	1997 Third Grade	208	209
1995 Fifth Grade	218	223	1997 Fifth Grade	219	222

Socioeconomic Rank: 677 of 750 possible

Applegate

Enrollment: 269

1995 Third Grade	197	200	1997 Third Grade	188	189
1995 Fifth Grade	208	211	1997 Fifth Grade	208	209

Socioeconomic Rank: 16 of 750 possible

Arleta

Enrollment: 438
1995 Third Grade	191	193	1997 Third Grade 194	196
1995 Fifth Grade	206	210	1997 Fifth Grade 209	211

Socioeconomic Rank: 77 of 750 possible

Astor

Enrollment: 380
1995 Third Grade	200	201	1997 Third Grade 210	202
1995 Fifth Grade	213	214	1997 Fifth Grade 214	219

Socioeconomic Rank: 270 of 750 possible

Atkinson

Enrollment: 521
1995 Third Grade	198	204	1997 Third Grade 197	198
1995 Fifth Grade	213	214	1997 Fifth Grade 214	217

Socioeconomic Rank: 301 of 750 possible

Ball

Enrollment: 299
1995 Third Grade	190	195	1997 Third Grade 194	194
1995 Fifth Grade	208	217	1997 Fifth Grade 214	219

Socioeconomic Rank: 34 of 750 possible

Beach

Enrollment: 722
1995 Third Grade	192	199	1997 Third Grade 194	191
1995 Fifth Grade	206	207	1997 Fifth Grade 204	207

Socioeconomic Rank: 56 of 750 possible

Boise-Eliot

Enrollment: 696
1995 Third Grade	195	198	1997 Third Grade196	195
1995 Fifth Grade	211	217	1997 Fifth Grade211	211

Socioeconomic Rank: 122 of 750 possible

1995 Statewide Average:			1997 Statewide Average:		
	Reading	Math		Reading	Math
Third Grade	203	201	Third Grade	209	204
Fifth Grade	216	214	Fifth Grade	218	217

Bridger

Enrollment: 261

1995 Third Grade	191	196	1997 Third Grade	195	201
1995 Fifth Grade	214	219	1997 Fifth Grade	213	222

Socioeconomic Rank: 333 of 750 possible

Bridlemile

Enrollment: 491

1995 Third Grade	209	212	1997 Third Grade	210	212
1995 Fifth Grade	222	231	1997 Fifth Grade	224	232

Socioeconomic Rank: 698 of 750 possible

Brooklyn

Enrollment: 211

1995 Third Grade	202	203	1997 Third Grade	193	193
1995 Fifth Grade	214	220	1997 Fifth Grade	214	224

Socioeconomic Rank: 112 of 750 possible

Buckman

Enrollment: 525

1995 Third Grade	205	199	1997 Third Grade	206	201
1995 Fifth Grade	217	218	1997 Fifth Grade	222	219

Socioeconomic Rank: 295 of 750 possible

Capitol Hill

Enrollment: 325

1995 Third Grade	202	205	1997 Third Grade	202	200
1995 Fifth Grade	215	219	1997 Fifth Grade	218	223

Socioeconomic Rank: 613 of 750 possible

Chapman

Enrollment: 547

1995 Third Grade	208	210	1997 Third Grade 212	214
1995 Fifth Grade	223	230	1997 Fifth Grade 223	234

Socioeconomic Rank: 515 of 750 possible

Chief Joseph

Enrollment: 373

1995 Third Grade	195	203	1997 Third Grade 199	203
1995 Fifth Grade	211	216	1997 Fifth Grade 212	216

Socioeconomic Rank: 303 of 750 possible

Clarendon

Enrollment: 439

1995 Third Grade	189	194	1997 Third Grade 190	190
1995 Fifth Grade	204	205	1997 Fifth Grade 207	207

Socioeconomic Rank: 6 of 750 possible

Clark

Enrollment: 553

1995 Third Grade	198	203	1997 Third Grade 200	200
1995 Fifth Grade	209	217	1997 Fifth Grade 214	218

Socioeconomic Rank: 137 of 750 possible

Creston

Enrollment: 378

1995 Third Grade	197	198	1997 Third Grade 198	198
1995 Fifth Grade	208	213	1997 Fifth Grade 211	215

Socioeconomic Rank: 115 of 750 possible

Duniway

Enrollment: 446

1995 Third Grade	203	204	1997 Third Grade 207	207
1995 Fifth Grade	218	225	1997 Fifth Grade 220	225

Socioeconomic Rank: 743 of 750 possible

1995 Statewide Average:			1997 Statewide Average:		
	Reading	Math		Reading	Math
Third Grade	203	201	Third Grade	209	204
Fifth Grade	216	214	Fifth Grade	218	217

Edwards

Enrollment: 228

1995 Third Grade	210	213	1997 Third Grade	205	208
1995 Fifth Grade	219	222	1997 Fifth Grade	224	234

Socioeconomic Rank: 427 of 750 possible

Faubion

Enrollment: 350

1995 Third Grade	200	203	1997 Third Grade	194	194
1995 Fifth Grade	211	217	1997 Fifth Grade	211	214

Socioeconomic Rank: 31 of 750 possible

Glencoe

Enrollment: 468

1995 Third Grade	206	207	1997 Third Grade	210	213
1995 Fifth Grade	223	228	1997 Fifth Grade	219	224

Socioeconomic Rank: 558 of 750 possible

Grout

Enrollment: 393

1995 Third Grade	197	200	1997 Third Grade	199	199
1995 Fifth Grade	214	222	1997 Fifth Grade	210	214

Socioeconomic Rank: 127 of 750 possible

Hayhurst

Enrollment: 360

1995 Third Grade	204	208	1997 Third Grade	206	209
1995 Fifth Grade	221	227	1997 Fifth Grade	216	221

Socioeconomic Rank: 171 of 750 possible

Hollyrood

Enrollment: 197
1995 Third Grade   211   217   1997 Third Grade   214   214
Socioeconomic Rank: 746 of 764 possible

Humbolt

Enrollment: 416
1995 Third Grade   193   192   1997 Third Grade   190   192
1995 Fifth Grade   202   209   1997 Fifth Grade   205   200
Socioeconomic Rank: 8 of 750 possible

Irvington

Enrollment: 576
1995 Third Grade   206   205   1997 Third Grade   203   201
1995 Fifth Grade   218   223   1997 Fifth Grade   214   221
Socioeconomic Rank: 573 of 750 possible

James John

Enrollment: 643
1995 Third Grade   196   198   1997 Third Grade   195   193
1995 Fifth Grade   204   209   1997 Fifth Grade   206   209
Socioeconomic Rank: 43 of 750 possible

Kelly

Enrollment: 578
1995 Third Grade   194   200   1997 Third Grade   195   192
1995 Fifth Grade   204   212   1997 Fifth Grade   208   211
Socioeconomic Rank: 95 of 750 possible

Kenton

Enrollment: 245
1995 Third Grade   198   205   1997 Third Grade   202   205
1995 Fifth Grade   209   219   1997 Fifth Grade   210   214
Socioeconomic Rank: 70 of 750 possible

1995 Statewide Average:			1997 Statewide Average:		
	Reading	Math		Reading	Math
Third Grade	203	201	Third Grade	209	204
Fifth Grade	216	214	Fifth Grade	218	217

King

Enrollment: 793

1995 Third Grade	198	201	1997 Third Grade	195	197
1995 Fifth Grade	209	215	1997 Fifth Grade	208	211

Socioeconomic Rank: 41 of 750 possible

Laurelhurst

Enrollment: 557

1995 Third Grade	203	208	1997 Third Grade	202	200
1995 Fifth Grade	220	224	1997 Fifth Grade	221	225

Socioeconomic Rank: 644 of 750 possible

Lee

Enrollment: 422

1995 Third Grade	191	192	1997 Third Grade	198	198
1995 Fifth Grade	207	213	1997 Fifth Grade	208	208

Socioeconomic Rank: 216 of 750 possible

Lent

Enrollment: 376

1995 Third Grade	198	204	1997 Third Grade	191	192
1995 Fifth Grade	205	211	1997 Fifth Grade	210	210

Socioeconomic Rank: 170 of 750 possible

Lewis

Enrollment: 281

1995 Third Grade	195	200	1997 Third Grade	201	198
1995 Fifth Grade	213	218	1997 Fifth Grade	215	218

Socioeconomic Rank: 283 of 750 possible

Llewellyn

Enrollment: 360
1995 Third Grade   201   204   1997 Third Grade   203   207
1995 Fifth Grade   216   228   1997 Fifth Grade   219   225
Socioeconomic Rank: 355 of 750 possible

Maplewood

Enrollment: 290
1995 Third Grade   208   207   1997 Third Grade   210   209
1995 Fifth Grade   219   226   1997 Fifth Grade   223   228
Socioeconomic Rank: 688 of 750 possible

Markham

Enrollment: 336
1995 Third Grade   206   209   1997 Third Grade   210   206
1995 Fifth Grade   218   223   1997 Fifth Grade   219   224
Socioeconomic Rank: 508 of 750 possible

Marysville

Enrollment: 397
1995 Third Grade   195   198   1997 Third Grade   193   194
1995 Fifth Grade   208   214   1997 Fifth Grade   212   220
Socioeconomic Rank: 39 of 750 possible

Meek

Enrollment: 249
1995 Third Grade   195   199   1997 Third Grade   206   208
1995 Fifth Grade   208   208   1997 Fifth Grade   213   214
Socioeconomic Rank: 104 of 750 possible

Metropolitan Learning Center

Enrollment: 169
1995 Third Grade   203   209   1997 Third Grade   205   202
1995 Fifth Grade   227   230   1997 Fifth Grade   220   219
Socioeconomic Rank: 718 of 750 possible

1995 Statewide Average:			**1997 Statewide Average:**		
	Reading	Math		Reading	Math
Third Grade	203	201	Third Grade	209	204
Fifth Grade	216	214	Fifth Grade	218	217

Northeast Community School (Grades 4-8)

Enrollment: 98

1997 Fifth Grade	225	232
1997 Eighth Grade	231	241
State Averages 8th Grade	231	231

Socioeconomic Rank: 693 of 750 possible

Peninsula

Enrollment: 301

1995 Third Grade	193	190	1997 Third Grade	201	201
1995 Fifth Grade	208	209	1997 Fifth Grade	212	212

Socioeconomic Rank: 171 of 750 possible

Richmond

Enrollment: 521

1995 Third Grade	206	212	1997 Third Grade	209	210
1995 Fifth Grade	217	226	1997 Fifth Grade	219	226

Socioeconomic Rank: 622 of 750 possible

Rieke

Enrollment: 281

1995 Third Grade	206	209	1997 Third Grade	207	213
1995 Fifth Grade	220	231	1997 Fifth Grade	223	236

Socioeconomic Rank: 709 of 750 possible

Rigler

Enrollment: 576

1995 Third Grade	198	203	1997 Third Grade	195	199
1995 Fifth Grade	208	216	1997 Fifth Grade	208	213

Socioeconomic Rank: 65 of 750 possible

Rose City Park

Enrollment: 551

1995 Third Grade	199	204	1997 Third Grade	205	204
1995 Fifth Grade	213	217	1997 Fifth Grade	214	218

Socioeconomic Rank: 511 of 750 possible

Sabin

Enrollment: 543

1995 Third Grade	192	192	1997 Third Grade	192	189
1995 Fifth Grade	210	216	1997 Fifth Grade	208	210

Socioeconomic Rank: 97 of 750 possible

Scott

Enrollment: 581

1995 Third Grade	196	201	1997 Third Grade	197	198
1995 Fifth Grade	210	216	1997 Fifth Grade	211	216

Socioeconomic Rank: 180 of 750 possible

Sitton

Enrollment: 417

1995 Third Grade	192	198	1997 Third Grade	200	200
1995 Fifth Grade	207	210	1997 Fifth Grade	207	208

Socioeconomic Rank: 15 of 750 possible

Skyline

Enrollment: 311

1995 Third Grade	202	206	1997 Third Grade	208	205
1995 Fifth Grade	219	232	1997 Fifth Grade	221	230

Socioeconomic Rank: 583 of 750 possible

Smith

Enrollment: 285

1995 Third Grade	206	212	1997 Third Grade	207	208
1995 Fifth Grade	215	223	1997 Fifth Grade	220	227

Socioeconomic Rank: 629 of 750 possible

1995 Statewide Average:			**1997 Statewide Average:**		
	Reading	Math		Reading	Math
Third Grade	203	201	Third Grade	209	204
Fifth Grade	216	214	Fifth Grade	218	217

Stephenson

Enrollment: 396

1995 Third Grade	210	214	1997 Third Grade	211	216
1995 Fifth Grade	222	232	1997 Fifth Grade	220	226

Socioeconomic Rank: 721 of 750 possible

Sunnyside

Enrollment: 331

1995 Third Grade	188	195	1997 Third Grade	206	201
1995 Fifth Grade	207	210	1997 Fifth Grade	209	210

Socioeconomic Rank: 175 of 750 possible

Vernon

Enrollment: 560

1995 Third Grade	188	194	1997 Third Grade	195	198
1995 Fifth Grade	205	210	1997 Fifth Grade	203	201

Socioeconomic Rank: 12 of 750 possible

Vestal

Enrollment: 284

1995 Third Grade	193	197	1997 Third Grade	194	194
1995 Fifth Grade	209	213	1997 Fifth Grade	212	218

Socioeconomic Rank: 73 of 750 possible

Whitman

Enrollment: 432

1995 Third Grade	195	198	1997 Third Grade	194	196
1995 Fifth Grade	207	215	1997 Fifth Grade	211	212

Socioeconomic Rank: 52 of 750 possible

Wilcox

Enrollment: 188
1995 Third Grade	198	208	1997 Third Grade	199	198
1995 Fifth Grade	207	217	1997 Fifth Grade	209	211

Socioeconomic Rank: 154 of 750 possible

WinterHaven

Enrollment: 139
1997 Third Grade	213	222
1997 Fifth Grade	228	229

Socioeconomic Rank: 749 of 750 possible

Woodlawn

Enrollment: 538
1995 Third Grade	196	200	1997 Third Grade	202	206
1995 Fifth Grade	207	218	1997 Fifth Grade	212	223

Socioeconomic Rank: 33 of 750 possible

Woodmere

Enrollment: 485
1995 Third Grade	192	197	1997 Third Grade	195	196
1995 Fifth Grade	208	217	1997 Fifth Grade	207	208

Socioeconomic Rank: 26 of 750 possible

Woodstock

Enrollment: 354
1995 Third Grade	202	203	1997 Third Grade	200	200
1995 Fifth Grade	213	218	1997 Fifth Grade	217	221

Socioeconomic Rank: 210 of 750 possible

Youngson

Enrollment: 220
1995 Third Grade	202	204	1997 Third Grade	201	202
1995 Fifth Grade	216	220	1997 Fifth Grade	216	220

Socioeconomic Rank: 244 of 750 possible

Chapter Three

Suburban School Districts

Beaverton School District

Located seven miles west of Portland, the city of Beaverton is one of the fastest growing communities in the nation. It's a young community. Nearly half of its residents are between the ages of 19 and 44, and children under 18 make up nearly a third of the population. It has a strong local economy, good schools, and excellent park and recreational facilities.

The schools have strong support from the business community through the Business/Education Partnership Program, which is a joint venture of the Beaverton Area of Chamber of Commerce and Beaverton School District. Beaverton is at the heart of Oregon's Tualatin Valley, which has attracted sufficient high technology industry to have been dubbed "Silicon Forest".

Beaverton School District is the third largest in the state. It has over 31,000 students in 42 schools — twenty-nine elementary (K-5), seven middle (6-8), and six high schools (9-12).

The average elementary teacher/ student ratio is 1:21. The secondary (6-12) teacher/ student ratio averages 1:26. The district made $62 million in cuts over the past few years and is now focusing on instruction.

Twenty-two percent of the students in the district are minority kids. Currently the largest of this group is Asian, but the Hispanic population is expected to become the largest minority group in the next few years. Students in the district speak over twenty languages. The percentage of students qualifying for free and reduced lunch is 16%. The district promotes cultural diversity in its goal to help students become productive members of society. All students entering the district who do not speak English as their native language are evaluated and placed appropriately in ESL courses and regular classes. The dropout rate for students in the district is 9%.

The district passed the second-largest school bond in Oregon history in 1996. (Only Portland's $197-million has exceeded it.) The $146-million will pay for land and construction of four new schools: two elementary schools, one middle school, and one high school. One of these new schools opened in 1997, and the other three opened in September of 1999. As a result of opening the new schools, district boundaries will change. Existing facilities have been upgraded, and classrooms have been added to existing schools. Six and a half-million dollars went toward new technology in the form of classroom computers, printers, scanners, computer projection equipment, expanded phone service and better public address systems.

Beaverton students score well above the national average on standardized testing and produce high SAT scores. Sixty-one percent of district seniors took the SAT in 1997. Beaverton Science and Technology School, a specialized alternative school with about 90 students, had among the states' best 1995 test scores despite a low socioeconomic ranking.

The district maintains an open enrollment policy, which gives parents the opportunity to apply to schools that have programs they feel will be best for their children. Admission is based on individual student application and is subject to certain conditions (i.e. available space). The alternative high schools (Arts & Communication and Merlo Station) are not part of this policy.

Several Alternate High School programs are available for students with special interests and special needs. In order to qualify for these options, students must work with their counselors, complete an application, and participate in an interview process. The Merlo Station Campus offers Community School, a full-day program for 9-12 graders who are having little success in their regular high schools. Currently 255 students are enrolled in Community School. Evening Academy is an individualized credit-recovery program for 10 students in grades 11 &12 who need help to graduate, and Continuing Education for Young Parents (CEYP) gives students the opportunity to continue their education and prepare for the responsibility of pregnancy and parenthood.

There are several career-enhancement opportunities at the Merlo Station Campus. Cascade Educational Corps is an all-day, semester-long program for students age 16-19 years who want to participate in community work/ service projects in an outdoor setting. Natural Resources Science & Technology, a program for students in grades 9-11, focuses on special areas or interests within a regular curriculum. The VA/ St. Vincent Career Focus is a half-day, one-semester program for 11th & 12th-grade students who are looking for opportunities to work with hospital personnel in various settings. The NIKE Student Internship Program offers elective credits through internships for students working outside the classroom in the company's retail stores.

The Arts and Communication High School at the C.E. Mason Campus is a full-day program for students in grades 9-12 who wish to develop skills in writing, speaking and visual design through independent projects. The school also offers the Common Ground Horticulture Program, which utilizes a greenhouse and the outdoors as classrooms for interested students.

Beaverton School district is dedicated to offering its students quality education. The Northwest Association of Schools and Colleges accredits its high schools. The district has a strong base of parent volunteers, and the community-at-large provides effective support.

Beaverton District High Schools

3

Aloha High School
18550 S.W. Kinnaman Road
Aloha, OR 97007
✆ **503/591-4670**

Grades: 9 through 12
Enrollment: 1,956
Faculty: 77
Founded: 1967
Middle Schools: Conestoga, Highland Park and Mountain View

Aloha offers college preparatory and standard classes. The school operates with a traditional eight-period day, with a typical schedule of six classes, lunch and a prep period. Students in the college prep program are encouraged to take a minimum of four years each of English, math and science and two years of German, Spanish, French or Japanese. The fine arts program covers performing arts (choral, strings and instrumental), theater arts and visual arts. Advanced Placement classes are available for interested students.

Aloha has a 2+2 Credit Program for students working toward special degrees in automotive service technology, building construction, business/ office technology, hospitality and tourism, and drafting. This program allows students to begin classes at Aloha and finish at Portland Community College.

The Network of Complementary Schools, Inc. provides a unique educational opportunity for eleventh and twelfth graders. This organization arranges exchange programs (four to six weeks in length) throughout the United States at twenty-six member schools. The schools, both public and private, share specialized programs. For example, a student might focus on space at NASA in Huntsville, Alabama, study the Grand Canyon with Colorado Springs students, become immersed in Quaker culture at Germantown French School or take training in fisheries and wildlife management in Beaverton. Programs vary from year to year.

SAT Scores 1997:	Verbal: 518	Math: 540
1995:	467	538
Percent of seniors taking the test: 58%		
OAT Scores 1997 (10th Grade):	Reading: 236	Math: 234
1997 Statewide Average:	236	233
1995 (11th Grade):	237	234
1995 Statewide Average:	235	232
Socioeconomic Rank: 226 of 254 possible		

The Arts and Communication High School at C.E. Mason

11375 S.W. Center Street
Beaverton, OR 97005
✆ **503/672-3700**

Grades: 9 through 12
Enrollment: 245
Faculty: 15
Founded: 1992

Admission to this magnet school is by application, interview, counselor referral and transcript review. Students interested in pursuing arts and communication find unique opportunities to write, paint, film, draw, design and create. They are encouraged to be self-directed learners. The program is based on Ted Sizer's work and the Coalition of Essential Schools' principle that teachers serve as coaches rather than lecturers. Students here get a solid academic core curriculum called "Integrated Thematic" that combines language arts, social studies, health and science to create in-depth project studies. They also receive instruction in mathematics and foreign language. Paula Kinney became Principal in 1998. She was Principal at Portland's magnet middle school, the da Vinci Arts Middle School and was connected to the award winning Jefferson High School dance program. Julia Stites, Artistic Director of the Jefferson Dancers, moved to Arts and Communication in the fall of 1999. Ms. Stites worked as a choreographer for the Jefferson dance company for 18 years and was director for the last six years.

She will start a new dance company called Dance West. This is very good news for Beaverton dancers.

Students in this four-year program can choose a liberal arts background or specialize in the areas of film/ video production, written communication, visual communication, or the fine arts. Students work with professionals in the arts and communications fields through the Artists-in-Residence Program.

SAT Scores 1997:	Verbal: 552	Math: 503
1995:	508	485
Number of students taking the test: 47		
OAT Scores 1997 (10th Grade):	Reading: 238	Math: 231
1997 Statewide Average:	236	233
1995 (11th Grade):	235	231
1995 Statewide Average:	235	232
Socioeconomic Rank: 235 of 254 possible		

Beaverton High School

13000 S.W. 2nd Avenue
Beaverton, OR 97005
✆ **503/591-4680**
Grades: 9 through 12
Enrollment: 2,039
Faculty: 98
Founded: 1902
Middle Schools: Conestoga, Highland Park and Whitford

Beaverton High School offers the standard high school requirement courses and a variety of college preparatory classes. Foreign language classes are given in French, Japanese, German, and Spanish. The business department has various activities to interest students, including a mock trial, a Japanese orientation unit, and the Portland Federation campaign. The school sponsors a Cooperation Work Experience Program and a DECA organization (business club).

Tech Prep, a vocational/ technical program that begins at Beaverton High School, is completed at PCC. It allows the student to obtain a two-year Associate of Applied Science Degree in Automotive Service Technology, Business/ Office Technology, Drafting Technology, Early Childhood Education and Mathematics. Other programs are directed toward health careers and restaurant careers.

Beaverton High School has a Resource Room to help special-needs students with living skills, communication skills and survival skills. An Independent Skills Center is designed to meet the needs of students with intellectual delays and multiple handicaps. The school also provides preparation for the GED exam.

SAT Scores 1997:	Verbal: 529	Math: 550
1995:	467	538

Percent of seniors taking the test: 66%

OAT Scores 1997 (10th Grade):	Reading: 239	Math: 237
1997 Statewide Average:	236	233
1995 (11th Grade):	239	238
1995 Statewide Average:	235	232

Socioeconomic Rank: 236 of 254 possible

Merlo Station

841 S.W. Merlo Drive
Beaverton, OR 97006
© **503/591-4492**

Grades: 9 through 12
Enrollment: Community School: 255, Science & Technology: 127
Faculty: 25
Founded: 1993

The Merlo Station campus houses several unusual educational programs. The Natural Resources Science and Technology High School allows students in grades 9 through 11 to focus on special-interest areas in addition to the required basics. Learning skills are developed through student projects, exhibits and demonstrations. Individuality and creativity are fostered as graduation and college requirements are met. Admission is by application, counselor referral and interview.

The Community School is for selected 9th-12th grade students who are not finding success in their regular high school programs. The 9th and 10th grade program focuses on teaching academic and social skills that will allow the student to successfully return to his or her high school. The 11th and 12th grade program focuses on academic skills with an emphasis on credit recovery, job exploration and internships. Other opportunities offered by the Merlo Station Campus: Evening Academy (grades 11-12), Continuing Education for Young Parents, NIKE: Student Internship Program, VA/ St. Vincent Career Focus (grades 11-12), and Cascade Educational Corps (ages 16-19).

The Natural Resources Science and Technology High School:

OAT Scores 1997 (10th Grade):	Reading: 241	Math: 240
1997 Statewide Average:	236	233
1995 (11th Grade):	238	238
1995 Statewide Average:	235	232

Socioeconomic Rank: 75 of 233 possible

The Community School:

OAT Scores 1997 (10th Grade):	Reading: 225	Math: 225
1997 Statewide Average:	236	233
1995 (11th Grade):	231	227
1995 Statewide Average:	235	232
Socioeconomic Rank: 109 of 254 possible		

Sunset High School
13840 N.W. Cornell Road
Portland, OR 97229
✆ **503/591-4690**

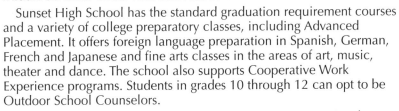

Grades: 9 through 12
Enrollment: 1,520
Faculty: 68
Founded: 1958
Middle Schools: Cedar Park and Meadow Park

Sunset High School has the standard graduation requirement courses and a variety of college preparatory classes, including Advanced Placement. It offers foreign language preparation in Spanish, German, French and Japanese and fine arts classes in the areas of art, music, theater and dance. The school also supports Cooperative Work Experience programs. Students in grades 10 through 12 can opt to be Outdoor School Counselors.

Freshman may apply for the four-year program in International Studies, which prepares students for understanding global history, geography and cultural issues. Interdisciplinary instruction and out-of-class activities fortify the program. At the completion of the four years, students will receive an International Studies endorsement on their diploma and receive special credits in this area. The program requires four years of foreign language, four years of language arts and four years of social studies/ global studies and one year in fine arts. Included are such electives as Model UN and Metro Congress.

For students who wish to focus on project- and lab-oriented learning, Sunset has a program called "SunTech." Students spend two periods of the day in academy classes. Much of the course work is done in teams, with sixteen Apple Macintosh LC II computers available for use. Sophomores may apply for this program, which is designed to prepare students for a college experience. The school also has an Independent Skills Center and a Resource Program to meet the needs of special education students. Courses are offered in basic life skills, communication skills, and job skills.

More than 400 parents are active in the Parent Volunteer Program. In addition to supporting sports activities and drama, parents staff the College and Career Center, where students may explore career interests, college selection and scholarship availability. A Career Information System (CIS) program is available in a computer lab completely devoted to this project. Parents also staff the Peer Tutor program, matching tutors with students seeking academic help.

SAT Scores 1997:	Verbal: 550	Math: 554
1995:	463	526
Percent of seniors taking the test: 74%		
OAT Scores 1997 (10th Grade):	Reading: 236	Math: 236
1997 Statewide Average:	236	233
1995 (11th Grade):	237	236
1995 Statewide Average:	235	232
Socioeconomic Rank: 233 of 254 possible		

Westview High School

4200 N.W. 185th Avenue
Portland, OR 97229
© 503/591-4180
FAX 503/259-5230
Grades: 9 through 12
Enrollment: 2,064
Faculty: 90
Founded: 1995
Middle Schools: Five Oaks and Meadow Park

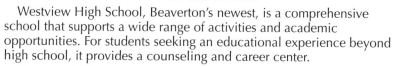

Westview High School, Beaverton's newest, is a comprehensive school that supports a wide range of activities and academic opportunities. For students seeking an educational experience beyond high school, it provides a counseling and career center.

The school offers a strong program in academics and extracurricular activities, including athletics. In addition to college preparatory course work, Westview supports a wide variety of electives in instrumental and vocal music, theater arts and visual arts. Students have the opportunity to become proficient in Spanish, French, Japanese or German. The business department sponsors DECA, a voluntary business club. Westview offers "honors" credits in the required core courses in the language arts, social studies and science curriculum areas and advanced placement courses.

Students at Westview register to take a maximum of six classes per semester; the school day is based on block scheduling. Students attend three academic classes for 95 minutes each and have a 45-minute prep time. The block system alternates schedules on different days, but allows the full schedule of classes to be given each week. A Resource Center and an Independent Skills Center meet the needs of special education students. Westview had no seniors in 1994-1995, so there are no 1995 SAT scores available.

SAT Scores 1997:	Verbal: 526 Math: 549	
Percent of seniors taking the test: 62%		
OAT Scores 1997 (10th Grade):	Reading: 239 Math: 235	
1997 Statewide Average:	236	233
1995 (11th Grade):	238	236
1995 Statewide Average:	235	232
Socioeconomic Rank: 242 of 254 possible		

Beaverton District Middle Schools

Cedar Park Middle School
11100 S.W. Parkway Street
Portland, OR 97225
© **503/591-4610**

Grades: 6 through 8
Enrollment: 1,012
Faculty: 47
Founded: 1965

Cedar Park's core classes are based on a thematic approach in the areas of language arts, mathematics, social studies, physical education/ health and science. The school features an Integrated Science Program focusing on critical thinking and problem solving. Students have a team of five teachers, who are responsible for the core classes. These teachers meet regularly to monitor the students' progress and track their grades on computers. If a student has performed particularly well, the parents will receive a postcard. If the student is not performing up to par, parents get a letter or phone call.

A variety of electives are available in the form of nine-week classes in keyboarding/ computers, technology (a hands-on lab approach), teen living, and introduction to music. Students can explore their interests in band, orchestra or choir. An after-school drama program and an after-school language program in Japanese, French, and Spanish as well as TAG options are also available. Elementary schools that feed into Cedar Park: Cedar Mill, Raleigh Park, Ridgewood, Terra Linda, West Tualatin View, and William Walker.

OAT Scores 1997 (8th Grade):	Reading: 234 Math: 233	
1997 Statewide Average:	231	231
1995 (8th Grade):	231	232
1995 Statewide Average:	228	230
Socioeconomic Rank: 337 of 355 possible		

Conestoga Middle School

12250 S.W. Conestoga Drive
Beaverton, OR 97008
℡ 503/591-4160
FAX 503/591-4379

Grades: 6 through 8
Enrollment: 1,057
Faculty: 50
Founded: 1994

Built with a pioneering spirit when Oregon was celebrating the 150th anniversary of the Oregon Trail, Conestoga was specifically designed to meet 21st Century goals for middle school education. In an effort to showcase Beaverton's newest school as an "important place" in the community, its integrated, interdisciplinary instruction is planned to celebrate diversity and allow for life-skill experiences, as well as providing strong academic instruction.

Classes begin at 9:15 and end at 3:30. Core classes include language arts, reading, social studies, math and science. Interdisciplinary teams work with the students during core learning time, and counselors work with assigned interdisciplinary teams to help meet each student's needs. An exploratory program allows students to take courses in art, media lab, multicultural studies, and foreign language. Music choices include orchestra and band. TAG options are also available. Elementary schools that feed into Conestoga: Greenway, Hiteon, McKay, Nancy Ryles and Sexton Mountain.

OAT Scores 1997 (8th Grade):	Reading: 235	Math: 234
1997 Statewide Average:	231	231
1995 (8th Grade):	231	234
1995 Statewide Average:	228	230
Socioeconomic Rank: 334 of 355 possible		

Five Oaks Middle School

1600 N.W. 173rd Avenue
Beaverton, OR 97008
℡ 503/591-4620

Grades: 6 through 8
Enrollment: 1,037
Faculty: 48
Founded: 1976

Five Oaks Middle School provides students with a rich educational atmosphere. The school encourages responsibility and respect among its students. The school's "Three Rs Program" stresses rigor, respect and responsibility. Interdisciplinary teaching teams teach core academic courses, with a strong focus on basic academic skills. Advanced concepts in math and reading are emphasized, and students are further challenged by access to fully equipped labs for computer skills and typing, applied technology, power mechanics, drama, music, art, woods, metals, plastics, crafts, jewelry, sewing and cooking. Three computer labs are equipped with laser printers and laser disc players. Spanish is the foreign language option.

Students perform above average on the statewide assessment in math, reading and physical education testing. A special education program and TAG program are incorporated into the school's curriculum. Low-achieving 8th graders are given help with learning skills in math and language arts. Elementary schools that feed into Five Oaks: Beaver Acres, Bethany, Elmonica, McKinley and Rock Creek.

OAT Scores 1997 (8th Grade):	Reading: 233	Math: 232
1997 Statewide Average:	231	231
1995 (8th Grade):	230	233
1995 Statewide Average:	228	230

Socioeconomic Rank: 291 of 355 possible

Highland Park Middle School

7000 S.W. Wilson Avenue
Beaverton, OR 97008
℃ **503/591-4630**
FAX 503/591-4659

Grades: 6 through 8
Enrollment: 1,073
Faculty: 51
Founded: 1965

Highland Park Middle School is dedicated to helping students become productive members of a changing society. The school is multicultural with a diversified student population (22 countries are represented and 16 languages spoken). The average class size was reduced to 32 students in 1995-1996. Highland Park students have the opportunity to attend English as a Second Language programs before and after school.

The curriculum is concentrated around interdisciplinary teaming, exploratory programs and homerooms. Teacher assistance teams include a counselor, administrator, resource teacher, and academic teachers. Instruction focuses on technology, leadership and multicultural education. Highland Park offers core courses in English, social studies, mathematics, science, and physical education. Exploratory classes are available in art, ceramics, crafts, teen living, drama and technology. Language courses are offered in French, Spanish and Japanese. Music options include orchestra and band. A TAG program is in effect.

The school has support staff that includes a school psychologist, five interpreters, three guidance counselors, school nursing services, and a police liaison officer. Special events and activities include a cultural fair, celebration of the arts/ arts fair, community service, intermurals, and school business partnerships. A strong volunteer parent group supports Highland Park. Elementary schools that feed into Highland Park: Chehalem, Cooper Mountain, Fir Grove and Sexton Mountain.

OAT Scores 1997 (8th Grade):	Reading: 234	Math: 234
1997 Statewide Average:	231	231
1995 (8th Grade):	229	231
1995 Statewide Average:	228	230
Socioeconomic Rank: 329 of 355 possible		

Meadow Park Middle School

14100 S.W. Downing Street
Beaverton, OR 97006
© 503/591-4640

Grades: 6 through 8
Enrollment: 1,108
Faculty: 49
Founded: 1963

Meadow Park Middle School is dedicated to preparing its students for a changing, complex world. It offers an integrated core curriculum taught by a team of teachers. Students are put in heterogeneous groups, which allows them to learn at their own rate and level. The use of stationary and mobile Macintosh labs, laptop computers, laser disk players and a variety of instructional hardware enhance technology instruction.

Electives are available in art, music, physical education, applied technology and personal development. Specialty classes allow students to explore various interest areas. An English as a Second Language program and a Spanish immersion program are available to students. TAG options are included in the curriculum. Academic assessment is made through portfolio development and outcome-based instruction.

Counselors work with teams to develop social skills, provide classroom guidance and counseling, and instruct the student body on drug and alcohol intervention. Specialists in the school serve students with special needs. Meadow Park is strongly supported by its Parent Teacher Organization and its parent volunteers. Various assemblies, projects, celebrations and fundraisers are held throughout the year. Elementary schools: Barnes, Bethany, Oak Hills, Ridgewood and William Walker.

OAT Scores 1997 (8th Grade):	Reading: 234	Math: 233
1997 Statewide Average:	231	231
1995 (8th Grade):	231	233
1995 Statewide Average:	228	230
Socioeconomic Rank: 324 of 355 possible		

Mountain View Middle School

7500 S.W. Farmington Road
Beaverton, OR 97007
© 503/591-4650

Grades: 6 through 8
Enrollment: 925
Faculty: 75
Founded: 1969

Sixth grade students at Mountain View are assigned to one teacher for the majority of the day. The core curriculum provides instruction in communications, reading, math, social studies, science/ health and physical education. Music options include general music, band and orchestra.

Seventh graders are assigned to a team of teachers for a language arts/ social studies block, science and math. Music options are orchestra, band, and chorus. Exploratory subjects include keyboarding/ technology. Eighth graders are also instructed in core subjects by a teaching team. Students in both grades are given options for studying Spanish or French.

Special education programs are provided, and the district sponsors a Title 1 Reading Program. Counselors are available for aid in conflict resolution skills and problem solving. TAG options are offered. Mountain View encourages participation in such school-wide activities as drama, chess club, Youth Crime Watch, Spirit/ Service, student store, student leadership, recycling, yearbook, RAPP (Resolve All Problems Peacefully), and OSSOM (Oregon Students On the Move). Elementary schools: Aloha Park, Errol Hassell, Hazeldale and Kinnaman.

OAT Scores 1997 (8th Grade):	Reading: 232	Math: 232
1997 Statewide Average:	231	231
1995 (8th Grade):	229	231
1995 Statewide Average:	228	230
Socioeconomic Rank: 251 of 355 possible		

Beaverton District Elementary Schools

Each of Beaverton's twenty-nine elementary schools has a Site Council, composed of parents and school personnel, which helps determine how the resources available to the school will be allocated. This makes each school unique and allows the schools to develop and support individual programs. Some schools foster art literacy, foreign language classes and/ or technology, where others may focus on lowering student/ teacher ratios. Students may be grouped together in multi-age classes. Many elementary schools have a "school-within-a-school" program, where children are placed in groups called "communities," "neighborhoods" or "families." The objective is to create smaller units so children get to know their teachers and each other.

The site councils at Bethany, Barnes, Raleigh Park, West Tualatin View, and William Walker have decided to focus on the development of technology in their schools. The following schools have after-school language programs (predominately Spanish) offered for a fee by "Passport to Languages": Barnes, Cooper Mountain, Elmonica, Fir Grove, Raleigh Park, Rock Creek, Terra Linda, West Tualatin View, and William Walker. Raleigh Hills School is part of the National Network of Mindful schools, which helps children develop multiple intelligences.

Special Education inclusion programs are found at Chehalem and Errol Hassell. The district implements a TAG (Talented and Gifted) program through which elementary students may take part in discovery classes, science fairs, Publishing House, Challenge reading and math, and Junior Great Books.

The district encourages Business/ School Partnerships, which link local businesses with schools so that resources are shared for mutual benefit. Beaverton schools also foster strong Parent/ Volunteer support groups.

Beaverton Elementary School OAT Scores

1995 Statewide Average:			1997 Statewide Average:		
	Reading	Math		Reading	Math
Third Grade	203	201	Third Grade	209	204
Fifth Grade	216	214	Fifth Grade	218	217

Aloha Park					
Enrollment: 544					
1995 Third Grade	199	203	1997 Third Grade	207	203
1995 Fifth Grade	214	213	1997 Fifth Grade	215	216
Socioeconomic Rank: 340 of 750 possible					

Barnes

Enrollment: 578
| 1995 Third Grade | 203 | 201 | 1997 Third Grade | 209 | 205 |
| 1995 Fifth Grade | 213 | 212 | 1997 Fifth Grade | 218 | 220 |

Socioeconomic Rank: 370 of 750 possible

Beaver Acres

Enrollment: 476
| 1995 Third Grade | 203 | 201 | 1997 Third Grade | 208 | 204 |
| 1995 Fifth Grade | 215 | 213 | 1997 Fifth Grade | 217 | 216 |

Socioeconomic Rank: 480 of 750 possible

Bethany

Enrollment: 581
| 1995 Third Grade | 207 | 204 | 1997 Third Grade | 215 | 210 |
| 1995 Fifth Grade | 221 | 220 | 1997 Fifth Grade | 223 | 222 |

Socioeconomic Rank: 686 of 750 possible

Cedar Mill

Enrollment: 368
| 1995 Third Grade | 209 | 202 | 1997 Third Grade | 216 | 210 |
| 1995 Fifth Grade | 219 | 219 | 1997 Fifth Grade | 225 | 220 |

Socioeconomic Rank: 560 of 750 possible

Chehalem

Enrollment: 463
| 1995 Third Grade | 204 | 201 | 1997 Third Grade | 213 | 205 |
| 1995 Fifth Grade | 214 | 213 | 1997 Fifth Grade | 222 | 220 |

Socioeconomic Rank: 606 of 750 possible

Cooper Mountain

Enrollment: 575
| 1995 Third Grade | 205 | 204 | 1997 Third Grade | 216 | 211 |
| 1995 Fifth Grade | 219 | 218 | 1997 Fifth Grade | 223 | 221 |

Socioeconomic Rank: 726 of 750 possible

1995 Statewide Average:			1997 Statewide Average:		
	Reading	Math		Reading	Math
Third Grade	203	201	Third Grade	209	204
Fifth Grade	216	214	Fifth Grade	218	217

Elmonica

Enrollment: 547

1995 Third Grade	210	207	1997 Third Grade	212	207
1995 Fifth Grade	220	219	1997 Fifth Grade	223	221

Socioeconomic Rank: 641 of 750 possible

Errol Hassell

Enrollment: 528

1995 Third Grade	207	206	1997 Third Grade	214	208
1995 Fifth Grade	219	218	1997 Fifth Grade	221	221

Socioeconomic Rank: 615 of 750 possible

Findley — Opened in September of 1997

Enrollment: 591
No scores yet available

Fir Grove

Enrollment: 606

1995 Third Grade	206	204	1997 Third Grade	213	206
1995 Fifth Grade	219	216	1997 Fifth Grade	221	221

Socioeconomic Rank: 605 of 750 possible

Greenway

Enrollment: 577

1995 Third Grade	203	201	1997 Third Grade	213	206
1995 Fifth Grade	214	213	1997 Fifth Grade	220	220

Socioeconomic Rank: 389 of 750 possible

Hazeldale

Enrollment: 533

1995 Third Grade	205	204	1997 Third Grade	212	208
1995 Fifth Grade	217	215	1997 Fifth Grade	220	219

Socioeconomic Rank: 568 of 750 possible

Hiteon

Enrollment: 588

1995 Third Grade	210	207	1997 Third Grade	216	211
1995 Fifth Grade	221	221	1997 Fifth Grade	225	224

Socioeconomic Rank: 730 of 750 possible

Kinnaman

Enrollment: 462

1995 Third Grade	204	202	1997 Third Grade	212	208
1995 Fifth Grade	215	216	1997 Fifth Grade	220	220

Socioeconomic Rank: 545 of 750 possible

McKay

Enrollment: 370

1995 Third Grade	204	203	1997 Third Grade	211	207
1995 Fifth Grade	215	215	1997 Fifth Grade	219	219

Socioeconomic Rank: 548 of 750 possible

McKinley

Enrollment: 491

1995 Third Grade	205	205	1997 Third Grade	213	209
1995 Fifth Grade	218	217	1997 Fifth Grade	218	218

Socioeconomic Rank: 546 of 750 possible

Montclair

Enrollment: 344

1995 Third Grade	207	205	1997 Third Grade	213	209
1995 Fifth Grade	217	216	1997 Fifth Grade	221	222

Socioeconomic Rank: 639 of 750 possible

Nancy Ryles

Enrollment: 855

1995 Third Grade	207	205	1997 Third Grade	212	207
1995 Fifth Grade	216	215	1997 Fifth Grade	224	222

Socioeconomic Rank: 741 of 750 possible

3

1995 Statewide Average:			1997 Statewide Average:		
	Reading	Math		Reading	Math
Third Grade	203	201	Third Grade	209	204
Fifth Grade	216	214	Fifth Grade	218	217

Oak Hills

Enrollment: 562

1995 Third Grade	208	206	1997 Third Grade	216	211
1995 Fifth Grade	221	222	1997 Fifth Grade	224	224

Socioeconomic Rank: 734 of 750 possible

Raleigh Hills

Enrollment: 418

1995 Third Grade	209	206	1997 Third Grade	211	205
1995 Fifth Grade	219	219	1997 Fifth Grade	223	225

Socioeconomic Rank: 566 of 750 possible

Raleigh Park

Enrollment: 442

1995 Third Grade	210	210	1997 Third Grade	218	216
1995 Fifth Grade	220	218	1997 Fifth Grade	223	223

Socioeconomic Rank: 604 of 750 possible

Ridgewood

Enrollment: 448

1995 Third Grade	209	205	1997 Third Grade	216	209
1995 Fifth Grade	220	219	1997 Fifth Grade	227	225

Socioeconomic Rank: 678 of 750 possible

Rock Creek

Enrollment: 488

1995 Third Grade	209	206	1997 Third Grade	215	211
1995 Fifth Grade	217	216	1997 Fifth Grade	225	223

Socioeconomic Rank: 720 of 750 possible

Sexton Mountain

Enrollment: 743
1995 Third Grade 205   204   1997 Third Grade 215   212
1995 Fifth Grade 219   217   1997 Fifth Grade 221   221
Socioeconomic Rank: 708 of 750 possible

Terra Linda

Enrollment: 484
1995 Third Grade 209   207   1997 Third Grade 214   208
1995 Fifth Grade 221   220   1997 Fifth Grade 224   223
Socioeconomic Rank: 682 of 750 possible

Vose

Enrollment: 520
1995 Third Grade 202   200   1997 Third Grade 209   206
1995 Fifth Grade 215   214   1997 Fifth Grade 219   220
Socioeconomic Rank: 291 of 750 possible

West Tualatin View

Enrollment: 379
1995 Third Grade 207   207   1997 Third Grade 217   213
1995 Fifth Grade 220   217   1997 Fifth Grade 222   223
Socioeconomic Rank: 628 of 750 possible

William Walker

Enrollment: 418
1995 Third Grade 207   205   1997 Third Grade 206   203
1995 Fifth Grade 217   214   1997 Fifth Grade 215   216
Socioeconomic Rank: 372 of 750 possible

Gresham-Barlow School District

The Gresham-Barlow School District educates 11,000 students in 18 schools. There are two high schools, five middle schools, ten elementary schools and one alternative school. Founded in 1852 by pioneers coming to Oregon by wagon train, Gresham is Oregon's fourth-largest city and one of the oldest. Several high tech industries, including Fujitsu Corp., LSI Logic and Boeing, have facilities in this rapidly growing district.

Voters approved a $32.1 million bond issue to repair and renovate virtually all schools in the district. Eight million will be spent to put all schools on-line and provide technology training for teachers, as well as professional-technical labs in all the middle and high schools and hundreds of new computers. There is a computer for every seven students in the district. The district maintains a Web site (http://district. gresham.k12.or.us). Bond funds will also be used to purchase land for additional growth. The district received $4,130 per student from the state in 1996-97. Because Gresham-Barlow is in better financial shape than many districts, it has been able to add programs.

An International Baccalaureate program is available at Gresham High School for students from either high school who wish to participate. Second language instruction begins in first grade. The elementary schools have a full-time counselor, music teacher and physical education teacher and a half-time media specialist. Middle schools offer a no-cut athletics program and students compete with other Mt. Hood Conference schools. The middle school student to teacher ratio is 27:1 and the high school ratio is 25:1. Student-led Benchmark conferences offered every spring in grades 3, 5, 8 & 10 help parents and students assess how the student is meeting Oregon's standards. The home page offers information on assessment.

The district's educational foundation is also in very good health. It raised $180,420 in 1996-97 and distributed over $60,000 in grants in 1997-98. Foundation publications are attractive and very informative. A Gresham High School alumnus donated $250,000 to the foundation in 1998. The district takes out-of-district students on a tuition basis ($4,500), and it currently has between 50 to 60 tuition students.

Gresham-Barlow District High Schools

Sam Barlow High School

5105 S.E. 302ⁿᵈ
Gresham, Oregon 97080-8927
✆ **503/663-4112**

Grades: 9 through 12
Enrollment: 1725
Faculty: 102
Founded: 1968

Sam Barlow offers a comprehensive academic program with a focus on college prep courses supported by technology. Beginning with the graduating class of 2001, students must earn 25 credits for graduation. Students are on block schedules and take seven classes per semester.

Funds from the bond passed in 1996 allowed the district to renovated the library, add a new gymnasium, a new track and field facility, science rooms and East Multnomah County's first Smart Lab (a $300,000 professional-technical computer facility) and 200-300 additional computers.

Sam Barlow's professional-technical offerings, which are filled to capacity each semester, are linked with Mt. Hood Community College through a 2+2 program. During the 1998-99 school year, Sam Barlow celebrated its 30-year anniversary as a high school serving the Orient, Damascus, Boring and Gresham communities. Ceremonies focused on the school's rich history of achievement academically, athletically, and in music, speech and the arts.

Students compete in athletics and music in the Mt. Hood conference, and the Bruins enjoy success in many areas. Large numbers of students participate in school activities.

SAT Scores 1997:	Verbal: 510	Math: 516
1996:	523	542
1995:	460	507
Number taking test in 1997: 167		
OAT Scores 1997 (10th Grade):	Reading: 238	Math: 234
1997 Statewide Average:	236	233
1995 (11th Grade):	234	233
1995 Statewide Average:	235	232
Socioeconomic Rank: 217 of 254 possible		

3

Gresham High School

1200 North Main
Gresham, Oregon 97030-3899
✆ 503/666-8033
Grades: 9 through 12
Enrollment: 1,555
Faculty: 89
Founded: 1914

Redbook magazine recognized Gresham High School in 1996 as a School of Excellence for its rigorous Senior Project program, which is now in its fourth year of refinement. Gresham High offers a broad range of instruction designed to provide a comprehensive academic program for all students. An International Baccalaureate program, advanced placement classes, and early entry college credit classes offered in conjunction with Mt. Hood Community College meet the needs of college-bound students.

The school's emphasis on technology is facilitated by over 500 computers serving the nearly 1,600 students. Eight new state-of-the-art science classrooms were added in 1998. The school provides instruction in four languages including four years of Japanese. The high school has one of the lowest drop out rates in Oregon for large high schools and offers a very successful school-within-a-school program for kids at risk of dropping out.

Classes are on a block schedule; students take seven or eight classes each semester. Twenty-five credits are required for graduation. The school offers a 2+2 program with Mt. Hood Community College in several career areas. There is a very good theater arts program. The Gophers compete in the Mt. Hood Conference, and there is a full range of athletic teams.

SAT Scores 1997:	Verbal: 487	Math: 495
1996:	502	513
1995:	424	487
Number taking test 1997: 136		
OAT Scores 1997 (10th Grade):	Reading: 237	Math: 233
1997 Statewide Average:	236	233
1995 (11th Grade):	234	232
1995 Statewide Average:	179	232
Socioeconomic Rank: 175 of 254 possible		

Gresham-Barlow District Middle Schools

Clear Creek Middle School

219 N.E. 219th
Gresham, OR 97030-8495
✆ **503/492-6700**
FAX 503/492-6707

Grades: 6 through 8
Enrollment: 689
Faculty: 42
Founded: 1993

Students at Clear Creek are divided into five teams. Each team has the same core teachers for all three years of the middle school program. This helps the teachers get to know their students well and to meet individual student needs. Electives offered include choir, band, art, technology, Internet, creative writing, yearbook, speech, math challenge, science challenge and flag and drill team.

OAT Scores 1997 (8th Grade):	Reading: 234	Math: 233
1997 Statewide Average:	231	232
Socioeconomic Rank: 274 of 355 possible		

Damascus Middle School

14151 S.E. 242nd
Boring, OR 97009-9398
✆ **503/658-3171**
FAX 503/658-6275

Grades: 5 through 8
Enrollment: 361
Faculty: 21
Founded: 1921

At Damascus students are taught by teams of math, science, language arts and social studies teachers. Electives include band, choir, art, technology and Spanish. Bond dollars will go to a new gymnasium in 1998-99 and additional remodeling.

OAT Scores 1997 (8th Grade):	Reading: 234	Math: 233
1997 Statewide Average:	235	232
Socioeconomic Rank: 320 of 355 possible		

Gordon Russell Middle School

3625 East Powell Blvd.
Gresham, OR 97080-1614
✆ **503/667-6900**
FAX 503/492-6708

Grades: 6 through 8
Enrollment: 825
Faculty: 45
Founded: 1977

The school is divided into five teams; two sixth grade interdisciplinary teams, and three 7th and 8th grade interdisciplinary teams. Math, science,

3

humanities and Spanish are taught in the teams. The thematic, interdisciplinary approach helps students see connections between subjects and helps them tie what they are learning in the classroom to real life situations. Emphasis is on hands-on and project-oriented activities. Specialists teach PE, health and electives. Students may choose science technology, art, keyboarding, band or choir. In addition, enrichment classes are offered in drama, journalism, yearbook, German and student government.

OAT Scores 1997 (8th Grade):	Reading: 232	Math: 228
1997 Statewide Average:	231	231
Socioeconomic Rank: 254 of 355 possible		

McCarty Middle School

1400 S.E. 5th
Gresham, OR 97080-8198
✆ 503/665-0148
FAX 503/669-1892

Grades: 6 through 8
Enrollment: 625
Faculty: 34
Founded: 1968

Sixth graders have two long blocks, humanities (writing, speaking, reading, listening and social studies) and math/ science/ health. They also take an exploratory program of electives; keyboarding/word processing, research skills, and art. They have PE every day. Seventh graders have a humanities teacher who stays with them for two years. Math, science and health/ PE are taught by specialists at the seventh and eighth grade levels. Algebra is available for eighth graders in addition to their regular eighth grade math class. McCarty encourages parent involvement through the PTC and parent volunteer program.

OAT Scores 1997 (8th Grade):	Reading: 234	Math: 233
1997 Statewide Average:	231	232
Socioeconomic Rank: 298 of 355 possible		

West Orient Middle School

29805 S.E. Orient Drive
Gresham, OR 97080-8816
✆ 503/663-3323
FAX 503/663-2504

Grades: 5 through 8
Enrollment: 399
Faculty: 18
Founded: 1854

West Orient emphasizes a strong parent-school partnership. Students are encouraged to become self-directed learners. The school philosophy is that pre-adolescents are most likely to achieve their personal best when there is a safe, nurturing and intellectually challenging environment that values individual contributions and progress. In addition to the regular academic program, Spanish is offered to all students in grades 5-8. There is also a band program and two technology labs. Enrichment classes in science, art, drama, chess and technology are available. Before and after school tutorials are available for students who need additional help. Students have been recognized for community service and leadership, as well as for band and choir performances.

OAT Scores 1997 (8th Grade):	Reading: 237	Math: 234
1997 Statewide Average:	231	231
Socioeconomic Rank: 292 of 355 possible		

Gresham-Barlow District Elementary Schools

The district is a combination of several smaller districts. When these small districts unified with Gresham-Barlow, some schools kept the same grades. For this reason, some of the elementary schools are K-4 and some are K-5. The student-teacher ratio is 27:1 in the elementary schools.

Second language instruction is introduced to all students in first grade. Spanish is available in all schools and Japanese at West Gresham. All of the elementary schools provide before and after-school care. There is also an after-school enrichment program at each of the K-5 schools.

Gresham-Barlow Elementary School OAT Scores

Statewide Average 1995:			Statewide Average 1997:		
	Reading	Math		Reading	Math
Third Grade	203	201	Third Grade	209	204
Fifth Grade	216	214	Fifth Grade	218	217

Deep Creek Elementary

Enrollment: 348 (Grades K-4)
1995 Third Grade 205 200 1997 Third Grade 215 209
Socioeconomic Rank: 724 of 764 possible

East Gresham Grade School

Enrollment: 585
1995 Third Grade 204 201 1997 Third Grade 209 205
1995 Fifth Grade 213 212 1997 Fifth Grade 219 220
Socioeconomic Rank: 379 of 764 possible

Statewide Average 1995:   **Statewide Average 1997:**

	Reading	Math		Reading	Math
Third Grade	203	201	Third Grade	209	204
Fifth Grade	216	214	Fifth Grade	218	217

East Orient Elementary

Enrollment: 379 (Grades K-4)

1995 Third Grade	203	204	1997 Third Grade	212	208

Socioeconomic Rank: 656 of 764 possible

Hall Elementary

Enrollment: 471

1995 Third Grade	203	201	1997 Third Grade	207	206
1995 Fifth Grade	215	213	1997 Fifth Grade	216	216

Socioeconomic Rank: 250 of 764 possible

Highland Elementary

Enrollment: 536

1995 Third Grade	206	202	1997 Third Grade	210	207
1995 Fifth Grade	216	215	1997 Fifth Grade	217	218

Socioeconomic Rank: 503 of 764 possible

Hollydale Elementary

Enrollment: 490

1995 Third Grade	201	202	1997 Third Grade	209	205
1995 Fifth Grade	216	216	1997 Fifth Grade	214	216

Socioeconomic Rank: 660 of 764 possible

Kelly Creek Elementary

Enrollment: 522

1995 Third Grade	206	202	1997 Third Grade	211	206
1995 Fifth Grade	216	216	1997 Fifth Grade	219	216

Socioeconomic Rank: 674 of 764 possible

North Gresham Grade School

Enrollment: 555

1995 Third Grade	201	200	1997 Third Grade	207	206
1995 Fifth Grade	215	212	1997 Fifth Grade	215	215

Socioeconomic Rank: 593 of 764 possible

Powell Valley Grade School

Enrollment: 547

1995 Third Grade	203	202	1997 Third Grade	207	203
1995 Fifth Grade	218	214	1997 Fifth Grade	217	216

Socioeconomic Rank: 599 of 764 possible

West Gresham Grade School

Enrollment: 429

1995 Third Grade	203	203	1997 Third Grade	210	207
1995 Fifth Grade	219	219	1997 Fifth Grade	223	222

Socioeconomic Rank: 691 of 764 possible

3

Hillsboro School District

Hillsboro is now Oregon's seventh largest city. It's located 20 minutes west of Portland in Washington County, which is Oregon's fastest growing county. The city was founded in the 1840's by pioneers arriving in wagon trains. It is named after David Hill, who established a post office here in 1843 and gave a portion of his land to be called "Hillsborough." Traditionally an agricultural area, Hillsboro is now home to several high-tech companies, including Fujitsu, Intel, Lattice and Logic. The Portland-Hillsboro Airport is the state's busiest general aviation airport and home to the Intel-sponsored Rose Festival Airshow, which attracts over 100,000 visitors. The area has nine golf courses, including two nationally ranked courses; Pumpkin Ridge and Reserve Vineyards. In 1997, the average home sale price in the Hillsboro area was $161,100. The westside light rail MAX train now takes residents of Hillsboro downtown in minutes.

The Oregon legislature mandated that school districts without a high school would have to merge with districts that had a high school by 1996. Hillsboro is a combination of seven small districts: Reedville Elementary, Groner Elementary, Farmington View, West Union, North Plains, Hillsboro Elementary and Hillsboro Union High. Hillsboro is the fifth largest school district in Oregon and educates over 17,000 students. Rapid growth in Washington County has created the need for more schools in the district.

The new Century High School opened in 1997. Intel Corporation donated 550 computers to the new high school. The district still has many students in portable classrooms and plans to build two additional elementary schools. A bond measure for $38 million passed in November of 1998. Funds will be used to renovate Hillsboro High School and build two new elementary schools set to open in September of 2000.

The district opened Net School in January of 1999. Net

School is an approved alternative school for elementary and secondary students in the district who are home schooled. Students can access science, math, history and English classes (www.netschool.hsd.k12.or.us). They can interact with the teacher and other online students, and use interactive multimedia technology. Thirty-one students enrolled in the first week!

Hillsboro District High Schools

Century High School

2000 S.W. 234 Avenue
Hillsboro, OR 97123
✆ **503/848-6500**
Grades: 9 through 12
Enrollment: 1,750
Faculty: 85
Founded: 1997

Century High School is a modern, comprehensive school that has standard graduation requirement courses and a variety of college prep courses, including Advanced Placement. It offers foreign language preparation in Spanish, German, French, and Japanese, as well as a wide variety of fine art electives in instrumental and vocal music, theater arts, and visual arts. The technology department will prepare students for the 21st Century through curricular offerings in the Discover Lab 2000, Beta Test Lab, Communication Lab, and seven other well-equipped computer labs.

Students at Century may register for a maximum of eight 90-minute classes during a semester, moving them toward the 22 credits required for graduation. A resource center, numerous inclusion opportunities and courses offered in basic life skills, communication skills, and job skills help meet the needs of special education students. For students seeking an education experience beyond high school, Century provides a complete counseling and career center. In the career center, students may explore career interests, college selection, and scholarship availability. Aptitude testing (ASVAB) and a Career Information System (CIS) program are available on numerous computers to assist students in making appropriate career decisions.

Century also offers an "honors" program for students wishing a college preparatory academic challenge. A complete extracurricular program, including athletics and activities, complements the curriculum program. Because Century opened for school year 1997-'98, no test scores are available.

Glencoe High School

2700 N.W. Glencoe Road
Hillsboro, OR 97124
© 503/640-8971
Grades: 9 through 12
Enrollment: 1,605
Faculty: 91
Founded: 1980

Glencoe High School is located at the northwest corner of Hillsboro, in an area of mixed open farmland and suburban housing. A complete, modern high school facility, Glencoe offers a comprehensive variety of classes and programs. Students take six classes each day on a traditional eight-period schedule. Advanced and college preparatory classes are offered in all subject areas, including Advanced Placement English, U.S. History, and Calculus. Foreign language classes are offered in Japanese, Spanish, German, and French through the fourth- and fifth-year levels.

Certificate of Advanced Mastery (CAM) programs are available in business and management, health services, science and engineering, natural resources, social services, education, and law. These are junior and senior year block programs of integrated, multi-disciplinary studies. Glencoe also participates in the Western Washington County School-to-Work Consortium through the Hillsboro Chamber of Commerce, the Portland Community College (PCC) Tech-Prep, and CAPITAL Center regional high school programs.

The school competes in the Metro League and has consistently fielded strong, competitive teams. State championships have been won in track and field, boys' and girls' basketball, football, dance team, cheerleading, and sportsmanship.

SAT Scores 1997:	Verbal: 523	Math: 519
Number of students taking the test: 201		
OAT Scores 1997:	Reading: 239	Math: 234
1997 Statewide Average	236	233
Socioeconomic Rank: 199 of 254		

Hillsboro High School

3285 S.E. Rood Bridge Road
Hillsboro, OR 97123
© **503/648-8561**
Grades: 9 through 12
Enrollment: 1,400
Faculty: 80
Founded: 1924

HillHi is located on the south side of Hillsboro on a 48-acre campus. The current facility was opened in 1969 and consists of 13 buildings on a community college style campus. The football field, baseball field, and track are located in the center of Hillsboro.

Hillsboro High School is a comprehensive high school and students may take six classes each day on a traditional schedule. Advanced Placement (AP) classes in English and History are available. Students may take Spanish, German, and French up to four or five years. Through cooperation with Portland Community College, credit is awarded for various professional-technical classes including Childrens Services, Drafting, and Automotives. The school, which is fully networked technologically, offers a computer refurbishing class.

Since 1989, Hillsboro International High School (IHS) has been an option for students who want to pursue an integrated program with a focus on global understanding. Students take specialized classes, are involved in outside international experiences, and complete a senior thesis. Currently, there are 100 students in IHS.

Service to school, community, and extracurricular activities are an important part of Hillsboro High School tradition. Half of the students are involved in clubs and more than 130 in-service activities on a regular basis. Hillsboro High School has a strong reputation in the Metro League and state-level athletics and activities. In recent years, Hillsboro athletes captured state trophies in baseball, wrestling, dance team, cross-country, volleyball, basketball, track and field, skiing, and sportsmanship. All sports are available.

SAT Scores 1997:	Verbal: 531	Math: 524
Number of students taking the test: 201		
OAT Scores 1997:	Reading: 236	Math: 233
1997 Statewide Average	236	233
Socioeconomic Rank: 217 of 254 possible		

Miller Education Center

1665 S.E. Enterprise Circle
Hillsboro, OR 97123

Upper School	Grades: 9 through 12
✆ 503/648-2117	Enrollment: 50
Middle School	Grades: 7 and 8
✆ 503/693-2922	Enrollment: 30
Twilight School	Grades: 9 through 12
✆ 503/648-2117	Enrollment: 75
Outreach Recovery Program	Ages: 16 through 20
✆ 503/648-2117	Enrollment: Unlimited

The Miller Education Center houses several schools focused on helping students to find the success they have not been able to achieve in the traditional school setting. An Upper School, Middle School, Credit Recovery Program, and Outreach Recovery Program to get dropouts back into school are options available to Hillsboro students. Students may be enrolled in any combination of programs that meet their individual educational and vocational needs.

The Upper School stresses core curriculum and includes community service projects, challenge courses and job training. Inventive activities and lessons help meet individual needs and learning styles. A nursery with facilities for ten children and a program for teen mothers that includes parenting skills, as well as an academic program leading to graduation rounds out the high school program. Admission is by application initiated by the home school counselor and includes a personal interview by staff.

The Middle School, which is located at 560 S.E. Third Avenue, has close ties to the Hillsboro Boys' and Girls' Club. The school day is comprised of core classes (English, math, social studies and science), along with an elective. Field trips and activities, such as rock climbing, provide opportunities for experiences beyond the classroom.

The Twilight School, located on the Upper School campus, focuses on providing seniors with credit-recovery opportunities for graduation. Classes are taught as independent study; students work at their own pace with individual instruction from staff members. Most students are enrolled at their home school and come to Twilight School following the regular school day. Ninety-minute sessions are offered in the afternoon and early evening to accommodate student schedules. Admission is by referral from the student's school counselor.

The Outreach Recovery Program seeks to reconnect discouraged learners with school options. Programs include General Equivalency Diploma (GED) preparation and testing, pre-employment training, and job placement assistance. Some students are eligible for a dual enrollment program with local community colleges. With this option, students can graduate and receive certain college credits. ORP also connects students with community agencies, including the Human Development Corporation and Adult and Family Services.

Hillsboro District Middle Schools

Brown Middle School

1505 S.W. Cornelius Pass Road
Hillsboro, OR 97123
✆ **503/693-4022**

Grades: 7 and 8
Enrollment: 709
Faculty: 36
Founded: 1962

The R.A. Brown faculty places high value on team teaching. Both the seventh and eighth grade are divided into two instructional teams for the core areas of math, science, social studies, and language arts. Additionally, seventh grade students select nine-week elective classes in physical education, industrial arts, fine arts, music keyboarding, vocal music, home living, and computers. Eighth grade students elect similar classes for a semester or choose yearlong classes in foreign language and instrumental music. A student-centered leadership program is open to seventh and eighth grade students.

Computer technology is supported across the curriculum by offering three classroom-sized computer labs, one of which offers Internet access, as well as an industrial arts computer-aided design (CAD) lab for special project design. The media center has a bank of computers with electronic resources and Internet access.

Student tutoring is available in the mornings and after school. Activities, such as National Junior Honor Society, Diversity Club, hobby clubs, intramural tournaments, snack bar, and socializing are offered during a twenty-minute "Panther Pause" three times a week within the Homeroom structure. Homeroom teachers serve as Certificate of Initial Mastery (CIM) file managers along with their student advocacy role that focuses on character education and diversity issues. Opportunities for reading and study round out the week in Homeroom. A vibrant after-school intramural athletic program offers volleyball and basketball as well as track and field events.

R.A. Brown Middle School is proud of its educational program that balances core curriculum, skill building, multiple elective offerings, and physical fitness in a student-centered middle school environment. Elementary schools that feed into R.A. Brown Middle School include: Indian Hills, Butternut Creek, Ladd Acres, L.C. Tobias, Witch Hazel, Brookwood, and Reedville.

OAT Scores 1997 (8th Grade):	Reading: 231	Math: 231
1997 Statewide Average:	231	231
Socioeconomic Rank: 297 of 355 possible		

Evergreen Middle School

29850 N.W. Evergreen Road
Hillsboro, OR 97124
© 503/640-8900

Grades: 7 and 8
Enrollment: 754
Faculty: 34
Founded: 1981

Evergreen Middle School is committed to success for all students. Respect for self, others, and the community is emphasized. The school is divided into teams to provide smaller communities of learning. Interdisciplinary teaching teams teach core academic courses, with a strong focus upon basic academic skills. Advanced concepts in mathematics, reading, and written language are emphasized. Students are provided with multiple opportunities to demonstrate mastery of the Oregon Content Standards. Evergreen provides students access to technology through computer applications. A strong exploratory elective program is available at grade seven, which includes nine-week sessions of art, computer keyboarding, applied technology, and home living. At grade eight, students have the opportunity for more in-depth study of art, foreign languages, technology, and home living. Choir and band are offered at both grades and are enjoyed by a large group of students. Learning opportunities are enriched and expanded into the community through a strong service learning program.

Special Education and Talented and Gifted (TAG) programs are incorporated into the school's curriculum. A strong English as a Second Language (ESL) program provides for the needs of students whose first language is not English. Evergreen students perform above average on the statewide assessment in math and reading. Elementary schools that feed into Evergreen: North Plains, West Union, Lenox, Mooberry, Jackson, and Peter Boscow.

OAT Scores 1997 (8th Grade):	Reading: 233	Math: 233
1997 Statewide Average:	231	231
Socioeconomic Rank: 295 of 355 possible		

Poynter Middle School

1535 N.E. Grant Street
Hillsboro, OR 97124
© 503/640-3691

Grades: 7 and 8
Enrollment: 630
Faculty: 35
Founded: 1959

Students study a strong core curriculum and enroll in a rich variety of exploratory electives, such as band, choir, Spanish, technology, home living, and computers. In preparation for high school, students learn how to use a daily planner, organize homework, and set goals. Each student has a Certificate of Initial Mastery (CIM) manager, and CIM groups meet throughout the year to monitor work towards the eighth grade benchmarks for the CIM.

Activities are important at Poynter, home of the Patriots. At the end of each quarter, there is a Patriot Party to celebrate achievement. Student groups include: the PATS (Poynter Activity Team), Natural Helpers, Peer Mediators, the International Club, MESA (Math, Engineering, and Science Achievement), AWSEM (Association of Women in Science, Engineering, and Math), the Student Diversity Committee, Thespians, and Ensemble Choir. A high percentage of students participate in intramural sports, featuring volleyball, basketball, and track.

Poynter has a diverse, yet cohesive, student body. Students come from eight elementary schools, and students leave to all three district high schools. There is an English as a Second Language (ESL) program, a program for developmentally-delayed students, and an Educational Service District (ESD) early intervention program for three- and four-year olds which is housed at Poynter.

OAT Scores 1997 (8th Grade):	Reading: 232	Math: 230
1997 Statewide Average:	231	231
Socioeconomic Rank: 101 of 355 possible		

Thomas Middle School

645 N.E. Lincoln Street
Hillsboro, OR 97124
☏ **503/640-8939**

Grades: 7 and 8
Enrollment: 520
Faculty: 32
Founded: 1929

Thomas Middle School has been known throughout the years as a high school, mid-high, junior high and, now, middle school. It serves a diverse population of students that are on a traditional school schedule. Students are scheduled into seventh and eighth grade teams made up of language arts, social studies, and science teachers. Teachers meet daily during their common prep period to monitor students' academics and behavior.

Thomas students participate in elective courses such as foreign languages, art, technology, computers, home living, physical education, music, and drama. Thomas is also known for its outstanding video production room that provides hands-on training in audio video technology. Teachers utilize the facility to teach script writing and editing, video filming and editing, eventually producing a finished audio video product. Great efforts are made in introducing the students to modern technology. In fact, all students are given an Internet ethics course that prepares them to use computers and the programs available.

OAT Scores 1997 (8th Grade):	Reading: 231	Math: 231
1997 Statewide Average:	231	231
Socioeconomic Rank: 194 of 355 possible		

Hillsboro District Elementary Schools

Average class sizes in the elementary programs are 25 for kindergarten and 26 in grades 1-6. Parent volunteers donate more than 90,000 hours to the schools annually. The curriculum is the same in all 20 elementary schools. A pilot program introduces Spanish instruction to students in kindergarten through second grades. It will eventually be available through the elementary grades. Specialists teach PE and music. A character education program emphasizes the importance of honesty, responsibility, respect, integrity, compassion and civic participation.

Hillsboro Elementary School OAT Scores

Statewide Average 1995:			Statewide Average 1997:		
	Reading	Math		Reading	Math
Third Grade	203	201	Third Grade	209	204
Fifth Grade	216	214	Fifth Grade	218	217

Brookwood

Enrollment: 540
1997 Third Grade   207   206   1997 Fifth Grade   219
219Socioeconomic Rank: 602 of 750 possible

Butternut Creek

Enrollment: 455
1997 Third Grade   212   206   1997 Fifth Grade   222   222
Socioeconomic Rank: 668 of 750 possible

David Hill

Enrollment: 330
1997 Third Grade   203   201   1997 Fifth Grade   211   211
Socioeconomic Rank: 15 of 750 possible

Eastwood

Enrollment: 605
1997 Third Grade   206   204   1997 Fifth Grade   219   221
Socioeconomic Rank: 540 of 750 possible

Farmington View

Enrollment: 355
1997 Third Grade   209   203   1997 Fifth Grade   216   216
Socioeconomic Rank: 404 of 750 possible

Groner

Enrollment: 225
1997 Third Grade   213   208   1997 Fifth Grade   217   214
Socioeconomic Rank: 413 of 750 possible

Indian Hills

Enrollment: 585
1997 Third Grade   208   203   1997 Fifth Grade   222   219
Socioeconomic Rank: 686 of 750 possible

Jackson

Enrollment: 620
1997 Third Grade   209   205   1997 Fifth Grade   220   222
Socioeconomic Rank: 666 of 750 possible

L.C. Tobias

Enrollment: 660
1997 Third Grade   209   205   1997 Fifth Grade   217   219
Socioeconomic Rank: 633 of 750 possible

Ladd Acres

Enrollment: 640
1997 Third Grade   213   210   1997 Fifth Grade   219   217
Socioeconomic Rank: 678 of 750 possible

Lenox

Enrollment: 445
1997 Third Grade   212   209   1997 Fifth Grade   221   222
Socioeconomic Rank: 731 of 750 possible

Minter Bridge

Enrollment: 445
1997 Third Grade   208   205   1997 Fifth Grade   218   219
Socioeconomic Rank: 406 of 750 possible

Statewide Average 1995:			**Statewide Average 1997:**		
	Reading	Math		Reading	Math
Third Grade	203	201	Third Grade	209	204
Fifth Grade	216	214	Fifth Grade	218	217

Mooberry

Enrollment: 640

1997 Third Grade	206	202	1997 Fifth Grade	214	215

Socioeconomic Rank: 407 of 750 possible

North Plains

Enrollment: 365

1997 Third Grade	214	207	1997 Fifth Grade	217	214

Socioeconomic Rank: 417 of 750 possible

Peter Boscow

Enrollment: 520

1997 Third Grade	205	203	1997 Fifth Grade	215	215

Socioeconomic Rank: 127 of 750 possible

Reedville

Enrollment: 220

1997 Third Grade	209	203	1997 Fifth Grade	218	215

Socioeconomic Rank: 351 of 750 possible

W.L. Henry

Enrollment: 610

1997 Third Grade	206	199	1997 Fifth Grade	213	212

Socioeconomic Rank: 89 of 750 possible

W. Verne McKinney

Enrollment: 600

1997 Third Grade	205	200	1997 Fifth Grade	220	218

Socioeconomic Rank: 296 of 750 possible

West Union

Enrollment: 350

1997 Third Grade	212	208	1997 Fifth Grade	220	219

Socioeconomic Rank: 527 of 750 possible

Witch Hazel

Enrollment: 200

1997 Third Grade	210	208	1997 Fifth Grade	214	212

Socioeconomic Rank: 205 of 750 possible

Lake Oswego School District

In 1850 Alonzo Durham of Oswego, New York built a mill and laid out the Oregon town that became Oswego. In 1913 the name of the lake was changed from Sucker Lake to Lake Oswego and in 1959 the cities of Oswego and Lake Grove merged to become Lake Oswego. It is one of Portland's closest suburbs. The average price of housing in 1998 was $271,000. Covering thirteen square miles, with a community population of 34,000, the Lake Oswego School District educates 7,207 students in nine elementary schools, two junior high schools, and two high schools. Although it receives only $4,606 per pupil from the state, the Lake Oswego District spends $5,211 per pupil. In addition to the money received from the state, revenue comes from tuition students, fees for athletics, federal monies, district reserves and foundation contributions. The city of Lake Oswego provides just under $1 million annually to fund the athletic programs and after school activities such as the band program. A bond measure passed in November of 1997 provides $1.5 million per year over three years. $300,000 per year will fund technology and $200,000 per year will fund field renovation and maintenance. The remaining $1 million provides classroom equipment, textbooks, and other instructional support.

The district functions as a college preparatory school system. Ninety-eight percent of the high school students graduate; eighty-five percent of these students go on to college. Lake Oswego and Lakeridge High School students consistently produce high scores on the SAT, the National Merit Scholarship competition, and Advanced Placement tests.

The city's location, six miles south of Portland's business district, adjacent to the southern boundary of Portland and west of the Willamette River, is attractive to large numbers of professionals, managers, and administrators who work in downtown Portland. The lake in Lake Oswego is surrounded by residential development.

The Lake Oswego School District is strongly committed to providing its students with a high standard of education. It continues to work on restructuring efforts in accordance with the Oregon Education Act of the 21st Century. The district has a strong supportive community to help implement its goals. It has made a commitment to focus internally to strengthen its curriculum and instruction. Student performance standards have been raised to meet increased graduation requirements. Unlike neighboring districts West Linn/ Wilsonville and Tigard/ Tualatin, Lake Oswego enjoys a stable enrollment with little major growth projected. There is little undeveloped land left in the district. No new schools are projected to be built, and the district can concentrate on improving programs already in place.

The U.S. Department of Education's National Secondary School Recognition Award program has recognized the two high schools as among the nation's most outstanding high schools. Both are accredited by the Northwest Association of Schools and Colleges. The National Commission of Excellence in Education named Lake Oswego Junior High as a School of Excellence. The Oregon Department of Education recognized the exemplary status of Waluga Junior High's Drug and Alcohol Abuse Prevention Program. Each of the elementary schools features a parent-taught Art Literacy Program.

Lake Oswego students scored consistently above the state average on the 1995 Oregon Statewide Assessment Test in basic skill areas (math, reading and science). The district continues to strengthen its program and requires high school students to have a third year of math and science to graduate. Eighty-one percent of the high school students take the SATs.

The Lake Oswego District's Community School offers fee-based programs to provide more opportunities for students in the face of a reduced budget for the district. Year around enrichment classes and sports are offered. A before- and after-school extended day care program is available at all nine elementary schools. Kindergartners who attend half-day classes can go by bus to one of five schools for supervision in a day care program. Twenty-five percent of Lake Oswego students are enrolled in these extended day programs. Other pay-for-service programs sponsored by the Community School include a youth basketball program, sports camps, and numerous classes: math, science, computers, driver's education, art, drama, dance, chess and languages. The Community School also offers enrichment programs on Teacher In-Service days.

Every school in the district has established a 21st Century School Council. A collaborative team of parents, teachers, staff, and principals work toward improvement in the district's instructional program. Several organizations help strengthen district policies. Lake Oswego has established a Business-Education Partnership Program, which fosters a bond between businesses and schools in the community. The district has also developed a partnership for advanced learners, the Scholars Alliance Program. During the high school years, parents, educators and students in the program work in a unique collaborative process that involves innovative teaching techniques, advanced interdisciplinary curricula and small-group activities. Lake Oswego High Schools are partnered with the Oregon Department of Education, Lewis and Clark College, Clackamas County Education Service District, and the Lake Oswego Community School program to give highly motivated students the opportunity for intellectual development.

The Lake Oswego School District Foundation is a non-profit organization governed by a volunteer board made up of parents, business, community and educational leaders. It was established to support programs and activities that tax dollars are unable to fund. The goal is to significantly reduce class sizes and to broaden educational program offerings. In the 1997-98 school year, the Foundation funded eight teaching positions.

The district recently approved an alternative school program to help at-risk secondary students. Students take electives at their regular high school and participate in an academic program from 3:15 to 6:15 p.m., Monday through Thursday, at Lake Oswego High School. They may participate in a work experience program for credit. These students are provided guidance and counseling to help them get back on track toward graduation. The district has an open enrollment policy. Students may enroll at any school in the district as long as that school has space.

Lake Oswego District High Schools

Lake Oswego High School
2501 Country Club Road
Lake Oswego, Oregon 97034
✆ 503/635-0313
Grades: 9 through 12
Enrollment: 1,100
Faculty: 79
Founded: 1951
www.loswego.k12.or.us

Lake Oswego High School offers a challenging academic program with a focus on college preparatory courses. The school day consists of four 90-minute class periods operating on alternate day rotation. Ninth and tenth graders are required to enroll in seven classes. Six classes are required of eleventh and twelfth grade students. The school offers a comprehensive academic curriculum. Students must earn 23 units of credit to graduate, and they need to show competency in reading, writing, listening, mathematics, reasoning, speaking and career awareness.

Intensive study is encouraged by the following advanced and honors classes: Honors English, chemistry, America and the World and advanced placement calculus, physics, biology, U.S. history and discrete math. Spanish, French, German and Japanese are offered up to fourth and fifth year levels. College preparatory electives include computer science, fine and performing arts (drama, musical theater, choir, choral groups, band and orchestra), advanced vocational/ technical study, professional skills in the 21st Century, and advanced interdisciplinary studies in the 11th & 12th grades.

LOHS also offers a strong interscholastic athletic program. More than half of the students participate in sports. Competitive sports for girls include cross-country, soccer, volleyball, softball, basketball, skiing, swimming, golf, tennis and track. Boys compete in cross-country, soccer, football, basketball, baseball, wrestling, track, skiing, swimming, golf, and tennis. The school has an athletic stadium, which it shares with Lakeridge High School. A member of the OSAA and Three Rivers League, the school has a baseball field, soccer/ track field and tennis courts. All schools in the district use the swimming pool on campus.

A counseling center in the school includes counselors and specialists for learning support and remedial assistance. The center gives students assistance in high school scheduling and guidance in college selection.

SAT Scores 1999:	Verbal: 558	Math: 572
1998:	555	563
1997:	557	561
1996:	559	557
1995:	554	566
Number of students taking the test ('95): 220		
OAT Scores 1997 (10th Grade):	Reading: 240	Math: 238
1997 Statewide Average:	236	233
1995 (11th Grade):	242	239
1995 State Averages:	235	232
Socioeconomic Rank: 251 of 254 possible		

Lakeridge High School

1235 Overlook Drive
Lake Oswego, OR 97034
✆ **503/635-0319**
www.loswego.k12.or.us
Grades: 9 through 12
Enrollment: 986
Faculty: 40
Founded: 1971

Lakeridge High School offers a comprehensive four-year academic program for a student body that is a predominately college-bound. The school day consists of four periods, rotating every other day through eight periods on a block schedule with 90-minute classes. Students must earn 23 units of credit in order to graduate, plus they must be able to demonstrate competency in reading, listening, writing, mathematics, reasoning, speaking, and career awareness.

Lakeridge offers a challenging academic curriculum. A variety of advanced placement (AP) and honors courses are offered, including honors English, chemistry and advanced placement biology, physics, calculus, discrete math, U.S. history, and French, Spanish, German, and Japanese up to fourth and fifth year levels. A large selection of elective options is open to students. College preparatory courses include computer science, professional skills for the 21st Century, and advanced disciplinary studies (11th and 12th grades).

The school's fine and performing arts classes include On Stage, Children's Theater, improvisational theater, choir, Company (a by-audition choral group for 11th and 12th grades), band and orchestra. Students may participate in a wide range of activities and clubs. More than 70 percent of the students take part in Lakeridge's outstanding athletic program, which is a member of the 4A Three Rivers League. Fall sports include cross-country, football, soccer, volleyball, rally, and dance team. Winter sports are basketball, skiing, swimming and wrestling. Baseball, golf, softball, tennis and track are offered in the spring. Water polo (fall) and lacrosse (spring) are played, but not school-funded. The school has a baseball field, soccer field, track and tennis courts.

Students are given assistance in scheduling and college/ career guidance by the counseling center. A Learning Support Center is available to students with special needs. The technology center is open to all students. Travel education opportunities have allowed students to visit Austria, Germany, Japan, Canada, and the rain forests of Costa Rica.

SAT Scores 1999:	Verbal: 555	Math: 571
1998:	572	574
1997:	567	581
1996	542	555
1995	567	579
Number of students taking test ('95): 182		
OAT Scores 1997 (10th Grade):	Reading: 242	Math: 239
1997 Statewide Average:	236	233
1995 (11th Grade):	242	240
1995 State Average:	235	232
Socioeconomic Rank: 252 of 254 possible		

Lake Oswego District Middle Schools

Lake Oswego Junior High

2500 Country Club Road
Lake Oswego, OR 97034
© **503/635-0335**

Grades: 7 and 8
Enrollment: 616
Faculty: 27
Founded: 1956

Lake Oswego Junior High requires students to enroll in seven courses. An interdisciplinary team of teachers teaches required courses. One teacher teaches language arts and social studies in a two-period block. Each student is assigned to a core team of teachers, a counselor, and an adult advocate/ advisor.

Required seventh grade core subjects include language arts, social studies, mathematics, science, physical education, and computer technology. Seventh graders also complete one fine arts course, which may be music, art or drama. One or two electives may be chosen to complete the schedule. Eighth grade core subjects that are required include language arts, social studies, mathematics, science, and physical education. Two to four electives may be selected.

Elective options in music include band, orchestra, general music, chorus (7th graders), and the Sail Mates, a vocal group for 8th graders (by audition). Students can study French, Spanish, Japanese or German. Two types of art classes are available; one includes ceramics, printmaking, sculpture and jewelry, and the other concentrates on calligraphy, drawing and painting. Other electives include drama, home economics (food science, textile arts, family living), communications media, publications/ yearbook, technology, and leadership. Eighth graders may take computer technology and/ or computer applications. A Learning Support Center serves students who have been recommended by their counselor and Resource Specialist.

The Junior High features Intramural/ Interscholastic Athletic Programs. Boys' sports include cross-country, basketball, wrestling, track and field. Girls can participate in cross-country, volleyball, basketball, track and field. Students pay a sports fee to play.

The school has "Mixers" every six to eight weeks, which give the students an opportunity to join in various social activities. Students involved in drama and music participate in school concerts, plays and assemblies during the year.

OAT Scores 1997 (8th Grade):	Reading: 237	Math: 236
1997 Statewide Average:	231	231
1995 (8th Grade):	233	236
1995 Statewide Average:	228	230
Socioeconomic Rank: 351 of 355 possible		

Waluga Junior High School

4700 Jean Road
Lake Oswego, OR 97035
© **503/635-0343**

Grades: 7 and 8
Enrollment: 549
Faculty: 26
Founded: 1964

Waluga Junior High requires seventh and eighth grade students to enroll in seven classes. An interdisciplinary team teaches language arts, science and social studies in a three-period block. Each student is assigned to a counselor and a core team of six teachers. Seventh graders take language arts, social studies, mathematics, science, physical education, computer technology, and one fine arts selection (music, art, or drama). One or two electives complete the seven-period schedule. Eighth grade core subjects are language arts, social studies, mathematics, science, physical education and electives.

Waluga offers a variety of electives. Music selections include band, orchestra, mixed choir, and 8th grade concert choir (by audition). Art classes focus on painting and sculpture or ceramics and printmaking. Seventh and eighth graders may take Spanish. French, German and Japanese are also available to eighth graders. Others electives include communications media, computer application, computer technology (8th grade), drama, home economics (food science, textile arts, family living), leadership, publications/ yearbook, and technology.

A Learning Support Center assists students who have been recommended by their counselor and Resource Specialist. Waluga encourages students to participate in their athletic programs. Girls compete in volleyball, cross-country, basketball, and track. Boys participate in cross-country, basketball, wrestling, and track. A sports fee is charged. Intramural activities (bowling, tennis, swimming, table tennis, floor hockey, gymnastics, and volleyball) are recommended for all students. Student council representatives are selected by vote. All students are invited to participate in mixers, concerts, plays, assemblies and intermurals.

OAT Scores 1997 (8th Grade):	Reading: 236	Math: 236
1997 Statewide Average:	231	231
1995 (8th Grade):	234	236
1995 Statewide Average:	228	230
Socioeconomic Rank: 353 of 355 possible		

Lake Oswego District Elementary Schools

Lake Oswego School District has nine elementary schools. All schools have developed a similar curriculum and have the same type of facilities (gymnasium, covered play area, field area, and playground). Students from Bryant, Hallinan, Palisades, River Grove, and Westridge attend Waluga Junior High. Students from Forest Hills, Lake Grove, Oak Creek and Uplands go into Lake Oswego Junior High. The district has an open enrollment policy, provided there is space available.

Students may be grouped together in multi-age classes. They also may receive instruction in various subjects from different teachers according to their abilities. The student teacher ratio is 1:25, and the curriculum focuses on language arts and mathematics skills. Instruction is given in reading, spelling, science, physical education, literature, written expression, social studies, art, mathematics, computer literacy, health, and music. Special attention is given to developing students' ability to think, communicate and solve problems. The school psychologist or counselor instructs all students on self-concept and getting along with others.

Each elementary school has a staff of specialists: a talented and gifted (TAG) specialist, a physical education teacher, general music instructor, speech clinician, learning specialist, counselor, school psychologist and nurse. Band instruction is available to sixth grade students before school. Strings instruction is available for grades 4,5, and 6. Elective foreign language classes are taught outside the school day. Students with special needs or disabilities are provided with services at Oak Creek and

Uplands or in their regular schools. Elementary students may participate in sport programs offered by organizations not connected with the schools. The sports offered include soccer, basketball, Little League, softball, and skiing.

The Lake Oswego District has a home page on the Internet (www.loswego.k12.or.us) that you can use to access more information on the elementary schools.

Lake Oswego Elementary School OAT Scores

Statewide Average 1995:			Statewide Average 1997:		
	Reading	Math		Reading	Math
Third Grade	203	201	Third Grade	209	204
Fifth Grade	216	214	Fifth Grade	218	217

Bryant

Enrollment: 335

1995 Third Grade	210	208	1997 Third Grade	215	209
1995 Fifth Grade	224	220	1997 Fifth Grade	225	223

Socioeconomic Rank: 734 of 764 possible

Forest Hills

Enrollment: 393

1995 Third Grade	211	207	1997 Third Grade	217	210
1995 Fifth Grade	222	221	1997 Fifth Grade	226	225

Socioeconomic Rank: 758 of 764 possible

Hallinan

Enrollment: 417

1995 Third Grade	209	208	1997 Third Grade	218	208
1995 Fifth Grade	222	218	1997 Fifth Grade	226	225

Socioeconomic Rank: 755 of 764 possible

Lake Grove

Enrollment: 472

1995 Third Grade	208	206	1997 Third Grade	215	209
1995 Fifth Grade	218	218	1997 Fifth Grade	224	223

Socioeconomic Rank: 713 of 764 possible

Statewide Average 1995:			Statewide Average 1997:		
	Reading	Math		Reading	Math
Third Grade	203	201	Third Grade	209	204
Fifth Grade	216	214	Fifth Grade	218	217

Oak Creek

Enrollment: 606

1995 Third Grade	210	208	1997 Third Grade	217	210
1995 Fifth Grade	216	215	1997 Fifth Grade	227	225

Socioeconomic Rank: 760 of 764 possible

Palisades

Enrollment: 317

1995 Third Grade	210	209	1997 Third Grade	217	209
1995 Fifth Grade	221	218	1997 Fifth Grade	226	221

Socioeconomic Rank: 737 of 764 possible

River Grove

Enrollment: 345

1995 Third Grade	210	205	1997 Third Grade	215	210
1995 Fifth Grade	223	222	1997 Fifth Grade	221	222

Socioeconomic Rank: 719 of 764 possible

Uplands

Enrollment: 495

1995 Third Grade	205	201	1997 Third Grade	214	211
1995 Fifth Grade	222	221	1997 Fifth Grade	221	220

Socioeconomic Rank: 726 of 764 possible

Westridge

Enrollment: 360

1995 Third Grade	215	208	1997 Third Grade	221	217
1995 Fifth Grade	222	222	1997 Fifth Grade	227	226

Socioeconomic Rank: 762 of 764 possible

North Clackamas School District

The North Clackamas School District is located southeast of downtown Portland. It covers forty square miles and includes the cities of Milwaukie, Happy Valley and Johnson City, as well as the neighborhoods of Oak Grove, Clackamas, Concord, Mount Scott, Sunnyside, Southgate and Carver. The fifth largest district in the state, it educates 14,000 students in three high schools, a technical education school, four junior highs and eighteen elementary schools. Fifty-six percent of its seniors go on to college after graduation. In the past eight years, 126 students have earned National Merit honors. The 1995 graduating seniors received more than $3.8 million in scholarships. North Clackamas participates in Odyssey of the Mind and has qualified more Talented And Gifted teams to the international competition than any other district in the country. The district is committed to technology. It has a home page on the Internet (www.nclack.k12.or.us) with up-to-date information on the schools.

Socioeconomically, North Clackamas is extremely diverse; affluent neighborhoods and pockets of genuine poverty exist within the district boundaries. More than 3,500 volunteers and 500 business contribute to educating students here. The North Clackamas Education Foundation seeks to provide scholarships, to support activity and athletic programs and to enhance education through added programs and services. It raised and distributed more than $26,000 last year. The district put a bond measure on the ballot in 1998 for technology equipment and facilities. The $94.4 million will be used to upgrade some facilities and build a new elementary school, which will open in September of 2000 and a new high school, which will open in 2001.

The district has been named as a national School-to-Work Benchmark Community. In partnership with Oregon Business Council, it offers internships at Sabin Skills Center.

The program gets very high marks from educators.

A great program for pregnant and parenting teens called "PACE" serves all of Clackamas County. Federally funded and housed in the Sabin Skills Center, the program offers parenting classes for both the mother and the father. An on-site daycare facility for the infants makes it possible for girls to finish their high school course work.

I've also heard good things about The Academy, the district's alternative high school program for students with a high rate of truancy who have been let go by the other high schools. The Academy is located in an office park off McLoughlin Boulevard.

The district operates a Community School program of after-school classes for children and adults. Among the classes offered are art, music, Spanish and the Red Cross Babysitting Class. Summer school classes are available for elementary, junior high and high school students. The district is affiliated with the Northwest Association of Schools and Colleges.

North Clackamas District High Schools

Clackamas High School

13801 S.E. Webster Road
Milwaukie, OR 97267
© **503/653-3722**

Grades: 9 through 12
Enrollment: 1400
Faculty: 65
Founded: 1957

Clackamas High School was recognized for Excellence in Education by the U.S. Department of Education in 1984. The campus is on a 34-acre site ten miles from downtown Portland. The school has a very good honors program. Sixty seven percent of the graduating seniors go on to college immediately after graduation. In addition to honors classes, students can take such courses as calculus, humanities, history of Western Civilization and economics at Portland State or Clackamas Community College for college credit.

Foreign languages offered are Spanish, German, French and Japanese. The PE Department offers gymnastics, aerobics, and strength and conditioning, as well as health and PE Drama, music and band are also available. Clackamas has a marching band.

SAT Scores 1997:	Verbal: 537	Math: 522
1996	522	536
1995	449	520
Number taking the test 1997: 192		
OAT Scores 1997 (10th Grade):	Reading: 238	Math: 234
1997 Statewide Average:	236	233
1995 (11th Grade):	237	235
1995 Statewide Average:	235	232
Socioeconomic Rank: 228 of 254 possible		

Milwaukie High School

11300 S.E. 23rd
Milwaukie, OR 97222
☎ **503/653-3750**
Grades: 9 through 12
Enrollment: 1280
Faculty: 63
Founded: 1925

Milwaukie High School has had its share of problems in the past few years. There have been some racial incidents between Hispanic students and white supremacist students. The facility itself is old and in need of upgrading. The school offers several good programs, however. Project Advance allows students to take classes at Clackamas Community College; the Challenge Program allows accelerated students to take classes at Portland State; the Sabin Skills Center provides technical classes to Milwaukie High School students. Electives are standard, with French, German Spanish and Japanese offered in the languages department.

Milwaukie has a football stadium, track, softball and baseball fields and tennis courts. Fall sports for boys are football, cross-country and soccer. Girls have volleyball, cross-country, soccer and dance team. Winter sports are basketball, ski team and swim team for both sexes and wrestling for boys. Spring sports are track, golf and tennis for both, softball for girls and baseball for boys. The school competes in the 4A Three Rivers League. The Girls' Dance Team took first place in the state in 1995-96.

SAT Scores 1997:	Verbal: 528	Math: 495
1996:	510	519
1995:	466	527
Number taking the test 1997: 81		

OAT Scores 1997 (10th Grade):	Reading: 233	Math: 232
1997 Statewide Average:	236	233
1995 (11th Grade):	235	231
1995 Statewide Average:	235	232
Socioeconomic Rank: 93 of 254 possible		

Rex Putnam High School

4950 S.E. Roethe Road
Milwaukie, OR 97267
✆ **503/653-3800**

Grades: 9 through 12
Enrollment: 1200
Faculty: 55
Founded: 1966

Rex Putnam is located ten miles from Portland on a thirty-seven-acre site south of the Milwaukie residential area. The school received national recognition in 1984-85 from the National Secondary School Recognition Program. The school's motto is "An Uncompromising Commitment to the Pursuit of Excellence." The administration encourages students to set high expectations for themselves. Accelerated students can take classes at either Clackamas Community College or Portland State.

Rex Putnam offers French, Spanish, German and Japanese. Advanced Placement classes are available, and there's a wide range of electives in drama and music. The school follows an eight-period alternating block schedule. Students are expected to have homework and many class listings tell students how much homework per week they can anticipate in that class. Students may also take classes at the Sabin Center.

Students have many options in athletics. Fall sports for boys are football, cross-country and soccer. Girls have volleyball, cross-country, soccer and dance team. Winter sports include basketball, ski team and swim team for both sexes and wrestling for boys. Spring sports are track, golf and tennis for both, softball for girls and baseball for boys. The girls' softball team won the state championship in the spring of 1995. The boys' golf team won the district title. Putnam competes in the 4A Three Rivers League. Athletic facilities include a gym, a stadium for football and soccer, and baseball and softball fields. The school is hoping to fund tennis courts from the bond measure.

SAT Scores 1997:	Verbal: 553	Math: 529
1996	529	546
1995:	438	519
Number taking the test 1997: 115		

OAT Scores 1997 (10th Grade):	Reading: 237	Math: 234
1997 Statewide Average:	236	233
Socioeconomic Rank: 202 of 254 possible		

Owen Sabin Occupational Skills Center and Land Lab

14211 S.E. Johnson Road
Milwaukie, OR 97267-2397
✆ **503/653-3812**

Grades: 9 through 12
Enrollment: 2080
Faculty: 50
Founded: 1967

The Sabin Center is a unique program in Oregon, offering professional technical training in 19 subject areas. It serves more than 2,000 high school students in the district. Sabin has programs in Applied Computer Technology, which includes MS DOS, WordPerfect, Windows, Lotus 1-2-3 and AutoSketch. The Advanced Information systems program prepares students for office support and administrative assistant positions, using Windows, WordPerfect, Excel, E-mail and other business communication skills.

Seniors get on-the-job experience. Animal science, soil and plant management, agricultural mechanics and agricultural leadership are taught "hands-on" at the Land Lab. The Building Construction program has been developed with the Associated General Contractors to teach students the basic skills of builders. Child Services trains future nursery school teachers, daycare providers and teachers. Computer aided drafting uses AutoCad to train students in mechanical and architectural fields. Electricity/ Electronic teaches students to build lasers, stereo amps and other projects. They design and test circuits using IBM 486 computers. Sabin offers programs in Financial Careers, Forestry/ Natural Resources, Graphics Technology, Hospitality/ Tourism/ Recreation, Industrial Mechanics, Law Enforcement, Manufacturing Technology, Marketing & Management, Nursery & Landscaping and Telecommunications.

Sabin has an outstanding Health Occupations program. The school also provides education in Health Services to students in several rural Oregon districts through Oregon's first Distance Learning Program. Students in Tillamook, Lakeview, North Lake, Enterprise, Paisley, Ontario, Gilchrist and John Day attend classes beamed to their districts on Oregon Ed-Net's satellite. The interactive program provides one-way video and two-way audio to the sites. This project has been named OPT-Net for Oregon Professional Technical Education network. The system was funded by a grant from the Oregon Legislature and Governor John Kitzhaber presided at the grand opening ceremonies. Students in the program can communicate with the instructor through a bulletin board service run by students in the Sabin Telecommunications program. The Center does not participate in the OAT or SAT testing.

North Clackamas District Middle Schools

McLoughlin Junior High School

14450 S.E. Johnson Road
Milwaukie, OR 97267
✆ 503/653-3704

Grades: 7 through 8
Enrollment: 480
Faculty: 25
Founded: 1968

Students at McLoughlin are assigned to a "house" of 25 students with one advisor. They meet every other school day and remain together for the two years the student is at McLoughlin. The philosophy is that the close peer relationships and the contact with an interested, involved adult adds to the student's sense of belonging. The House teacher serves as the advisor, working with the student's parents to help them understand the goals of the program and the student's progress. All seventh graders are part of an interdisciplinary team and the teams stay together for the year. The teams use integrated thematic instruction to teach geography, language arts, science and math. Eighth graders take humanities, an integrated U.S. history and language arts class. There are two teachers in the humanities teams, and again the team stays together for the entire year. McLoughlin offers Odyssey of the Mind. Its 1995 team went to the state competition.

Electives are divided into the fine arts and the applied arts. Seventh graders must choose one of each. Eighth graders can select among any electives offered. Fine arts include the music program, drawing, painting, drama and dance. McLoughlin has a great drama department. The drama teacher was a professional actress and choreographer who starred in a TV series made for the Japanese market, "From Oregon with Love." Applied arts include technology, family and consumer studies, Understanding Children, fabric arts, creative writing, calligraphy, French and Spanish. Eighth graders can also choose to be an office assistant, instructional helper or cafeteria helper. Intramurals include girls' basketball, boys' basketball and coed volleyball. As a result of the bond measure, a new technology center is scheduled to open here in 2002.

OAT Scores 1997 (8th Grade):	Reading: 230	Math: 231
1997 Statewide Average:	231	231
1995 (8th Grade):	229	233
1995 Statewide Average:	228	230
Socioeconomic Rank: 156 of 355 possible		

Milwaukie Junior High School

2300 S.E. Harrison　　Grades: 7 through 8
Milwaukie, OR 97222　　Enrollment: 388
☎ **503/653-3709**　　Faculty: 25
　　　　　　　　　　　Founded: 1936

Milwaukie Junior High was built by the WPA in 1936. The school has a new student population of Russian-speaking children who are beginners in English. There is also an English as a Second Language program, which serves mostly Spanish-speaking students. The school divides students into teams of 25. Humanities are taught as a block. The foreign language elective is German. Other electives include home economics, art, computers, technology, band, and choir.

OSSOM is a group of students willing to commit to no personal use of drugs or alcohol. Milwaukie also offers a peer mediation program. Intramural sports available include basketball, volleyball, soccer and track.

OAT Scores 1997 (8th Grade):	Reading: 230	Math: 230
1997 Statewide Average:	231	231
1995 (8th Grade):	227	229
1995 Statewide Average:	228	230
Socioeconomic Rank: 169 of 355 possible		

Rowe Junior High School

3606 S.E. Lake Road　　Grades: 7 through 8
Milwaukie, OR 97222　　Enrollment: 680
☎ **503/653-3718**　　Faculty: 42
　　　　　　　　　　　Founded: 1963

Rowe is the only district junior high that follows the eight-period block schedule used by the high schools. This means that students attend four classes per day on alternating days. Teachers feel that the longer period day helps kids learn. Students are also organized into teams, and each team has a group of teachers for most of the required classes. This allows teachers to integrate the curriculum and makes the learning more meaningful. Rowe offers Intensified Language Arts for 7th and 8th graders who have demonstrated exceptional abilities in language arts. TAG/ pre-algebra and TAG/ algebra are available also.

Electives are divided into fine arts, practical arts, foreign language and others. Fine arts include band, choir, literature, graphic arts, ceramics and art. Foreign languages offered are French and Spanish. Practical arts include technology, family and consumer studies and a class called "Foreign Foods Sampler." Other electives include computer classes, journalism, publications, gymnastics, weight training, dance and study hall. Rowe has an English as a Second Language program for about twenty students who publish their newsletter in Spanish. Intramural sports are also offered.

Rowe has several leadership opportunities in addition to student council. The Builder's Club is for students who do community service. Rowe Pals are eighth graders who provide support for incoming seventh graders during the first month of school. OSSOM is a group of students willing to commit to no personal use of drugs or alcohol. Rowe also offers a peer mediation program. Twenty seventh and eighth graders are trained to help other students work through conflicts in a positive manner.

OAT Scores 1997 (8th Grade):	Reading: 234	Math: 231
1997 Statewide Average:	231	231
1995 (8th Grade):	228	231
1995 Statewide Average:	228	230
Socioeconomic Rank: 138 of 355 possible		

Sunrise Junior High School

14331 S.E. 132rd Avenue　　　Grades: 7 through 8
Clackamas, OR 97015　　　Enrollment: 607
✆ **503/698-2040**　　　Faculty: 30
　　　Founded: 1991

The curriculum is divided into CORE (language arts, social studies, reading and study skills), PE/ health, science and electives for seventh grade. CORE is a three-period class with an integrated curriculum. Seventh graders who have demonstrated exceptional ability can opt for an accelerated CORE program. Eighth graders take language arts, social studies, PE/ health, math, science, Careers and Communication and electives.

An "Exploratory Wheel" includes nine weeks of computer education and introduces seventh graders to technology, Family and Consumer Studies and art. Additional electives include French, Spanish, music, art, creative writing, band/ orchestra and technology. Intramurals offered to both boys and girls include flag football, soccer and volleyball. Track and girls' and boys' basketball teams round out the sports program.

OAT Scores 1997 (8th Grade):	Reading: 234	Math: 233
1997 Statewide Average:	231	231
1995 (8th Grade):	230	232
1995 Statewide Average:	228	230
Socioeconomic Rank: 335 of 355 possible		

North Clackamas District Elementary Schools

The elementary schools emphasize the basics in academic instruction. There is strong parent involvement throughout the district. The schools offer a unique program in character education that teaches honesty, compassion, respect and courtesy. The program is used as a model for the state and nation. All of the eighteen elementary schools offer the same general academic program as well as PE and music classes. Before- and after-school care is available for a fee at all school locations.

North Clackamas Elementary School OAT Scores

Statewide Average 1995:	Reading	Math	Statewide Average 1997:	Reading	Math
Third Grade	203	201	Third Grade	209	204
Fifth Grade	216	214	Fifth Grade	218	217

Ardenwald

Enrollment: 340

1995 Third Grade	207	203	1997 Third Grade	212	205
1995 Fifth Grade	218	214	1997 Fifth Grade	224	220

Socioeconomic Rank: 430 of 750 possible

Bilquist

Enrollment: 534

1995 Third Grade	206	203	1997 Third Grade	213	207
1995 Fifth Grade	218	214	1997 Fifth Grade	219	218

Socioeconomic Rank: 634 of 750 possible

Clackamas

Enrollment: 374

1995 Third Grade	202	199	1997 Third Grade	208	201
1995 Fifth Grade	216	212	1997 Fifth Grade	217	217

Socioeconomic Rank: 198 of 750 possible

3

Statewide Average 1995:   **Statewide Average 1997:**

	Reading	Math		Reading	Math
Third Grade	203	201	Third Grade	209	204
Fifth Grade	216	214	Fifth Grade	218	217

Concord

Enrollment: 376

1995 Third Grade	206	204	1997 Third Grade	214	212
1995 Fifth Grade	218	213	1997 Fifth Grade	222	218

Socioeconomic Rank: 631 of 750 possible

Happy Valley

Enrollment: 348

1995 Third Grade	209	205	1997 Third Grade	213	209
1995 Fifth Grade	221	221	1997 Fifth Grade	224	224

Socioeconomic Rank: 714 of 750 possible

Hector Campbell

Enrollment: 332

1995 Third Grade	207	204	1997 Third Grade	209	203
1995 Fifth Grade	216	212	1997 Fifth Grade	219	216

Socioeconomic Rank: 612 of 750 possible

Linwood

Enrollment: 399

1995 Third Grade	205	204	1997 Third Grade	212	205
1995 Fifth Grade	217	214	1997 Fifth Grade	219	217

Socioeconomic Rank: 600 of 750 possible

Lot Whitcomb

Enrollment: 471

1995 Third Grade	208	210	1997 Third Grade	214	211
1995 Fifth Grade	219	218	1997 Fifth Grade	218	218

Socioeconomic Rank: 145 of 750 possible

Milwaukie

Enrollment: 378

1995 Third Grade	205	205	1997 Third Grade	210	208
1995 Fifth Grade	216	213	1997 Fifth Grade	220	221

Socioeconomic Rank: 541 of 750 possible

Mount Scott

Enrollment: 498
1995 Third Grade   206   205   1997 Third Grade   211   205
1995 Fifth Grade   220   219   1997 Fifth Grade   223   220
Socioeconomic Rank: 689 of 750 possible

North Oak Grove

Enrollment: 299
1995 Third Grade   202   199   1997 Third Grade   212   213
1995 Fifth Grade   213   213   1997 Fifth Grade   217   217
Socioeconomic Rank: 317 of 750 possible

Oak Grove

Enrollment: 299
1995 Third Grade   203   203   1997 Third Grade   212   207
1995 Fifth Grade   216   215   1997 Fifth Grade   219   220
Socioeconomic Rank: 438 of 750 possible

Oregon Trail

Enrollment: 565
1995 Third Grade   209   208   1997 Third Grade   212   207
1995 Fifth Grade   218   216   1997 Fifth Grade   225   224
Socioeconomic Rank: 669 of 750 possible

3

Riverside

Enrollment: 483
1995 Third Grade   203   200   1997 Third Grade   213   206
1995 Fifth Grade   215   210   1997 Fifth Grade   218   215
Socioeconomic Rank: 497 of 750 possible

Seth Lewelling

Enrollment: 433
1995 Third Grade   202   201   1997 Third Grade   209   206
1995 Fifth Grade   214   211   1997 Fifth Grade   217   218
Socioeconomic Rank: 488 of 750 possible

Sunnyside

Enrollment: 498
1995 Third Grade   211   209   1997 Third Grade   212   209
1995 Fifth Grade   220   217   1997 Fifth Grade   225   225
Socioeconomic Rank: 722 of 750 possible

Statewide Average 1995:			Statewide Average 1997:		
	Reading	Math		Reading	Math
Third Grade	203	201	Third Grade	209	204
Fifth Grade	216	214	Fifth Grade	218	217

View Acres

Enrollment: 515

1995 Third Grade	206	202	1997 Third Grade	214	209
1995 Fifth Grade	220	216	1997 Fifth Grade	222	220

Socioeconomic Rank: 614 of 750 possible

Wichita

Enrollment: 305

1995 Third Grade	207	202	1997 Third Grade	214	213
1995 Fifth Grade	220	221	1997 Fifth Grade	220	224

Socioeconomic Rank: 316 of 750 possible

Riverdale School District

The Riverdale School District was established in 1888. As one of Portland's oldest districts, it has a long tradition of community support for excellence in education. In 1998-99, residents donated over $200,000 to the Riverdale Foundation, which was founded to offset revenue shortfalls caused by Measure 5 cuts. Six hundred fifty families live in this district, which is located between Lewis and Clark College and the Willamette River. The schools are the center of the community.

In the past, Riverdale students attended the K-8 grade school and the district paid tuition at one of the neighboring public high schools: Wilson, Lake Oswego, Lincoln or West Linn. The Oregon legislature mandated that all districts without a high school must either begin a high school program by the fall of 1996 or merge with a district that has a high school. Neighborhood residents decided that rather than merge with the Lake Oswego or Portland School Districts, they would start a small, college preparatory high school. Many families with children are moving into the district because of the quality of the K-12 program. Enrollment at the grade school is up over ten percent since 1995.

Committees were formed and the process of creating a high school began several years ago. Parents, teachers, school administrators and staff from the graduate school at Lewis and Clark worked to put together a high school curriculum plan. The decision was made to adopt the Coalition of Essential Schools model. The Coalition research and information comes from Brown University, and its program supports integrated curriculum, personalized teaching, and student-as-worker rather than teacher as deliverer of instructional services. Teachers are expected to be generalists first (scholars) and specialists second (experts in one particular discipline).

The Coalition supports the small schools research and believes teachers should instruct no more than 80 students, which is substantially fewer than most area high school teachers now encounter during the school day. The Riverdale District offers small classes with an integrated curriculum that includes a lot of teacher contact and feedback.

The mission of the Riverdale School District is to provide an environment where students gain knowledge, grow in wisdom and character, develop confidence and value learning. Riverdale does just that. The faculty and staff are outstanding, the community is very involved in the school, and the school is a community of learners. Just over 20% of the students at the grade school have been identified as gifted. The district is in the process of revising its gifted program. The needs of gifted students are met through individualized instruction and access to special programs and weekend classes offered through Multnomah County Education Service District.

The high school is located on the Marylhurst College campus. It is now in its fourth year and is expected to enroll about 300 students when the facility is completed. Riverdale School District accepts tuition students into the grade school on a space-available basis, and it recruits qualified high school students seeking a thought-provoking, supportive learning environment.

Riverdale High School

Marylhurst College Campus
17600 Pacific Highway (Hwy 43)
P.O. Box 2
Marylhurst, OR 97036-0002
✆ 503/699-9707
FAX 503/699-9431

www.riverdale.k12.or.us

Grades: 9 through 12
Enrollment: 100 in 98-99 projected at 300 by 2001
Faculty: 10
Founded: 1996
Tuition for 1998-99: $7,500

Riverdale School District opened its high school in September of 1996 with grades 9-12. A small, college preparatory program using the Coalition of Essential Schools format was developed to correlate with the values of the community: learner-centered, personalized, committed to lifelong learning, and academically rigorous. Three core disciplines — language arts, history and philosophy, and math and art — are taught in extended block periods. Electives include foreign languages, drama, publications and choir. Sports include volleyball, soccer, basketball, and golf. Students are encouraged to explore the world beyond school walls through community service and field studies.

The high school has developed a unique partnership with Marylhurst College. Students have access to the college library with over 100,000 volumes, a media specialist and the college science labs. They also eat in the commons, a step up from the average high school cafeteria. Riverdale High School is experiencing some of the problems new schools go through as they find their identity and market niche. The school will be moving off the Marylhurst Campus once the school board has secured a permanent site. The program has a great deal of promise as an alternative to the large urban high schools in the area.

SAT Scores 1999:	Verbal: 667 Math: 670

OAT Scores 1997 (10th Grade):	Reading: 245 Math: 246

1997 Statewide Average:	236	233

Socioeconomic Rank: Riverdale had too few 10th graders to be ranked in this category in 1997.

Riverdale Grade School

11733 S.W. Breyman Avenue
Portland, OR 97219-8409
© **503/636-4511**
FAX 503/635-6342
www.riverdale.k12.or.us

Grades: K through 8
Enrollment: 320
Faculty: 26
Founded: 1888
Tuition (1998-99): $7,310

Riverdale Grade School is a public school that looks very much like an independent school. Located in the wooded Portland suburb of Dunthorpe, the grade school has an excellent academic program with an average class size of only 20 students. Riverdale offers an outstanding field studies program for all grade levels that allows students to travel throughout the Northwest. The school's library and media center are computerized; book fairs and author visits to the school are organized annually. In 1995, Marian Creamer, the Media Specialist, was named Media Specialist of the Year in Oregon. The school's Web site has a terrific Salmon Page (Dedicated to all things salmon: how to catch them, cook them, buy them and save them) that has won national recognition. The school has a state-of-the-art Macintosh computer lab connected to Internet and computers are networked throughout the grade school. All teachers and students in grades 4-8 have e-mail accounts. Shannon McBride was named Elementary Art Teacher of the Year in 1995 and Roxanne Malter, 7th & 8th grade math teacher, received the prestigious American Electronics Association Secondary Mathematics Teacher of the Year Award in 1997. In 1986, Riverdale received a National Elementary School award for excellence.

The school offers a competitive sports program for 6-8th grades in soccer, basketball, volleyball, tennis and track, competing with other small middle school programs. The band program is great. Riverdale has a marching band, a jazz band and a concert band. Specialists teach drama, foreign language, art, music and PE.

Riverdale Elementary School OAT Scores

Statewide Average 1995:	Reading	Math	Statewide Average 1997:	Reading	Math
Third Grade	203	201	Third Grade	209	204
Fifth Grade	216	214	Fifth Grade	218	217
Eighth Grade	228	230	Eighth Grade	231	231

Riverdale Elementary School

1995 Third Grade	206	202	1997 Third Grade	214	212
1995 Fifth Grade	222	222	1997 Fifth Grade	225	220
1995 Eighth Grade	238	242	1997 Eighth Grade	243	242

Socioeconomic Rank: 759 of 764 possible

Tigard-Tualatin School District

The Tigard-Tualatin School District serves 10,589 students in nine elementary schools, three middle schools and two high schools. A $20.5 million bond measure passed in May 1995 with $3.1 million to fund new computers and computer networking. About $4 million went to build Deer Creek Elementary School in the Bull Mountain area. Proceeds from the sale of Phil Lewis Elementary School, which is located in a commercial area off Highway 217, also helped fund the new elementary school. Phil Lewis closed in June of 1997 and Deer Creek opened in September of 1997. The bond measure also funded a ten-classroom addition to Durham elementary school.

The district offers a school choice program, which allows parents to select the school their children attend, provided that the school has space. A cap of 710 students has been put on enrollment at Mary Woodward Elementary. New students moving into that attendance area will be temporarily assigned to C.F. Tigard. Bridgeport is also near capacity and students moving into the Forest Rim or Orchard Hill apartments in the Bridgeport attendance area may be assigned to attend Byrom Elementary, if Bridgeport is full. Parents are responsible for providing transportation to the school of their choice (if it is not their neighborhood school) or providing transportation to a bus stop serving that school.

There are two kindergarten options. Half-day programs are available at Bridgeport, Durham, Byrom, and Templeton. Full-day, every-other-day, programs are available at C.F. Tigard, Mary Woodward, Tualatin and Metzger elementary schools. Breakfast is available at all district schools. The YMCA and other private providers run after-school care programs in all of the elementary schools.

Special education is an inclusive program and individual schools provide specialists to work with identified students. The district offers an alternative school for students ages 14 to 21 who are unlikely to complete a regular high school program. Individualized instruction and flexible hours help students earn GED certificates, transition back into high school or into a job. The needs of students who have been identified as talented and gifted (TAG) are met with activities that supplement the regular curriculum.

The Northwest Association of Schools and Colleges accredits the schools. The International Baccalaureate program is available at the high school level for academically strong students. English as a Second Language programs are available in the individual schools. The district has a music program, which begins in elementary school. Durham Elementary School has mixed-age groupings in all classes except kindergarten and first grade. The Tigard Swim Center is open to district residents for swim classes, lap swimming, family swimming and competitive swimming.

All of the schools in the district have site councils called "21st Century School Councils." Composed of staff, parents and community members, these councils serve as site-based decision-making teams. They have limited authority; they do not hire and cannot make decisions that would cost more money than the school is allocated. Like site councils throughout the metropolitan area, they hope to gain more authority as they become better established.

The district encourages parents to volunteer in the schools. It is actively seeking business partnerships with internship opportunities for students. A program called "The Community Experiences for Career Education" allows high school students to fulfill graduation requirements by working and exploring career opportunities in the community.

Tigard-Tualatin District High Schools

Tigard High School
9000 S.W. Durham Road
Tigard, OR 97281
℡ **503/684-2255**
Grades: 9 through 12
Enrollment: 1579
Faculty: 65
Founded: 1953

Tigard has an Honor School program that "encourages students to take risks, to stretch their intellectual potential, to assume responsibility for their studies and to make demands upon themselves academically." Honors-level course work includes upper division courses, many of which qualify for advanced placement and the International Baccalaureate.

Twenty-two credits are required for graduation. Those students in college preparatory are encouraged to take four years of language arts, three of math, two of science, three of social studies, two of foreign language and two college preparatory electives. French, Spanish, German and Japanese are offered. Electives include art, theater and music. Tigard has a cadet band, concert band, symphonic band, marching band, jazz ensemble, orchestra, guitar and four choirs. Facilities at the 50-acre site were completely remodeled in 1992.

A child services program with Portland Community College allows students to work three days a week in the preschool and two days week studying early childhood education and child development for PCC credit. The auto tech program offers six classes. Tigard has an English as a second language program to assist students and a GED program. A special services program is in place for students who have been identified and referred to the program.

SAT Scores 1999:	Verbal: 540	Math: 554
1998:	551	563
1997:	544	542
1996:	528	540
1995:	536	552

OAT Scores 1997 (10th Grade):	Reading: 240	Math: 237
1997 Statewide Average:	236	233
1995 (11th Grade):	235	235
1995 Statewide Average:	235	232
Socioeconomic Rank: 237 of 254 possible		

Tualatin High School

22300 S.W. Boones Ferry Road
Tualatin, OR 97062
© **503/598-2800**

Grades: 9 through 12
Enrollment: 1418
Faculty: 61
Founded: 1992

Tualatin High School's first class graduated in 1994. Built for 1500 students on a 64-acre site at a cost of $18 million, the school features eight science classrooms with greenhouse windows, a 12,000-square-foot library and a large computer center. Its athletic facilities include two gyms, team rooms, wrestling room, weight room, football, baseball, softball and soccer fields, an eight-lane all weather track, six tennis courts and practice fields.

The school offers a college preparatory program, an Honors School, and the International Baccalaureate. Twenty-two credits are required for graduation. Those in college prep are encouraged to take four years of language arts, three of math, two of science, three of social studies, two of foreign language and two college prep electives. Students who complete a comprehensive program of honors level courses in their junior and senior years and meet the Honors school requirements will have an "Honors Graduate" seal on their diploma and will be awarded a hood at Graduation.

Electives include art, theater and music. The school sponsors a concert band, symphonic band, wind ensemble, jazz ensemble orchestra and several choirs.

SAT Scores 1995:	Verbal: 540	Math: 554
1998:	551	563
1997:	544	542
1996:	528	540
1995:	536	552

OAT Scores 1997 (10th Grade): Reading: 240 Math: 237		
1997 Statewide Average:	236	233
1997 (11th Grade):	235	235
1995 Statewide Average:	235	232
Socioeconomic Rank: 237 of 254 possible		

Tigard-Tualatin District Middle Schools

Fowler Middle School

10865 S.W. Walnut Street
Tigard, OR 97223
© **503/684-2244**

Grades: 6 through 8
Enrollment: 849
Faculty: 37
Founded: 1973

In addition to its regular curriculum, Fowler offers an environmental studies program that uses Summer Creek as its laboratory. Here students determine the causes of its problems, work at restoration, and will eventually reintroduce fish. Field trips and guest speakers help relate the students' work to regional and global watershed problems.

The school also has a strong music program with woodwinds and brass and an eighth grade band. Orchestra and choir are available for seventh and eighth grade students. French and Spanish, various theater and art classes are also provided as electives. The leadership class works on school projects, service projects and runs the student store. Eighth graders can take computer classes in desktop publishing and multimedia.

OAT Scores 1997 (8th Grade): Reading: 232 Math: 232		
1997: Statewide Average:	231	231
1995:	229	231
1995 Statewide Average:	228	230
Socioeconomic Rank: 294 of 355 possible		

Hazelbrook Middle School

11300 S.W. Hazelbrook Road　Grades: 6 through 8
Tualatin, OR 97062　Enrollment: 823
✆ **503/598-2900**　Faculty: 35
　Founded: 1992

Hazelbrook was the first Tigard school designed and built as a middle school. Its classrooms are organized into three "school within a school" clusters. Students spend most of their day with one team of teachers, which allows teachers to offer integrated subject matter, such as science and math or language arts and social studies. Projects and assignments may involve several subject areas. Computer technology was "built in."

Electives include critical thinking, art, drama, home economics, and keyboarding/ word processing. Band and choir rooms accommodate a large music program. The student commons area has an elevated stage. Other special facilities include a media center, a gym and a covered play area. French and Spanish are taught as language electives.

OAT Scores 1997 (8th Grade):	Reading: 233	Math: 233
1997 Statewide Average:	231	231
1995 (8th Grade):	227	232
1997 Statewide Average:	228	230
Socioeconomic Rank: 330 of 355 possible		

Twality Middle School

14650 S.W. 97th Avenue　Grades: 6 through 8
Tigard, OR 97224　Enrollment: 857
✆ **503/684-2323**　Faculty: 37
　Founded: 1960

Twality Middle School was remodeled in 1996. Sixth graders here study language arts, reading, math and social studies daily, plus a health/ science unit that incorporates Outdoor School. Students alternate every other day between physical education and music. They must choose between band, orchestra or a general music/ choir class. A class called "Wheel" provides an introductory look at subjects they may choose to take as electives in grades 7 and 8, including computers, art, leadership, drama, and communication.

Seventh and eighth graders take social studies, language arts, math, science, wellness and a choice of electives — French or Spanish, band, orchestra, choir, computer programming, keyboarding/ word processing, art and drama.

OAT Scores 1997 (8th Grade):	Reading: 233	Math: 232
1997: Statewide Average:	231	231
1995:	Reading: 229	Math: 233
1995 Statewide Average:	228	230

Socioeconomic Rank: 327 of 355 possible

Tigard-Tualatin Elementary School OAT Scores

Statewide Average 1995:			Statewide Average 1997:		
	Reading	Math		Reading	Math
Third Grade	203	201	Third Grade	209	204
Fifth Grade	216	214	Fifth Grade	218	217

Bridgeport

Enrollment: 694

1995 Third Grade	206	205	1997 Third Grade	212	206
1995 Fifth Grade	221	219	1997 Fifth Grade	222	221

Socioeconomic Rank: 668 of 750 possible

Charles Tigard

Enrollment: 590

1995 Third Grade	203	203	1997 Third Grade	210	204
1995 Fifth Grade	216	214	1997 Fifth Grade	219	220

Socioeconomic Rank: 668 of 750 possible

Deer Creek

Enrollment: 547
New in 1997

Durham

Enrollment: 471

1995 Third Grade	209	208	1997 Third Grade	211	206
1995 Fifth Grade	218	218	1997 Fifth Grade	220	221

Socioeconomic Rank: 702 of 750 possible

Edward Byrom

Enrollment: 619

1995 Third Grade	208	204	1997 Third Grade	212	207
1995 Fifth Grade	220	220	1997 Fifth Grade	222	218

James Templeton

Enrollment: 594

1995 Third Grade	206	204	1997 Third Grade	215	208
1995 Fifth Grade	217	215	1997 Fifth Grade	219	218

Socioeconomic Rank: 684 of 750 possible

Mary Woodward

Enrollment: 715

1995 Third Grade	209	206	1997 Third Grade	213	207
1995 Fifth Grade	220	220	1997 Fifth Grade	223	222

Socioeconomic Rank: 731 of 750 possible

Metzger

Enrollment: 488

1995 Third Grade	204	202	1997 Third Grade	210	205
1995 Fifth Grade	212	211	1997 Fifth Grade	218	218

Socioeconomic Rank: 582 of 750 possible

Tualatin

Enrollment: 521

1995 Third Grade	208	206	1997 Third Grade	212	206
1995 Fifth Grade	216	214	1997 Fifth Grade	220	219

Socioeconomic Rank: 577 of 750 possible

West Linn-Wilsonville School District

Another of the state's fastest growing school systems, the West Linn-Wilsonville District educates 6,900 students in eleven schools. By the year 2010 the enrollment is projected to have increased to over 11,000. The farmlands that once covered much of the area are rapidly becoming upscale housing developments. Schools are crowded. The teacher/student ratio is 1:28.

Wilsonville has two primary schools, Boeckman Creek and Wilsonville, at near capacity. A new elementary school is needed, and soon. A new middle school, Rosemont Ridge, opened in September of 1999 with a capacity of 700 students. Bolton Middle School will house West Linn High School students while the high school undergoes renovation in the 1999-2000 school year. Students who would have attended Bolton will be at Rosemont Ridge along with a few Athey Creek students. When the construction is finished at the high school, Bolton is expected to become a primary school or possibly a K-8 school.

Ninety-six percent of district high school seniors go on to college, which is not surprising since the district is home to a number of Oregon's high tech companies and their employees. The new Wilsonville High School is a technological dream, genuinely a school for the 21st century. Every classroom is equipped with computers, TVs, VCRs and Internet hookups. Students can check out PowerBook computers in the school library. The initial budget for technology was $600,000, and computer companies donated much of the equipment.

The district meets the needs of talented and gifted students primarily though individualized programs in the classroom. Sixteen to twenty percent of students in the district have been identified as gifted.

Gifted middle school students are offered a number of classes designed to meet their needs. Accelerated eighth graders who have teacher and parent approval can also attend high school classes. The needs of special education students are attended through a range of opportunities from total classroom involvement to home instruction. The district supports inclusion of disabled students in the regular classroom and neighborhood school wherever possible.

In cooperation with Clackamas Community College, the district offers a Community Education and Recreation program with classes ranging from Embroidery to Sign Language. Such classes as Driver's Education and Dog Obedience are taught at the schools in the evenings. There's an adult volleyball league, plus Tae-Kwon-Do classes, tennis, yoga and dance. There are even classes on caring for your horse.

West Linn High School has an excellent Japanese program. Hitomi Tamura won the Confederation of Foreign Language Teacher's Teacher of the Year in 1995. Unfortunately, the district does not have the funding to hire more Japanese teachers for the elementary and middle schools. Spanish is the only language offered at middle school.

The district has an innovative and committed group of administrators who are concerned about what kids learn and how they learn it. The district provides a very good staff development program and a supportive environment for teachers. Teachers who become tenured after three years in the district are celebrated. An in-house memo to school leadership teams quoted Margaret Mead's statement, "Small groups of thoughtful, concerned citizens can change the world. Indeed, it is the only thing that ever has." The district believes in its staff members and their ability to create a learning environment in each school and for the district as a whole.

The West Linn-Wilsonville Education Foundation was created to help cover budget gaps. The school board has been asked to explore the idea of funding teacher positions through the foundation to alleviate some of the overcrowding.

The District's "Partnerships Program" is designed to find educationally enhancing partnerships among teachers, students and the professional/business community. Its stated goals are: to integrate learning with relevant experience; have common understanding of learning goals; involve students and adults in personally satisfying, life long learning; provide role models for students; expand resources and create synergy; and develop a work ethic that embraces individual and collaborative effort, engaged thinking and quality craftsmanship. The Northwest Association of Schools and Colleges accredits schools.

West Linn-Wilsonville District High Schools

West Linn High School
5464 West A Street
West Linn, OR 97068
✆ **503/673-7800**
FAX 503/657-8710
Grades: 9 through 12
Enrollment: 1360
Faculty: 68
Founded: 1911

West Linn bestows an "Honors Graduate" designation on the diplomas of students with advanced course work who maintain a cumulative GPA of 3.5 through the end of the second trimester in grade 12. Ninth, tenth and eleventh graders who excel in their classes are also honored through the Academic Awards programs. Through arrangements with Portland State and Clackamas Community College, students may earn college credit for advanced work in second languages, mathematics, language arts and history. The high school offers eight advanced placement courses and second language instruction through the fifth year level in French, German, Spanish and Japanese. The Fine Arts programs include art, photography, drama, dance, choral, band and orchestral music. Introductory professional technical education courses are provided on the school campus; advanced work continues at the Owen Sabin Skills Center in Milwaukie.

West Linn High School received a National School of Excellence Award from the U.S. Department of Education. West Linn High School offers special education, a comprehensive guidance department, and alternative education.

SAT Scores 1999:	Verbal: 558	Math: 567
1998:	549	559
1997:	555	556
1996:	531	553
1995:	531	545
Number of students taking the test: 328		
National Merit Commended Students (1996): 5		

OAT Scores 1997 (10th Grade):	Reading: 241	Math: 238
1997 Statewide Average:	236	233
1995 (11th Grade):	239	237
1995 Statewide Average:	235	232
Socioeconomic Rank: 246 of 254 possible		

Wilsonville High School

6800 Wilsonville Road
Wilsonville, OR 97070
✆ **503/673-7600**
Grades: 9 through 12
Enrollment: 479
Faculty: 46
Founded: 1995

This new school designed by Edward Vaivoda, Jr. of Thompson Vaivoda & Associates and built at a cost of $19 million looks like a traditional red brick high school. It is anything but traditional. Each classroom is equipped with a TV, VCR, overhead projector, telephone, three to five computers and 16 data drops for access to the school network and Internet. Local companies donated much of the computer technology.

The school has an initial capacity of 750 students; classrooms will be built to accommodate an additional 750 students. The cafeteria, gym, auditorium, library and athletic facilities are designed for 1,500 students. Facilities for arts include a small theater for audiences of less than 75 and a larger auditorium that seats 300. The area also supports a video projection room and rooms for vocal and instrumental music. Athletic facilities include a gym, wrestling room, aerobics room, weight room, locker rooms and a tunnel leading to the football field and track.

SAT Scores 1999:	Verbal: 532	Math: 537
1998:	524	531
1997:	527	524
OAT Scores 1997 (10th Grade):	Reading: 239	Math: 237
1997 Statewide Average:	236	233
Socioeconomic Rank: 243 of 254 possible		

West Linn-Wilsonville District Middle Schools

Athey Creek Middle School

2900 S.W. Borland Road
West Linn, OR 97068
© **503/673-7375**

Grades: 6 through 8
Enrollment: 746
Faculty: 30
Founded: 1990

Students take a core curriculum of language arts, literature, social studies, math, science and physical education. Additionally, they may choose one elective per semester; some electives are yearlong, others are for the single semester. Electives encompass choices in art (calligraphy, art survey, cartooning, drawing or sculpture) and music (band, strings and choir). Other electives include drama, Spanish, HyperCard, video productions, yearbook and fitness/ nutrition. Sixth graders have a special elective called "Exploratory Wheel" that introduces art, computers, music and foreign language in nine-week blocks. Athey Creek also offers a class for sixth graders called "Learning Strategies," which is encouraged for students on Individualized Education Programs. It provides an introduction to middle school, teaches organizational skills and goal setting, and social skills. The needs of gifted students are met primarily in the regular curriculum.

Athey Creek has an award-winning choir program. They attended a national choir contest and came home with "Overall Best Choir" and first place honors in Mixed Chorus and Women's Choir. In 1995 the Select Choir was Oregon's representative to the American Musical Salute to the Veterans of World War II in the Bay Area. Girls compete in volleyball, basketball and track, and boys in basketball, track, football and wrestling. Facilities include a track, tennis courts and football field.

Cluster: West Linn High School

OAT Scores 1997 (8th Grade):	Reading: 236	Math: 236
1997 Statewide Average:	231	231
1995 (8th Grade):	232	235
1995 Statewide Average:	228	230
Socioeconomic Rank: 338 of 355 possible		

Bolton Middle School

5933 S.W. Holmes Street
West Linn, OR 97068
© 503/656-3842

Grades: 6 through 8
Enrollment: 440
Faculty: 20
Founded: 1950

Bolton is being used to house West Linn High School programs in the 1999-2000 school year as the high school undergoes major renovations. Students will move to the new Rosemont Ridge Middle School at the corner of Rosemont and Salamo.

OAT Scores 1997 (8th Grade):	Reading: 236	Math: 233
1997 Statewide Average:	231	231
Socioeconomic Rank: 345 of 355 possible		

Wood Middle School

11055 S.W. Wilsonville Road
West Linn, OR 97070
© 503/673-7450

Grades: 6 through 8
Enrollment: 526
Faculty: 31
Founded: 1980

Students at Inza R. Wood Middle School take Core instruction in language arts/ literature, social studies, science, math and PE. Sixth graders are also taught organizational skills, study skills, art, and word processing, and they choose strings, band or Spanish as full year electives. If they are not enrolled in one of those three, they must select a semester of choir and another semester-long elective from Art Discovery, Video Productions, Hypermedia, Oceanography, Journalism/ Yearbook, Leadership, Science Projects, Learning Strategies, Classic Literature, Advanced Writing, Choir, Computer Graphics, Foreign Cultural Studies or Technology Exploration. The school has two computer labs.

An Educational Resource Center assists students with academic problems. Teachers and/ or parents can refer students for testing. The test results and the child advisory study team determine whether a student is eligible for the ERC. Competitive sports for girls are volleyball, basketball and track. Boys compete in basketball, track, football and wrestling. Sports facilities include an outdoor track and football field.

Cluster: Wilsonville High School

OAT Scores 1997 (8th Grade):	Reading: 236	Math: 234
1997 Statewide Average:	231	231
1995 (8th Grade):	230	233
1995 Statewide Average:	228	230
Socioeconomic Rank: 315 of 355 possible		

West Linn-Wilsonville District Elementary Schools

The district has six K-5 primary schools, and the ones I visited were truly cheerful places. Hallways are covered with student's work and awards they've earned. Students and teachers were busily engaged in learning activities. Parent volunteers helped in the classrooms and in the offices.

A before- and after-school care program is provided in the schools by the YMCA, which also offers morning care for children who are in afternoon kindergarten. All of the primary schools offer before- and/or after-school enrichment classes in computer science, the arts, foreign language and other subjects. Hands-on activities are emphasized, as is divergent thinking and creativity. Students who have been identified TAG have first priority for enrichment classes. Then, these classes are open to all students on a place-available basis. (There is a small charge for some.) The primary schools have computer labs, and all primary school students have weekly instruction in music from a specialist. The district also offers Saturday Enrichment Activities for gifted primary students K-5. These include field trips and offer kids the chance to meet students from other schools in the district who share their interests.

The only problem is that classes in the primary schools are large, and the district is meeting the needs of special education students in the classroom. This means that teachers are stretched to provide quality-time for all of the children in the classroom. The district is aware of the problem, but the student population is growing rapidly and budget constraints make it difficult to reduce class sizes.

Currently Boeckman Creek and Wilsonville Primary feed into Inza Wood and Athey Creek Middle schools and on to Wilsonville High. Cedaroak, Stafford, Sunset and Willamette feed into Rosemont Ridge and Athey Creek and on to West Linn High School. The Tualatin River forms the boundary between the two high school districts.

West Linn-Wilsonville Elementary School OAT Scores

Statewide Average 1995:			Statewide Average 1997:		
	Reading	Math		Reading	Math
Third Grade	203	201	Third Grade	209	204
Fifth Grade	216	214	Fifth Grade	218	217

Boeckman Creek

Enrollment: 524

1995 Third Grade	204	203	1997 Third Grade	218	213
1995 Fifth Grade	220	217	1997 Fifth Grade	222	220

Socioeconomic Rank: 694 of 750 possible

Cedaroak Park

Enrollment: 511

1995 Third Grade	207	204	1997 Third Grade	212	212
1995 Fifth Grade	220	218	1997 Fifth Grade	221	222

Socioeconomic Rank: 729 of 750 possible

Stafford

Enrollment: 638

1995 Third Grade	208	205	1997 Third Grade	216	211
1995 Fifth Grade	220	218	1997 Fifth Grade	224	221

Socioeconomic Rank: 738 of 750 possible

Sunset

Enrollment: 576

1995 Third Grade	207	206	1997 Third Grade	215	212
1995 Fifth Grade	221	220	1997 Fifth Grade	221	222

Socioeconomic Rank: 705 of 750 possible

Willamette

Enrollment: 539

1995 Third Grade	207	204	1997 Third Grade	214	209
1995 Fifth Grade	219	218	1997 Fifth Grade	223	222

Socioeconomic Rank: 676 of 750 possible

Wilsonville

Enrollment: 531

1995 Third Grade	203	202	1997 Third Grade	207	203
1995 Fifth Grade	216	215	1997 Fifth Grade	219	217

Socioeconomic Rank: 616 of 750 possible

Chapter Four
Private Schools

With the exception of parochial schools, which can be traced back to the mid-nineteenth century, Oregon does not have a long tradition of private education. There were only thirteen independent elementary and high schools listed in 1994-'95 summary of Private and Parochial Schools in Oregon that were neither religiously affiliated nor founded to serve one specific population (Tucker-Maxon Oral School for the Deaf or Mount Olive School for Dyslexic Children, for example).

Many families that have the economic means are now choosing private schools. Enrollment in independent and religiously affiliated schools has increased by 20% since 1991. The growth can be traced to several factors. Measure 5, which has forced increasing class sizes and declining options in our public school programs, has been a contributing factor to increased enrollment in independent schools. Also, people are moving to Portland from areas where independent schools have long been an alternative to public schools, and many families, especially evangelical Christians, are turning to religiously based schools.

How to Select a Private School

When choosing an independent or religiously-affiliated school there are several things you should know in addition to the information given in Chapter One, "What Every Parent Should Expect from a Public School." Values, governance, accreditation and mission are important in deciding if a certain school will fit your family and your child. Each school's publications will tell you a lot about its curriculum and facilities and about what the school values. Send for materials and read them carefully.

Admissions Policies

All independent schools have admission policies and deadlines. While it is not yet necessary to send a birth announcement to the school of your choice, you should plan ahead. Schools have points of entry, where the largest numbers of new students are enrolled. Usually this is at the prekindergarten, kindergarten, middle school and high school level. Numerically, this is the point at which your child will have the best chance of gaining admission to the school you have selected. The admissions process begins in the fall and early winter. It will probably involve tours, open houses, interviews and testing. The process is usually completed in January or February, and placements will be offered to new students in March or April for the following September. Schools also fill spaces that come available during the year when a child moves away. Most schools have a wait-list, but they may not be wait-listed for all grades, so if half way through the year you find that your child is not thriving in his or her current environment, it never hurts to call the admission's office and ask about openings.

Accreditation

Oregon does not accredit independent schools. The schools are simply registered with the state. Ask who accredits the program. The National Association of Independent Schools (NAIS) is a respected organization that accredits schools and provides training for school administrators, trustees and faculty. NAIS requires that member schools meet rigorous academic and ethical standards. The organization upholds "Principles of Good Practice for Member Schools" that spell out high standards and ethical behaviors for admissions, fund raising, financial management, instruction and administration. The cost of membership is high and usually only high schools or very large schools will belong. However, a regional association, Pacific Northwest Association of Independent Schools (PNAIS), also accredits schools and provides training and support services. Catlin Gabel, Oregon Episcopal, the French American International School, The International School, and Portland Jewish Academy are members or candidate members.

Governance

Ask about school governance. Is the school a non-profit or for-profit enterprise? Who are the trustees — parents or outsiders? What portion of the annual cost of educating your child comes from tuition and what are the school's other sources of revenue? Will you be expected to contribute to the school in other ways besides tuition? Some schools ask for volunteer hours, annual fund contributions, etc. How much input into the decision-making processes of the school will you as a parent have?

Staff

What are the qualifications and academic credentials of the administrators and faculty? Are they Oregon certified? Private school administrators and teachers do not have to be certified, although many are. Often they are highly qualified, with degrees from some of this country's best colleges and universities. However, occasionally you will find people who have worked their way up through the ranks without appropriate academic qualifications. Schools should offer profiles of their staff, listing degrees, experience and credentials. They should also offer written information about the curriculum.

Stability is another issue. If there is high staff turnover, ask why. How long has the present school head been there? Where were staff members employed before they came to this school? What are their qualifications? Does the school fund staff-development? Teachers need to be up-to-date on issues and research in education. Learning never stops, and good schools fund continuing education, or a portion of it, for their staff.

Environment

Facilities are very different in independent schools and run the gamut from urban schools with no outdoor playgrounds to beautiful campuses with lots of green spaces like Catlin Gabel. Assess your child's needs when looking for a match. Check the athletic facilities, the computer rooms, and the library. Is there a space for performing arts? If the school is lacking in something your child wants, can you provide it in an enrichment setting after school?

In selecting a private school you need to consider your child's academic, social and emotional needs. How much nurturing does your child need? Will he or she do better with a fast-paced stimulating environment? Does your child need special help that the school may not provide? As parents, you will also be a part of this school's community. Attend the schools' fundraisers and talk to parents to see if the school is a good fit for you and for your child. When you tour the school, notice how it looks and how it feels. Would you want to be in this environment for six hours a day? Would your child? All schools convey a "culture" that you can sense when you visit. Interactions among the staff and students will tell you a lot about the school and what it feels like to be a student there.

Class Size

Class sizes and teacher-student ratios are important. Ideally there will be no more than 14 to 22 students in a class. With fewer students your child will have less opportunity for cooperative learning and socialization. More than twenty-two children in a classroom with a single teacher suggests that the teacher might spend too much time on behavior and not enough on instruction. Preschool and prekindergarten should have a ratio of one staff member to ten students. If the class has an assistant, ask if that assistant is assigned full-time to the class or is expected to carry out other duties as well.

Test Scores

Private schools have different ways of listing their test scores. For such tests as the SAT, which a student is likely to take more than once, the school can publish the highest math score from one test and the highest verbal from another. Public schools don't have the time to do this, so this may skew the comparison between the various schools' average scores. Some schools, Catlin Gabel for example, prefer to declare a range of scores. They throw out the top and bottom 25% and list the middle range. Some private schools will not publish SAT scores and we have so noted.

In the listings that follow, we have included the schools we know from personal experience or the recommendations of knowledgeable parents and educators. Many independent schools are new, and we will be adding some of these in our next edition.

Independent Schools

Arbor School of Arts and Sciences

4201 S.W. Borland Road
Tualatin, OR 97062
✆ 503/638-6399
FAX 503/638-5636
Grades: K through 8
Enrollment: 150
Faculty: 10
Founded: 1989
Tuition 1999-2000: $7,000

ARBOR SCHOOL OF ARTS & SCIENCES

Arbor School was founded by Kit Abel Hawkins, who spent eighteen years at Catlin Gabel School. The Arbor philosophy is to approach learning as an integrated, interdisciplinary process. The curriculum is based on the interrelationships among intellect, character and creativity. "We believe that in order to be well-prepared for the future, children must have a solid intellectual foundation, must develop their capacities for inventiveness, and must participate in a community that builds self-confidence and interpersonal skills."

Mixed-age groupings and small classes help focus on individual talents. Students remain with one teacher for at least two years. Arbor believes this kind of continuity sustains the teacher-student partnership. The school is located on a ten acre rural setting with creeks, woods, gardens, fields and farm animals.

The program is organized into Primary (kinders and first graders), Junior Program, (second and third graders), Intermediate Program (fourth and fifth graders), and the Senior Program (sixth, seventh and eighth graders). Arbor cultivates a buddy system. Older students meet weekly with their younger buddies at reading time, sit with them at assemblies and undertake shared projects frequently. Community service is a part of the program. As their on-going service project, seniors have adopted Annie Ross House, a temporary shelter for families.

Facilities include a library, a large covered play area, a design studio, a music studio and La Casa Espanol, in addition to four classroom buildings. The classrooms are equipped with computers. Co-curricular classes are offered several days a week in an extended day program.

Carden School of Portland

19200 Willamette Drive
West Linn, OR 97068
℃ **503/635-8314**
www.teleport.com/~carden

Carden School of Portland

Grades: Pre-K through 6
Enrollment: 65
Faculty: 13
Affiliation: Carden Schools
Founded: 1994
Tuition 1998-'99: $5,000 (K-4); $5,555 (Grades 5 & 6); $2,500 (5-day preschool); $1,750 (3-day preschool)

Carden schools all follow a curriculum developed by the founder, Mae Carden. The curriculum, methodology and teaching materials are common to Carden Schools throughout the United States. Teachers are trained in the Carden method and regularly attend Carden Foundation courses. Schools are locally owned and operated, but the Foundation provides the educational programs and materials.

This is a new program in Portland, but Carden Schools were founded in New York in 1934. If you are looking for a school that feels like an eastern "Prep" school, this may be a fit for you. The school values a sense of family and a formal, calm, quiet, and supportive classroom environment.

The curriculum adheres to the Carden Reading Method, which uses phonics and decoding. Classical literature, poetry and music enrich all grade levels. Carden provides "the highest academic standards possible." In addition to the strong academic curriculum, the Portland school offers art, dance, computer science, drama, French, physical education and public speaking.

The school limits class size to 15 (the average is 12), and uniforms are required. It promotes high standards of dress, courtesy, good manners and thoughtful conduct. Preschoolers have the option of a three-day or a five-day program. Pre-kinders attend five mornings a week. Extended care is available from 7:30 to 6:00. The elementary program runs from 8:30 until 3:00, with extended care also available. Carden will be adding a grade level each year to become a K-8 program.

The Catlin Gabel School

8825 S.W. Barnes Road
Portland, OR 97225
© **503/297-1894**
FAX 503/297-0139
www.catlin.edu
Grades: Pre-K through 12
Enrollment: 670
Faculty: 80
Affiliation: National Association of Independent Schools; Pacific Northwest Association of Independent Schools
Founded: 1957
Tuition 1999-'00: $11,160 full-day kindergarten to $13,990 for high school (depending on grade level)

Miss Catlin's School, founded in 1911, and The Gabel Country Day School, founded in 1936, merged to form Catlin Gabel. The best-known independent school in Portland, Catlin Gabel has a national reputation for excellence. Seniors in 1998 were offered admission to Colby, Harvard, MIT, Oberlin, Pomona, Princeton, Stanford, Williams, and Yale among others. A low teacher-student ratio (1:15), off campus learning experiences and a strong extra-curricular program are the benefits of a Catlin education. The school has a philosophy of cultivating awareness of the feelings and rights of individuals, concern for public and private property and for the rules of the school. Catlin is committed to ethnic, religious, and socioeconomic diversity. The school has done extensive training within its community on issues of diversity and sexual orientation. Catlin offers a program called "Summerbridge," designed to help prepare students for challenging high school and college curricula. The program serves ethnically and economically diverse middle school students from the Portland area. The Catlin Gabel Annual Rummage Sale takes up 60,000 square feet of space at the Expo Center for three days each year and raises $200,000 for financial aid.

The Cabell Center, a 600-seat theater on campus, is used for performing arts. The lobby is an art gallery where the Exhibition Committee presents exhibits and gallery talks by artists. A Distinguished Writers Program brings authors like Maya Angelou, Robert Bly and Craig Lesley to the campus. Athletic facilities include a gym, weight room, indoor and outdoor tennis courts, soccer fields, baseball diamond and track. Catlin has a competitive interscholastic sports program. Exchange programs are encouraged, community service is part of the program. The computer resources include Sequent and Alpha server systems. There are two computer centers as well as computers in classrooms and in clusters around the campus. The school is on Internet and BITNET.

After-school care is available from 3:00 to 6:00. Catlin also runs a summer program with classes and fun camps. The preschool admits children who turn four by the first of September. There are 74 students in preschool through kindergarten, 201 in first through fifth, 172 in middle school and 243 in high school. Catlin lists its SAT scores as a range of the mid-50%. The top 25% and the bottom 25% are thrown out.

SAT Scores 1998:	Verbal: 620-710	Math: 610-690
1997	600-740	610-670
1996:	580-690	560-690
Number of students taking the test (1998): 56		
National Merit Scholars (1999): 7 semifinalists and ten commended scholars;30% of the class was so recognized		

The French American International School
8500 N.W. Johnson
Portland, OR 97229
✆ **503/292-7776 (FAIS)**
✆ **503/292-9111 (Gilkey Middle School)**
FAX 503/292-7444

the
**FRENCH
AMERICAN
SCHOOL**

www.fas.pps.k12.or.us
E-mail: fas@server.fas.pps.k12.or.us
Grades: Preschool through 7; eighth grade opening in 2000
Enrollment: 340
Faculty: 30
Affiliation: Accredited by the French Ministry of Education; Association of French Schools in America; Candidate Member Pacific Northwest Association of Independent Schools
Founded: 1979
Tuition 1998-99: $7,385 (Preschool through Grade 6, full-day program)

FAIS has just moved to its new 10-acre campus. The site will accommodate a preschool through grade eight program for 350 to 400 students. The elementary program is called the French American School and offers a European curriculum with instruction in English and French. The Gilkey Middle School offers an international middle years program for students who speak French, Spanish, and for those students who come into the sixth grade with no previous second language experience. The middle school programs attracts students from other elementary immersion programs- French and Spanish- and students with no previous language experience looking for an internationally focused middle school program.

FAIS is the largest immersion program in Portland and the oldest. The class size limit is 20. The early childhood program is excellent and offers full French immersion. The elementary program offers instruction in both French and English. It is an academically rigorous curriculum, emphasizing language arts, math and science. The French American International School belongs to a network of more than 400 French schools worldwide, and its the pilot school for technology among the Association of French Schools in America. The school offers before- and after-school care, a hot lunch program and a summer camp. Fifth graders participate in an exchange program with a fifth grade class in France. Field studies are also part of the curriculum for grades two through four. ACE Weeks (Art and Cultural Enrichment) bring a wide variety of Portland-area artists into the school two weeks each year for workshops and performances. The computer lab is connected to the Internet, and the school has a home page. FAIS also runs AFSANET, a computer network for the Association of French Schools in America. French children are eligible for French government scholarships. FAIS offers financial aid and a 10% discount for the second child and 15% discount for a third child.

OAT Scores 1997 (3rd Grade):	Reading: 219	Math: 210
1997 State Average:	209	204
OAT Scores 1997 (5th Grade):	Reading: 235	Math: 231
1997 State Average:	218	217

The German-American School

1849 S.W. 58th Avenue
Portland, OR 97221
© 503/293-3131

Grades: Preschool through 4
Enrollment:85
Faculty: 13
Tuition 1998-'99: $6,195 (K); $6,570 (Grades 1-4); Preschool varies depending upon how many days of the week the child attends.
Founded: 1993

The German-American School is a language immersion school. The school moved into the old Sylvan School when the French American International School moved to its new campus. The school follows a German curriculum, with a multi-age kindergarten of three to five-year-olds.

German is used as the language of instruction; English is introduced for 20% of the instructional time from second grade up. The grade school program is based on a curriculum from Germany with additions that meet Oregon standards, so that children can successfully transition into public schools. Teachers are native speakers trained in early childhood or elementary education. A nurturing environment is central to the school's vision, along with collaborative and cooperative learning. Teachers are encouraged to continue their professional development. The school encourages parent participation in the classroom, on school projects and as voting members of the community. The school has a before- and after-school care program, and it supports a summer program.

The International School

025 S.W. Sherman Street
Portland, OR 97201
℡ **503/226-2496**
FAX 503/525-0142

THE
INTERNATIONAL SCHOOL

Grades: Preschool through 5
Enrollment: 200
Faculty: 25
Founded: 1990
Tuition 1998-'99: $5,950 (Grades 1-3); $5,850 (Kindergarten)

The International School began a bilingual immersion Spanish program in September of 1990 with nine students. It now offers preschool through grade 5 in Spanish. In September of 1995, a Japanese track opened. A full immersion Chinese program opened in 1997 and extends through kindergarten.

The school is located in downtown Portland near River Place. The preschool runs half-day or full-day, from two to five days a week. Low Kindergarten, the four-year-old program, is five days a week, full or half-day. Kindergarten and the elementary grades are full-day programs. Teachers are Spanish, Japanese or Chinese native speakers. The Spanish Ministry of Education and Culture accredits the Spanish track. Before- and after-school care is available.

Montessori of Beaverton

MONTESSORI
SCHOOL
OF BEAVERTON

17415 N.W. Walker Road
Beaverton, OR 97006
℡ **503/645-5247**

Grades: Pre-K through 6
Enrollment: 168
Faculty: 12 full-time and 1 part-time
Affiliation: Association Montessori Internationale
Founded: 1977
Tuition 1998-'99: $4,985 (Grades 1-6); $4,630 (Full-day kindergarten); $3,570 (4-hour Preschool); $3,041 (3-hour Preschool)

This is a traditional Montessori program with a "Children's House" and an elementary program. For three to six year olds there are several options: a three-hour program, four-hour program or a six-hour program for kinders. I have spoken to parents whose children have been in the

188

Children's House and they were very happy with it. Montessori of
Beaverton seeks to nurture a child's self esteem and natural curiosity. The
Montessori learning environment allows children to work individually or
in group activities. It seeks to help children by supporting self-
development with Montessori methods and equipment.

Lower elementary is a mixed-age grouping of six to nine year olds.
Upper elementary is a mixed-age group of nine to twelve year olds. The
elementary program is highly individualized. Children develop their
own projects, based on the concepts they have learned. The
interconnectedness of things children are learning is emphasized rather
than pigeonholing knowledge into categories; earth science, geometry,
etc. The Montessori method is designed to teach children to learn on
their own, so they are not dependent on the teacher. The teacher
introduces the subject then guides the students as they develop
individual projects to explore the subject.

The school has two locations. Five classrooms are located in the
Westside Church of Christ on Walker Road. One classroom for the 9 to
12 year olds is at St. Bartholomew's at 11265 SW Cabot in Beaverton.
Both facilities have playgrounds. The Westside location has an apple
orchard, and St. Bartholomew's is a wooded environment. Tuition is for
the school year, from September through mid-June. There are several
payment plans, and a 20% discount for a second child in the program.

Mount Hood Academy
P.O. Box 189
Government, OR 97028
© 503/272-3503
FAX 503/272-3642
E-mail: hoodacad@cerfnet.com
www.teleport.com/~hoodacad/
Grades: 9 through 12
Enrollment: 24
Faculty: 4 full-time and 4 part-time
Affiliation: Pacific Northwest Association of Independent Schools
Founded: 1985
Tuition 1998-'99: $10,800 (including school, room & board and ski
training)

Mt. Hood Academy was founded by Bill and Mary Gunesch to meet
the needs of Northwest students who are serious skiers. Bill is a former
U.S. Ski Team coach and Mary is a former National Junior Champion.
Designed as a high school program for ski racers, the PNAIS- accredited
school offers training and competitions as well as a full academic
program. The average class size is only 4, and all Mt. Hood alumni go
on to college. The school has had five Junior Olympic Gold Medals to its
credit.

The academy plans to offer a year-round program capitalizing on
summer training opportunities on Mt. Hood. Bryan Burke, who designed

the Warm Springs museum, has designed tw[...]
academy. MHA envisions an enrollment of 4[...]
new facilities are completed.

Northwest Academy

THE NORTHWEST ACADEMY
...a new vision in education

1130 S.W. Main
Portland, OR 97205
© 503/223-3367
FAX 503/402-1043
www.nwacademy.org
Enrollment: 40
Faculty: 20-25 part time
Founded: 1996
Tuition 1998-'99: $9,800

Visualize a program that integrates an exciting academic curriculum
with the visual arts, performing arts and media arts. Imagine a lunch
time speaker's roster of filmmakers, performing artists, musicians and
civic leaders that would be the envy of the City Club. Think about a
faculty that includes Greg McKelvey, the man who made Wilson High
School's jazz band famous, and Andrei Kitaev, critically acclaimed jazz
pianist. You are beginning to see Mary Folberg's dream of a performing
arts high school. The school opened with about 30 full time students in
September 1997 in the Galleria. It moved into a new 10,000-sq.-ft.
permanent site in June of 1998 at 12th and Main.

The schedule consists of five 90 minute blocks, and the school day is
from 8:00am to 5:00pm. Class sizes are small, with 12 to 15 students.
The curriculum is structured in a sequential manner. Students will not be
age grouped, but grouped by the proficiencies they have mastered.
When their knowledge, skills and understanding demonstrates they are
ready for the next level, they will move on. Their day will consist of a
foreign language/computer block, an English/ Humanities block a Math/
Science block and an Arts Sampler block. The curriculum is based on
the work of Howard Gardner, integrating different kinds of intelligences.
Northwest Academy received a $142,000 grant from the Meyer Trust to
develop its curriculum and programs. Elective courses will be offered
from 3:40 to 5:00 and these will be open to part time students as well.
Professionals such as Horatio Law, PNCA teacher and visual artist,
Adrienne Flagg of Toad City Productions, and opera singer Susan St.
John teach arts courses. The Northwest Academy Jazz Band, under the
direction of Greg McKelvey, has already won two regional jazz
competitions.

4

...st Community School

...29th Avenue
...nd, OR 97232
...503/234-2826
FAX 503/234-3186

Grades: 6-12
Enrollment: 70
Faculty: 7
Affiliation: Northwest Association of Schools and Colleges
Founded: 1993
Tuition 1998-'99: $5,500

Pacific Crest Community School is a small private school serving 70 students. Each student pursues his or her own academic goals through a flexible but rigorous curriculum. In addition to course work, every student is expected to make a significant contribution to the school community. The school's curriculum is designed around essential skills: literacy, cognition, numeracy, and personal and social responsibility. Pacific Crest students are required to volunteer 8 hours per month in the service learning program.

Pacific Crest offers solid fundamentals along with a wide variety of non-traditional courses. The curriculum is enriched by students initiating classes and playing an integral role in school governance. There is an emphasis on hands-on learning opportunities. Environmental studies may involve hiking, camping, rock climbing and cross country skiing. Writing, public speaking and drama are part of the Mock Trial Team experience and cross-cultural experiences are shared through the Russian Exchange Program. Pacific Crest is a lively school that welcomes all types of motivated, community-oriented students.

Portland French School

6318 S.W. Corbett Avenue
Portland, OR 97201
© 503/233-3963 or 452-4160
Grades: Preschool through 5
Enrollment: 110
Faculty: 14
Affiliation: accredited by the French Ministry of Education and member Oregon Federation of Independent Schools
Founded: 1989
Tuition 1998-'99: $5,610 (Pre-kindergarten full-day); $5,370 (Kindergarten-Grade 2); $5,950 (Grades 3-5)

The Portland French School follows the French curriculum, and classes are taught in French. English language arts are introduced in the second grade. The school moved in September of 1998 from the eastside to the Terwilliger School near John's Landing. This will give the program room to grow and some badly needed outdoor play space.

Quest Academy

8955 S.W. Commercial Street
Tigard, OR 97223
© **503/620-8770**
FAX 503/684-8019
Grades: 9 through 12
Enrollment: 140
Faculty: 11

Affiliation: Northwest Association of Schools and Colleges
Founded: 1983
Tuition: $30 per day (Regular curriculum); $50 per day (Special education)

Quest is an alternative program for students who are not succeeding in a traditional program or for students who need to pick up a specific credit. The school employs performance-based learning contracts and offers such core curriculum courses as earth science, biology, health, general math, pre-algebra, algebra I & II, geometry, English 9, 10, 11 & 12 and United States history. A course entitled "It's the Law," is among the electives available, along with art appreciation, geology, global studies, government, personal finance, personal psychology, current events and economics. Students can earn high school credit or a GED. As summer school programs are cut in the metropolitan area because of Measure 5, more students are attending Quest for classes they might have taken in summer during years past.

The school also maintains a middle school program. Quest holds high expectations for its students. Absences are verified with the parent by phone. Students who show signs of substance abuse or behavior problems are referred to counseling, and parents are called in to develop a plan for intervention. Five local school districts refer students to Quest. The average class size is 18, with a limit of 23.

Thomas Edison High School

9020 S.W. Beaverton-Hillsdale Highway
Portland, OR 97225
© **503/297-2336**
FAX 503/297-2527
Grades: 9 through 12
Enrollment: 65
Faculty: 12
Founded: 1973
Tuition 1998-'99: $9,950

A program for students with dyslexia, attention deficit disorder and other learning disabilities, Thomas Edison High School is located on the Jesuit High School Campus. Founded as Tree of Learning, the program offers small classes with individualized expectations and instruction. Students must want to attend, and many area schools refer students to

Edison. Grades are non-competitive. A full-time counseling staff works with students and provides parenting classes.

The curriculum includes reading, language arts, math, social studies, science, health and personal finance. Art, drama, yearbook and community service are available as electives. Parents are mailed weekly progress reports and are required to attend scheduled parent meetings. All parents work on the annual scholarship benefit.

Some students remain at Edison throughout their high school years. The goal for others is to make a transition back into a public or private high school or to a high school completion program at a community college. Edison offers a summer program for middle school students with basic classes in reading, writing, math and study skills. The program is open to all students with learning challenges entering grades 6, 7 or 8.

Touchstone School

2 S.W. Touchstone
Lake Oswego, OR 97035
☎ 503/635-4486
FAX 503/635-6254
Grades: Preschool through 6
Enrollment: 175
Faculty: 27
Affiliation: National Association for Education of Young Children, Northwest Association of Schools and Colleges
Founded: 1982
Tuition 1999-'00: $7,155

Touchstone was one of the first early childhood programs in Oregon to be accredited by NAEYC. Touchstone provides a strong foundation in the traditional disciplines in an atmosphere that encourages creativity and fosters individual growth. The curriculum includes interdisciplinary and multi-cultural learning experiences. Instruction in Spanish, physical education, and computer literacy is part of the program. The school has an indoor swimming pool and gym space. The teachers are excellent and staff turn over is very low. Pediatric residents from Oregon Health Sciences University do a rotation at Touchstone to observe well children in a developmentally appropriate program.

The school offers before- and after-school care programs, a school lunch program, and a range of after school classes including swimming and choir. The preschool program accepts children who are three by September 1 of the academic year. There are full-day and half-day options available. Each class has a teacher and an assistant. Preschool classes average 18 to 20 children per class. The curriculum is developmentally appropriate and provides for the physical, emotional, social and cognitive growth of the child. Spanish instruction begins in the prekindergarten program at age four. Kindergarten is a full-day program with 16 students per class. All children in the early childhood program have swim instruction during the school day.

The elementary program offers small class sizes, an integrated curriculum, and hands-on learning. The curriculum incorporates interdisciplinary, thematic, project-based instruction with an emphasis on critical thinking and problem solving skills. All students are regularly assessed and their instructional program is geared to their current developmental level. Students are encouraged to take responsibility for their behavior. Student discipline is based on the Teaching with Love and Logic model developed by Foster Cline and Jim Fay. Touchstone will add a seventh grade in September of 2000 and an eighth grade in September of 2001.

Tucker-Maxon Oral School for the Deaf

Tucker-Maxon
Oral School
for
Hearing-Impaired
Children

2860 S.E. Holgate
Portland, OR 97202
© 503/235-6551
FAX 503/235-6973
E-mail: pstone@tmos.org
www.tmos.org
Grades: Birth through 12th
Enrollment: 55
Faculty: 10
Founded: 1947
Tuition 1998-'99: $8,200

Tucker-Maxon teaches deaf children to lip-read and talk. Sign language is not used at home or in the school. Elementary students are instructed in classes of four to six children, and the school teaches the same reading, writing, social studies, math and science skills these children would learn in a regular classroom. Students are mainstreamed into regular classrooms as soon as possible and given continuing support. Parents are taught how to help their infants develop speech and language. Children using cochlear implants are provided pre- and post-surgery audiological services. The program attracts interested families who move to Portland from other parts of the country.

Three-fourths of the Tucker-Maxon alumni have graduated from colleges, universities and technical schools. Financial aid is available. The main campus is on Holgate near Grout School, but twelve students are mainstreamed in neighborhood or private schools in the metropolitan area.

WoodHaven School

8470 S.W. Oleson Road   Office at 13816 S.W. Fanno Creek Dr. #1
Portland, OR 97223   Tigard, OR 97223
© 503/684-4850
Grades: Preschool through 3
Enrollment: 60
Faculty: 3 full-time and 1 part-time

Affiliation: NAEYC and Parent/Child Preschools of Oregon
Founded: 1998
Tuition 1998-'99: $5,950 (Grades 1-3); $4,550 (Full-day kindergarten);
$1,550-$2,400 (Preschool)

WoodHaven was founded as Magic Garden School by a group of six families in 1994 as a cooperative preschool. It has grown to 60 students and plans to expand through grade six by the year 2000. The elementary program is called "WoodHaven," and the preschool program retains the name "Magic Garden." The school seeks to develop each child's potential through small classes, individual attention, and a well-rounded program that connects learning with life. Education is viewed as a collaborative effort that involves teachers, children and parents. Parents are encouraged to participate and rotate as classroom assistants, as well as fill other volunteer opportunities in the school. The school values the spirit of community among its families. Curriculum is a blend of core academics, which include Spanish, enrichment activities — art, crafts, music and drama, and life skills. WoodHaven uses Howard Gardner's theory of multiple intelligences as well as collaborative learning, individualized instruction, and authentic assessment. Student work is evaluated on portfolios and narrative reports rather than letter grades. The classrooms are located in the West Hills Unitarian Fellowship.

Woodmont School for Dyslexics

8660 S.E. Foster Road
Portland, OR 97226
© 503/771-0002
FAX 503/771-2350
Grades: 1 through 9
Enrollment: 74
Faculty: 9
Affiliation: Slingerland Institute, Oregon Federation of Independent Schools
Founded: 1993
Tuition 1998-'99: $7,000 (Grades 6-8); $9,600 (Grades 9-12)

Woodmont is an independent school for Specific Language Disabled and Dyslexic children. Woodmont uses the classroom Slingerland Adaptation of the Orton-Gillingham Multi-Sensory One-on-One approach to language arts. A highly structured, sequential, simultaneous multi-sensory approach integrates auditory, visual and kinesthetic learning. A typical day includes a 2-hour block of this language arts method, followed by math, science, PE, electives and history. Students are taught learning strategies to cope with difficulties in language learning. Woodmont has a very good home page on the Internet accessible through citysearch.com. An explanation of dyslexia and how the program works are available on the Web site, as well as from the school's brochure.

Religiously Affiliated Schools

Francis Norbert Blanchet, the first Catholic priest in Oregon, arrived at Fort Vancouver in 1838. In the years that followed, he settled in St. Paul and became archbishop of the diocese of Oregon, the second oldest archdiocese in the United States. There have been parochial schools in Oregon ever since. Now called the Archdiocese of Portland, it extends from the Washington to the California border, west to the Pacific and east to the Cascades. Eleven thousand students are enrolled in the 42 elementary schools and eight high schools in the archdiocese.

Catholic schools have changed, but the schools continue to produce very well educated students. The philosophy of the parochial school system maintains that parents are the primary educators of their children. Schools that once drew almost exclusively from their parishioners, now draw students from many neighborhoods. The schools have more lay teaching staff, are less structured, less rigid and more nurturing than the author remembers.

Other faiths and denominations have also founded fine schools in Portland over the years. Their purpose is to teach the beliefs and values of their religion as well as to offer a good education. The percentage of the student's day that is devoted to the study of religion varies tremendously. In some programs there may be chapel once a week, in others students study the Bible daily. Some schools have an interdenominational student population and others attract predominately students of one faith. Information about the student population is given in the school brochures.

I have selected the schools I believe have good, established academic programs. There are many new religiously affiliated programs, and I'll include some of the newer schools in the next edition. Admissions policies vary, so contact the individual school for information

Archbishop Howard

ARCHBISHOP
HOWARD
SCHOOL

5309 N.E. Alameda
Portland, OR 97213
✆ 503/281-1912
FAX 503/281-0554
www.teleport.com/schools/ahs
Grades: Pre-K through 8
Enrollment: 275
Faculty: 12
Affiliation: Archdiocese of Portland
Founded: 1986

Tuition 1998-'99: $2,280 (Catholic subsidized by Parish); $3,360 (Catholic non-subsidized and non-catholic); $3,089 (prekindergarten). Archbishop Howard serves the parishes of St. Rose and St. Charles. About 69% of the students are Catholic; another 22% come from different cultures. The school offers full-day prekindergarten and kindergarten classes with 25 students per class. In addition to the teaching staff, the school has a media specialist and five full-time instructional aides. Students have library and computer education weekly. There is a Learning Lab computer-based program to help students struggling in math and reading.

Before- and after-school care are also offered at $2 per hour. Hours are 7:00 to 8:15 and 3:00 to 6:00. A hot lunch is available daily, as is a snack. Archbishop Howard participates in Catholic Youth Organization sports. Students in grades 4-8 have interscholastic competition in volleyball, basketball, track and field. The elementary program features band for grades four through eight. Foreign language is available as an after-school elective. Sixth graders participate in Outdoor School. Uniforms are required.

Parental involvement is also required. A portion of the cost of educating each child comes from fund raising. Two-parent families contribute 30 hours per year and single parents give 15 hours per year. The annual fund drive supports the financial aid program, curriculum enhancements, playground improvement and technology. The goal for the 1997 school year is $30,000.

Cathedral School

110 N.W. 17th Avenue
Portland, OR 97209
© 503/275-9370
FAX 503/275-9379
Grades: K through 8
Enrollment: 225
Faculty: 12
Affiliation: Archdiocese of Portland
Founded: 1896
Tuition 1998-'99: $3,300 (non-Catholic); $2,475 (Catholic)

Cathedral has been educating children in Portland for over a century, and the National Catholic Education Association has recognized its faculty for excellence. Specialists teach music, computer technology, and PE. The school's mission is "to provide an excellent academic education grounded in Catholic religious principles and values, thereby creating a lifelong love for learning and a respect for each person and all creation as gifts of God." Students are encouraged to participate in the community through service, cultural projects and social interaction.

Parents are actively involved in the school community, volunteering in the classroom and for other activities. After-school care is available through a private contractor on the school campus. There is a waiting list for some classes, especially for places in the sixth grade, because many parents bring their children in for the middle school years. Parents I talked to are very happy with the school.

Uniforms are required. Cathedral students participate with other Catholic schools in the area in CYO athletics. The school offers basketball and volleyball. It has both a gym and a playground.

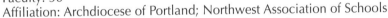

Central Catholic High School

2401 S.E. Stark
Portland, OR 97214
✆ **503/235-3138**
FAX 503/233-0073

Central Catholic High School

Grades: 9 through 12
Enrollment: 800
Faculty: 50
Affiliation: Archdiocese of Portland; Northwest Association of Schools and Colleges; National Catholic Education Association
Founded: 1939
Tuition 1998-'99: $5,200 (non-Catholic); $4,450 (Catholic)

Central Catholic is a co-educational college preparatory high school. Its mission is to educate students from diverse backgrounds in "an environment built on academic excellence, Christian values, and community spirit, and in a manner consistent with the teachings of the Catholic Church."

The school has a strong academic program and competes in the 4A Mt. Hood League. It offers a wide range of athletics, a speech team, choir, band and two drama productions annually. A group of parents, alumni and students, called Friends of the Fine Arts provides personal and monetary support to the fine arts program at Central. Students make one-day retreats as freshmen and sophomores to reenergize and reflect. Juniors and seniors also have some retreat options. Students are required to perform at least eighty hours of community service to graduate. Central Catholic is no longer publishing SAT scores.

SAT Scores 1995:	Verbal: 454 Math: 504
Number taking test 1995:126	

Franciscan Montessori Earth School & St. Francis Academy

14750 S.E. Clinton Street
Portland, OR 97236
✆ **503/760-8220**
FAX 503/760-8333

Franciscan Montessori
Earth School

Grades: Preschool through 12
Enrollment: 375
Faculty: 70
Affiliation: Association Montessori Internationale; Oregon Montessori Association

Founded: 1977
Tuition 1998-'99: $4,269 (Children's House full-day program); $4,627 (Lower Elementary); $4,968 (Upper Elementary); $5,871 (St. Francis Academy Junior Division) $6,329 (Senior Division)

The school is on a nine-acre campus with flower and vegetable gardens, fields and playgrounds. A respect for the earth is part of the school's mission and recycling and gardening are part of the program at all age levels. The youngest children visit parks, older students participate in overnight camping trips. High school students have an annual earth study tour, and earth-learning experiences are integrated into the regular curriculum in science, biology and history. The school is an independent Catholic school, which means that it is not tied to a parish. The program offers Catholic-based religious study, non-denominational religious study or parents may choose to exclude religion from their child's course of study. Class sizes range from 20 to 25.

The curriculum follows the Montessori method. Children's House is the program for preschool through age-six. There are four classes with twenty to twenty five children in each class. They can experiment and explore, working individually or in small groups. Or they can work on specifically designed tasks. Elementary is divided into Lower Elementary (ages six to nine) and Upper Elementary (ages nine to twelve). The elementary school follows the integrated experiential Montessori approach. There are four classes of each Upper and Lower, with twenty to twenty five children in a class. Language study in Spanish or Japanese, field trips, camping and hiking are part of the Earth School experience. Extracurricular activities include Independent study, Junior Great Books, Scouts, 4H Club, community service projects and gardening.

St. Francis Academy is the middle and high school extension of the Franciscan Montessori Earth School. The middle school years provide a broad overview of subjects with a hands-on approach. The high school is more academically and college preparatory oriented. Many of the high school students attend community college classes. Experiential learning includes "Business Discovery," a two-week work experience in the spring and the fall; "Drama Workshop," an academically integrated three to four-week program; and a three-week rural life experience called "Erdkinder." A spring Study Tour, which includes a service project and cross-cultural lessons, completes the course of study for seniors. The average class size ranges from 15 to 20.

Before- and after-school care for the two-and-a-half to twelve-year-olds is called "Montessori Aspect." Children are grouped by age to interact in a family-like setting. After school care is $3.00 per hour.

Jesuit High School

9000 S.W. Beaverton-Hillsdale Highway
Portland, OR 97225-2491
© 503/292-2663
FAX 503/291-5464
Grades: 9 through 12
Enrollment: 1010
Faculty: 67
Affiliation: Northwest Association of Schools and Colleges; National
Association of College Admission Counselors; National Catholic
Education Association
Founded: 1956
Tuition 1997-'98: $5,500

Jesuit is a Catholic college preparatory high school located on a 34-acre campus in southwest Portland. It became coeducational in 1993 and now has an enrollment of 40% women. The Jesuits were founded by St. Ignatius to be the intellectual branch of the Church. They've been in the education business for 450 years and have 47 high schools and 28 universities in this country. The mission of the school is to prepare students to become leaders. As part of their graduation requirement, students contribute a minimum of 65 hours of community service. Ninety-seven percent of the graduating class goes on to colleges and universities. Jesuit offers a college prep curriculum with honors and advanced placement courses. Students must complete a two-year foreign language requirement in French, Spanish or Japanese.

Jesuit won an exemplary school award from the U.S. Department of Education in 1989. It is expanding to meet the needs of a larger and coeducational population, but the average class size remains at 18. New facilities include a performing arts center, physical education center, library, classrooms and tennis courts. The Jesuit Crusaders play in the 4A Metro league, and the school has won numerous titles. Two-thirds of the students participate in one or more sports. The school has a football field, two full basketball courts, weight room, all weather track, soccer field, baseball and softball diamonds and six tennis courts. There are a number of extracurricular activities, clubs and opportunities for community service.

SAT Scores 1997:	Verbal: 574	Math: 574
1996:	568	580
1995:	480	533
Number of students taking the test in 1997: 246		

LaSalle High School

LA ⚜ SALLE
COLLEGE   PREPARATORY

11999 S.E. Fuller Road
Milwaukie, OR 97222
☏ 503/659-4155
FAX 503/659-2535
E-mail: janrose@teleport.com
www.teleport.com/~janrose
Grades: 9 through 12
Enrollment: 607
Faculty: 28 full-time and 1 part-time
Affiliation: Northwest Association of Schools and Colleges; National Education Council of Christian Brothers; National Catholic Education Association
Founded: 1966
Tuition 1998-'99: $4,111

LaSalle is located on a thirty-acre campus, two blocks west of Clackamas Town Center. It is a college preparatory school and ninety-five percent of graduates go on to colleges and universities. In addition to the challenging curriculum, LaSalle students and staff spend a day each fall volunteering for local charities and agencies. With its average class size of 20 students, the school has a philosophy of valuing the individual. It strives to provide a nurturing environment for students while teaching them to respond to poverty and injustice. Seventy-five to eighty percent of LaSalle students are Catholics.

The drama department puts on two productions annually. Harvard Model Congress, Service Club, International Club, National Honor Society and REACH America are among the extra-curricular activities available to students. There is a full sports program, including swimming, tennis and golf. LaSalle received a grant in May of 1995 to add a computer lab for math and science and to add electronic media to the library. ESL classes are available for foreign exchange students. A 2.5 GPA and behavior recommendations are required for admission. Twenty-five percent of the student body receives some financial aid.

SAT Scores 1997:	Verbal: 532	Math: 530
1996:	523	517
1995:	453	498

Number of students taking the test in 1997: 80

The Madeleine School

3240 N.E. 23rd Avenue
Portland, OR 97212
☏ 503/288-9197
Grades: K through 8
Enrollment: 242
Faculty: 25

Affiliation: Archdiocese of Portland; National Catholic Education Association
Founded: 1911
Tuition 1998-'99: $3,000 (non-parishioner); $2,500 (in parish)

Madeleine has a very good academic program with a strong computer component. Music, Toastmaster's Speech Club and community service opportunities are also encouraged. Students participate in citywide Catholic Youth Organization sports programs in volleyball, basketball and track. The school is in the process of upgrading the gymnasium.

Eighty-seven percent of the students come from Catholic families. Twelve percent are minority children. Madeleine extends a sliding tuition scale for each additional child in the school. Families are expected to volunteer at least 30 hours per year, and an enthusiastic parent body responds with school activities and elaborate fund raising events. Madeleine has an endowment of $250,000, which it is seeking to increase to $1 million. Sixty-two percent of the cost of educating a student comes from tuition; the remainder from the parish, fund raising and donations. Financial aid is available to qualified parishioners. After-school care is offered. Uniforms are required and the buildings are wheel chair accessible.

Mount Olive School for Dyslexic Children

15351 S.E. Johnson Road
Clackamas, OR 97015
© 503/650-8277
FAX 503/656-7358
Grades: 1 through 6
Enrollment: 50
Faculty: 8
Affiliation: Oregon Federation of Independent Schools
Founded: 1982
Tuition 1998-'99: $6,500

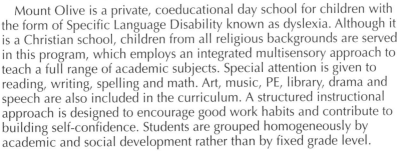

Mount Olive is a private, coeducational day school for children with the form of Specific Language Disability known as dyslexia. Although it is a Christian school, children from all religious backgrounds are served in this program, which employs an integrated multisensory approach to teach a full range of academic subjects. Special attention is given to reading, writing, spelling and math. Art, music, PE, library, drama and speech are also included in the curriculum. A structured instructional approach is designed to encourage good work habits and contribute to building self-confidence. Students are grouped homogeneously by academic and social development rather than by fixed grade level.

The purpose of the school is to return students to a regular classroom as soon as possible. The average enrollment time at Mount Olive is four years. A final mainstreaming class prepares students for making the transition to another school with developed competence in reading, writing and spelling. A student interested in attending Mount Olive must be evaluated by the school to determine whether his or her learning problem is one of Specific Language Disability. (The dyslexic child may experience learning difficulties in more than one of the language areas or in math.) An application must be completed before the child is given a battery of tests to determine placement. Every teacher at Mount Olive is Oregon certified and has received special training in the Slingerland Multisensory Approach. The staff includes a professional counselor.

Oregon Episcopal School

6300 S.W. Nicol Road
Portland, OR 97223
☏ **503/246-7771**
FAX 503/768-3140
admit@ad.oes.edu
Grades: Pre-K through 12
Enrollment: 710
Faculty: 100
Affiliation: Pacific Northwest Association of Independent Schools; National Association of Independent Schools
Founded: 1869
Tuition 1998-'99: $10,475 (Lower School); $11,990 (Middle School); $12,510 (Upper School); $22,725 (Boarding)

OES is located in southwest Portland on a 59-acre site, which includes 15 acres of wetlands. This all-grade, college preparatory school maintains a strong tradition of academic excellence. The school honors diversity in both its student and faculty populations. Its mission is to prepare students with promise for higher education and lifelong learning.

The school has a boarding program in the Upper School and a population of international students from twelve countries. "Winterim" provides a week to explore subjects not on the regular curriculum, from archeological digs to bread making. Community service has been a traditional part of the OES experience. Students in the Upper School are required to complete a specific number of hours of service both on and off campus.

Classes are small, with an average of only 16 or 17 students. Upper School graduates attend some of the best colleges in the country. The Middle School provides field studies, interscholastic sports and a rich curriculum. The Lower School offers a Global Studies Focus Program in which the entire school studies a chosen country. Faculty members are encouraged to pursue professional and personal development, and an endowment has been set up to support summer stipend work, travel and graduate education as well as workshops and conferences.

SAT Scores 1997:	Verbal: 540-690	Math: 580-690
1995:	556	614

Number taking the test (not including international students): 50

Our Lady of the Lake

716 A Avenue
Lake Oswego, OR 97034
© 503/636-2121
FAX 503/635-7760
Grades: K through 8
Enrollment: 250
Faculty: 19 full-time and 3 part-time
Affiliation: Archdiocese of Portland
Founded: 1938
Tuition 1998-'99: $2,500 (in parish); $4,900 (out of parish)

Our Lady of the Lake fosters value-based Catholic education. The school won an U. S. Department of Education School of Excellence award in 1989-'90. Its curriculum emphasizes the basics, with enrichment and accelerated courses encouraged. The media center is equipped with computers, providing Internet access and CD ROM capacity. Specialists teach physical education, computers and music. In the middle school grades, specialists instruct in math, science, language arts, social studies and art.

Uniforms are required. Students can purchased hot lunches twice a week. Our Lady of the Lake participates in Catholic Youth Organization sports. The school has volleyball, basketball, and swim teams and competes in track and field events. Our Lady of the Lake has a very good reputation, and it can be difficult to get into.

Portland Jewish Academy

6651 S.W. Capitol Highway
Portland, OR 97219
© 503/244-0126
FAX 503/452-7001
www.teleport:com/~megaines/index.html
Grades: Pre-K through 8
Enrollment: 209
Affiliation: Jewish Education Service of North America; Candidate Member Pacific Northwest Association of Independent Schools
Founded: 1986
Tuition 1998-'99: $6,225

PJA is located in the Mittleman Jewish Community Center. Having opened a new wing in 1995, the school now occupies 15 classrooms. It's a wonderful facility, full of colorful children's work and child-friendly decor. The library is exceptional, with children's books in both Hebrew and English as well as a section for teachers. The computers are also bilingual. The classrooms are large and light, and the teachers I visited clearly loved working with kids. The class size limit is 20.

The school has a lovely chapel, and it shares the athletic and auditorium spaces of the MJCC. MJCC staff conducts physical education classes twice weekly, and the program includes two six-week swimming sessions per year for each class. The curriculum emphasizes knowledge acquisition and processing, critical thinking, social interaction and personal development. Students are also taught Hebrew and Jewish studies. The school's goal is to develop the values and ideals needed to be committed citizens of the American-Jewish and world communities. Parents are very involved in the school. After-school Hebrew classes are offered for students in grades two through twelve at a cost of $345 to $635, and an adult Hebrew language class is offered once a week.

Portland Lutheran School

740 S.E. 182 Avenue
Portland, OR 97233
℃ 503/667-3199
FAX 503/667-4520
Grades: Pre-K through 12
Enrollment: 450
Faculty: 27
Affiliation: Northwest Association of Schools and Colleges
Founded: 1905
Tuition 1998-99: $3,790 (Grades 1-8); $5,161 (Grades 9-12)

This school was founded as Concordia Academy. In 1986 the name was changed, and in 1990 the school moved onto its new campus. The mission of the school remains to "proclaim Jesus Christ and His Word, inspire excellence in learning, nurture the whole child and build a caring Christian community." Over half of the student body is Lutheran.

The high school curriculum is designed to be college preparatory with a strong liberal arts base. German and Spanish are offered, as is computer education. Electives include choir, drama, student government and yearbook. In the elementary school a traditional, structured program puts emphasis on the total development of the student. Grades 5-8 have an athletic program that includes flag football, volleyball and basketball, and the school competes in the Metro Christian League. There is a half-day kindergarten program.

Tuition varies; members of Portland Lutheran Association for Christian Education churches pay a reduced rate. International students pay more, but their education includes an English as a Second Language program. A co-op plan and financial aid are available. Before- and after-school care are offered for students in K-5. Admission requirements include an interview, grade transcripts and possible testing. Portland Lutheran does not publish SAT scores.

St. Anthony's School

12645 S.W. Pacific Highway
Tigard, Oregon 97223
℡ 503/639-4979
FAX 503/639-4979
Grades: K through 8
Enrollment: 405
Faculty: 15 full-time and 4 part-time
Affiliation: Archdiocese of Portland
Founded: 1878
Tuition 1998-'99: $3,075 (non subsidized); $2,100 (Parish subsidized)

St. Anthony's is housed in a large brick building just west of Highway 217. Affiliated with St. Anthony's Church parish in Tigard, St. Francis Church in Sherwood, and St. Cyril Church in Wilsonville, the school offers a full-range academic program. Enrollment is based on priority status, but it is also open to non-Catholics from the areas of Tigard, Tualatin, Sherwood and Wilsonville. A placement test is given to all new students admitted to St. Anthony's in grades 2-8.

The school has a full-day kindergarten, elementary program (grades 1-5), and middle school program (grades 6-8), which is departmentalized in a separate building. Each classroom is equipped with a computer lab. All students are instructed in music, physical education and art. Language classes are offered in Spanish to grades 5-8. St. Anthony's provides unique opportunities in science and history. The 5th grade makes a trip to Newport and the 6th grade goes to Bend, Oregon to study science. The 7th grade goes to Vancouver B.C., and the 8th grade goes to Washington D.C. to study history.

St. Anthony's has a gym and a large outdoor playground. Students take swim instruction at the Tigard High School Swim Center. The school competes in volleyball, basketball and track, and it provides soccer with the Tigard Soccer Association, CYO basketball, and baseball with Tigard Little League. An extended on-campus care program is available before and after school for a fee. Before-school hours are 7:00-9:00 a.m.; after-school hours from 3:30 to 6 p.m.

St. Cecilia School

12250 S.W. 5th Avenue
Beaverton, OR 97005
℡ 503/644-7647
FAX 503/626-7204
Grades: K through 8
Enrollment: 270
Faculty: 12 full-time and 4 part-time
Affiliation: Archdiocese of Portland
Founded: 1876
Tuition 1998-99: $2,060

This parish school promotes excellence in education, with the conviction that high expectations lead to better results. The school's philosophy is to educate "the whole person by helping each child see the power of reason and imagination and to understand the importance of spiritual and human values." The core academic curriculum is enriched with computer education, foreign languages, community service projects, Outdoor School, band, science camp and speech club. Upper grade students serve as buddies to primary grade students. Grades six through eight are organized as a middle school. Self-discipline, good study habits and responsibility are encouraged as tools to prepare students to become lifelong learners.

St. Cecilia's offers an extended-day program and is open from 7 a.m. until 6 p.m. Catholic Youth Organization sports are available after school. Uniforms are required. There is a hot lunch program. Parents are very involved in the school, participating in the Auction, Family Math, board meetings, and as volunteers in the school. Parents praise the school because it has been able to maintain a community feeling among the students. Middle school girls are not divided into small cliques, and the group dynamics are good.

St. Ignatius School

3330 S.E. 43rd Avenue
Portland, OR 97206
℡ **503/774-5533**
Grades: K through 8
Enrollment: 250
Faculty: 8 full-time and 9 part-time
Affiliation: Archdiocese of Portland
Founded: 1908
Tuition 1998-'99: $2,490 (in-Parish); $3,140 (out-of-Parish)

St. Ignatius is a parish school located just off 39th at Powell, across from Creston Park. It offers two half-day kindergartens with 14 children per class. The elementary program has computer education, a social outreach component and art and music in addition to the core curriculum. A special reading/math teacher is on staff for primary students needing some extra help. The school has a Title 1 program. The middle school offers departmentalized classes. Teachers are Oregon Certified. Before- and after-school care is available; scouting and athletics are offered after school. Uniforms are required in grades 1-8. The school has a hot lunch program.

St. John Fisher

7101 S.W. 46th Avenue
Portland, OR 97219
℡ **503/246-3234**
FAX 503/246-4117

Grades: K through 8
Enrollment: 267
Faculty: 14 full-time 3 part-time
Affiliation: Archdiocese of Portland
Founded: 1959
Tuition 1997-98: $1,900 (in-Parish); $2,750 (out-of-Parish)

Located a block from Gabriel Park, St. John Fisher offers a very good program in an attractive facility. In addition to the academic curriculum, students can take band and vocal electives. The school has good facilities for basketball, volleyball, track and field. A new wing completed in December of 1995 houses the library (with views of fields and Fanno Creek), a teacher's workroom and a kindergarten space. A new computer lab now occupies the old library space.

This is a parish school, and the parish provides about a quarter of the school's operating budget. The parents and parishioners are actively involved, having raised $830,000 for the new wing. Eighty-eight percent of the students are Catholic. After-school care is available, and hot lunches are offered on certain days.

St. Mary of the Valley
4440 S.W. 148th Avenue
Beaverton, OR 97007
℗ 503/626-7781
FAX 503/643-6979
Grades: K through 6
Enrollment: 380
Faculty: 16 full-time, 6 part-time
Affiliation: Northwest Association of Schools & Colleges, Western Catholic Education Association
Founded: 1902
Tuition 1998-99: $3,420 (families not supporting a parish); $2,720 (families supporting a parish)

St. Mary of the Valley has an outstanding elementary program that incorporates an advanced math program and "Odyssey of the Mind." The music program includes singing, orchestra and hand bells. All fourth graders learn the violin. Swimming is a regular part of the physical education program. After-school sports include volleyball, basketball and track as well as swimming. A specialist is available to offer assistance with reading problems.

The school has high expectations for students. It values self-discipline, respect for people and property, honesty, responsibility, courtesy, helpfulness and academic seriousness. Test scores are above average for diocesan schools. Parents are required to give forty hours of volunteer service per family per year. There's a sliding tuition scale for additional children in the school. Students wear uniforms.

St. Mary's Academy

ST.MARY'S
A C A D E M Y

1615 S.W. Fifth Avenue
Portland, OR 97201
© 503/228-8306
FAX 503/223-0995
E-mail: sma@sma.rain.com
Grades: 9 through 12
Enrollment: 560
Faculty: 30 full-time, 10 part-time
Affiliation: Northwest Association of Schools and Colleges
Founded: 1859
Tuition 1998-99: $5,425

St. Mary's is the oldest continuously operating high school west of the Rockies, and it is also the only remaining single-sex high school in Oregon. St. Mary's has long been known for excellence. The school received the U.S. Department of Education Exemplary School Awards in 1984 and 1989. It was the first school in the nation to received Apple Computer's Golden Apple Distinguished School Award for leadership and innovative integration of technology with a strong liberal arts curriculum. A Sequent mainframe computer (Marie) gives students and their families access to Internet.

Ninety-eight percent of St. Mary's graduates go on to colleges and universities. Fifty percent of the juniors and seniors take advanced placement classes for college credit or honors classes. Three years of science (conceptual physics, chemistry and biology) are required, while public schools require only two. The school draws from throughout the metropolitan area. Seventeen percent of students are women of color. All students participate in the Community Service Program, and a large number compete in at least one of the ten 4A Metro League sports. St. Mary's shares the record for the most basketball championships of any school in Oregon. The Meyer Trust awarded the school a $1.5 million matching challenge grant, which was matched on schedule and made possible the new Information Science Center and other upgrades. These funds, plus grants from the Wiegand Foundation, paid for the Wiegand Physics, Chemistry and Biology Lab, adjoining math classrooms and started the Wiegand Women-in-Science Network on Internet (WWISNET).

The mission statement reads in part "St. Mary's Academy exists to educate the young woman through a comprehensive and rigorous program of study which prepares her for higher education." It does so, and does it with class. Sixty-six percent of these women return to the Portland metropolitan area to live and work. St. Mary's lists the mid-50% of SAT scores.

SAT Scores 1998	Verbal: 520-660	Math: 490-610
1997:	530-620	490-610
1996:	520-620	490-590
1995:	450-540	400-550
Number of students taking test 1997: 125		

St. Thomas More

3521 S.W. Patton Road
Portland, OR 97221
✆ **503/222-6105**
FAX 503/222-2055
Grades: K through 8
Enrollment: 225
Faculty: 10 full-time and 6 part-time
Affiliation: Northwest Association of Schools and Colleges; Western Catholic Education Association
Founded: 1948
Tuition 1998-99: $4,056 (non parishioner); $2,388 (parishioners)

St. Thomas More is located in Portland Heights and is the parish school for this area. The school has an excellent program, which was accredited in 1995 by NASC "with merit." It is committed to preparing students for the 21st century. Computer education, leadership training, music, band and Spanish supplement the regular subjects. The school and its community value education as a lifelong process.

Extended care is available and the school is open from 7:30 a.m. until 5:30 p.m. Kindergarten is a morning-only program. However, there is a special afternoon-care program for kinders. Uniforms are required, and a hot lunch program is provided. Teachers are Oregon Certified. Students participate in Catholic Youth Organization sports, Outdoor School for sixth graders and a variety of activities and field trips.

Parents are actively involved as volunteers, members of the Board and 21st Century School Council, and in fundraisers. The community sponsors social events for the parents as well as the students. It is not easy to get into St. Thomas More. Parish siblings have first priority, then other parishioners. There is a sliding tuition scale for families with more than one child in the school. If I lived in the parish and had no older children at the school, I would give serious thought to sending the admissions office a birth announcement! The school welcomes diversity, but it not wheelchair accessible. Admissions information is updated and published annually.

4

Trinity Lutheran

5520 N.E. Killingsworth
Portland, OR 97218
© 503/288-6403
Grades: Pre-K through 8
Enrollment: 240
Faculty: 9
Affiliation: National Lutheran School Accreditation
Founded: 1959
Tuition 1999-2000: $3,240 (Grades 1-8)

Owned and operated by Trinity Evangelical Lutheran Church, this school provides a Christ-centered education. The congregation's children receive first priority, and there is a sliding tuition scale based on church membership. Admission procedures include an interview with the principal; transcripts and testing may also be required. All students participate in the religion program and attend weekly chapel.

The curriculum includes art, music, choir, band and computer. Prekindergarten is a three-day-per-week, half-day program. Kindergarten is offered half-day, with both morning and afternoon sessions. Before- and after-school care is available.

Valley Catholic High School & Middle School

4275 S.W. 148th Avenue
Beaverton, OR 97007
© 503/644-3745
FAX 503/646-4054
Grades: 7 through 12
Enrollment: 480
Faculty: 52
Affiliation: Northwest Association of Schools and Colleges
Founded: 1902
Tuition 1998-'99: $5,250 (high school); $4,070 (middle school)

Valley Catholic is a coeducational college preparatory high school located on a 15-acre campus. The school's mission is to prepare young men and women to be lifelong learners in the 21st Century. Over 95% of graduates go on to college and universities. An honors curriculum is offered in addition to regular classes. Students can take four years of music, art, Japanese and science. Beginning in the middle school, students can get in five years of French, Spanish and math. Electives include Pacific Rim Studies, Mock Trial, and film. An excellent fine arts program is in place, and the success of the music department can be judged by the fact that music students competing for college scholarships have had a ninety-eight percent success rate! The performing groups, including band, orchestra, choir, jazz band, handbells and ensemble groups, participate in numerous competitions, tours and festivals. The drama department stages two major productions each year.

The school has extensive athletic facilities, including a 400-meter rubberized track, gym, tennis courts, softball diamonds and a new athletic center with weight training equipment. Cross-country, soccer, basketball, swimming, tennis golf and track are available to both boys and girls. Valley Catholic competes in the 3A Tri-Valley league.

Students come to Valley Catholic from its sister school in Japan, Shukutoku School. The International Studies program offers trips to France, Japan and Spanish-speaking countries. The school sponsors a variety of clubs and organizations for students.

The middle school shares teachers with the high school, and its program is a similar. Applications for admission to either must to be in by January.

Westside Christian High School

Westside
Christian
High School

4565 Carman Drive
Lake Oswego, OR 97035
© 503/697-4711
FAX 503/697-4605
Grades: 9 through 12
Enrollment: 300
Faculty: 18 full-time and 5 part-time
Affiliation: Northwest association of Schools and Colleges and Association of Christian Schools International
Founded: 1981
Tuition 1998-'99: $5,000

Westside Christian High occupies space in the Lake Bible Church building in Lake Oswego. It sustains a college preparatory curriculum, and ninety percent of its seniors go on to college. Eighty-percent take the SAT. The school offers the option of a Standard Diploma, which meets state requirements or a College Prep Diploma. The school's mission is to provide an intimate and nurturing atmosphere for training the next generation of Christian leaders. Electives include performing arts, graphic arts, business courses, yearbook and computer science. Westside competes in the AA West Valley League, and students participate in ten varsity sports.

SAT Scores 1997:	Verbal: 559	Math: 518
1996:	518	499
1995:	485	479

Number of Students taking the test in 1997: 37

Chapter Five
Portland Area Preschool Programs

Finding the right preschool is difficult for most parents. It is particularly difficult for working parents, who often need extended care in addition to a nurturing school program. High-quality preschools have a well-trained staff, a rich learning environment and good learning materials. There is a balance between active learning, outdoor and gym time, and quiet learning, stories, puzzles and projects. The percentage of children enrolled in programs for three- and four-year-olds has increased in the past 30 years. Since there are very few public school pre-kindergarten programs, most parents will have to find a private school for these important early years.

Play is children's work. Through play they develop their social, emotional, physical and intellectual skills. They learn colors, numbers and the alphabet. New research points out the need for a rich learning environment at the preschool level. Kids need cognitive, as well as physical and emotional experiences, and a healthy, nurturing environment for their brains to develop to full potential.

Preschool is also primarily a time for learning how to get along with others. The title of Robert Fulghum's charming book, *Everything I Need to Know I Learned in Kindergarten* says it all. Your preschool child will be forming a value system that will govern his or her life. A preschool program that is a good fit for your child and for your family is also one where you will meet other families with young children who share your values. Many families I know met their best family friends at their child's preschool. So, the choice you make is important.

How to Judge a Preschool

Look for an environment that promotes the total development of your child. Developmentally appropriate programs are staffed by teachers who understand children's growth patterns and individual differences. The classrooms should be bright and cheery with lots of kids' work on display and lots of equipment to facilitate play. The classroom should have centers for housekeeping play, science, writing, art, sensory exploration, computers and a reading corner. Students should have some structured activities, and some free time to pursue what interests them in the classroom.

In terms of equipment, there should be lots of picture books and materials for art projects. Coloring books, worksheets and workbooks are not appropriate for children under six. Look for musical instruments, and puppets, dolls, "cooking" equipment and "dress-up clothes" for pretend play. Children at this stage also need to develop fine motor skills, so there should be lots of puzzles, building blocks and other toys designed for improving dexterity.

Music should be an important part of the curriculum. According to researchers at the University of California Irvine who observed two groups of three-year-olds, the group that took piano lessons and sang in a chorus scored 80% higher than their playmates in spatial intelligence, which translates into mathematical abilities at a later age.

Much research has been done on the study of music in preschool and the research demonstrates how important it is. The Music School in Providence, Rhode Island gave kindergarten students seven months of extra music and arts training. Their test scores improved significantly on math achievement tests over a control group of children who did not receive the special training. Music contributes to a child's ability to reason abstractly, particularly in spatial areas. Spatial-temporal reasoning is what we use to understand relationships between objects, such as calculating proportions or playing chess. It is used in mathematics, physics and engineering. Early music education is important to cognitive development and good early childhood programs know this.

If the school has television in the classroom, find out what the children watch and how long they watch it. TV does not facilitate creating one's own imagination and should not be a big part of your young child's day. Story-telling and reading to children enables them to create images they cannot see and teaches them to think in the abstract.

It is in preschool and pre-kindergarten that children begin their exposure to language that will help them learn to read in first and second grade. Read to your child and choose an early childhood program where listening to stories is a part of the day. Libraries are important places to take preschoolers. Kids should engage in word play and nursery rhymes. They need to understand that speech is made up of sounds. Educators call this "phonemic awareness." By the age of four, children should begin to understand that letters stand for sounds. They should know the letters in their name and begin to print these letters. If you read a well loved story, leave out key words and let the child fill in the blanks. Show them how we read left to right, by following the text with your finger. Talk about the meaning of the story and the sequence of events. Help your child make connections between stories in books and real life. Look for a teacher to do the same. Far too many kids in this country arrive at first grade without a basic grounding in language, written and spoken, and this makes learning to read difficult.

And because young children learn a second language much more readily than older ones, a preschool second language program is a definite plus. An immersion preschool program will have all of the elements of a good preschool and the teacher will speak another language. A child cannot learn a second language by hearing it spoken for an hour a day. To be effective, they must be immersed in the language for at least half of their day. Portland has several very good immersion preschool/ pre-kindergarten programs. Most are at independent schools.

As a component of a good preschool, an outdoor playground with age-appropriate play equipment is as significant as the classroom. Much more than "letting off steam," exercise actually feeds the brain and increases the nerve connections that facilitate learning. Children must be free to run, climb, crawl, swing and slide. The play equipment should be designed to provide lots of options; excessive turn-taking is difficult for small children. There should be sand and water for manipulative play; opportunities for construction with hammers and nails; places to hide and wheel toys to ride. Children need to learn to take risks, but the risks must be balanced with a concern for safety.

Check the equipment carefully. Look for sturdy swing structures with soft strap seats; check the chains for any dangerous open S-hooks. Check for protruding bolts on climbing structures, and verify that the platforms of climbing structures are enclosed with protective railings. The ground surface beneath play structures causes most play injuries. Therefore, all play equipment should be surrounded by a safety surfacing. Falls from play equipment will occasionally happen, but if the "fall-zone" is properly cushioned (with a thick layer of pea gravel, bark chips or rubberized padding), serious injuries can be avoided.

Important Questions to Ask

Visit the classrooms and observe how the teacher interacts with the children. Does the teacher truly like kids? You can usually tell what kind of rapport a teacher has with the students. Ask how discipline problems are handled. Will you, the parent, be welcome to drop in anytime? Does the school have a system in place to determine who is authorized to pickup your child? Are there opportunities for you to volunteer in the classroom or on field trips? What kinds of snacks are served? Is there a lunch program? When you visit the school, check out the bathrooms, the nap area and the lunchroom. They should be clean, orderly and attractive.

Ask about the staff members' credentials and the teacher to student ratio. How long have the staff members been employed in the school? A high rate of teacher turnover is one of the most frequent complaints about preschool programs. Children bond with their teachers, and it is upsetting when a teacher leaves. If teachers come and go at an alarming rate it's usually an indication that salaries are low or management is not what it should be.

What kind of a community is the teacher building in the classroom? Look for programs that teach respect for diversity of opinions and maintain diversity in the student population. Do the teachers model respect for others, empathy, fairness and curiosity about other cultures? These are values a preschooler needs to learn.

Is the program accredited or is it certified by Oregon Child Care Division? Not all preschool programs fall under CCD jurisdiction. Programs lasting more than four hours per day will have to be CCD-certified annually. The National Association for the Education of Young Children (NAEYC) accredits early childhood programs. Their address is 1509 16th Street NW, Washington, DC 20036. There is a great deal of very useful information for parents of young children on this organization's Web site (www.naeyc.org). It lists NAEYC accredited programs in the Portland area, and I have listed many of these in this book. You might check the Web site to see if new programs have become accredited since we went to press.

The well-established schools we have listed are not daycare facilities, but rather preschool programs in which students are expected to learn specific skills. Some also offer classes for parents.

Preschool Programs in Private Schools

The following private and religiously affiliated elementary programs listed in Chapter 4 also offer good preschool programs:

Archbishop Howard
The Catlin Gabel School
Franciscan Montessori Earth School
The French American International School
The German American School
The International School
Montessori of Beaverton
Oregon Episcopal School
Portland French School
Portland Lutheran School
Touchstone School

Preschools and Kindergartens

A Child's Way

12755 N.W. Dogwood Street
Portland, OR 97229
© **503/644-8407**

Grades: Preschool and Kindergarten
Enrollment: 334
Faculty: 21
Affiliation: NAEYC accredited
Founded: 1982
Tuition 1998-99: $236 per month (half-day kindergarten)

A Child's Way offers a developmentally appropriate curriculum based on NAEYC guidelines. The learning environment includes art, music, play, science, math and language learning activities. Spanish is offered in the kindergarten program, and there is a Spanish lunch and play program for four-year-olds. There are many options in each age group: two mornings a week, three mornings a week, etc. Most classes are from 9:00 a.m. to 11:30 a.m. or 3:30 p.m. A Child's Way offers a class for parents of two-year-olds. The school has a large outdoor playground and a covered play area.

Child's View Montessori School, Inc.

4729 S.W. Taylor's Ferry Road
Portland, OR 97219
© **503/293-9422**

Grades: Preschool and Kindergarten
Enrollment: 49
Faculty: 4 full-time, 4 part-time
Affiliation: Oregon Montessori Association
Founded: 1988
Tuition 1998-'99: $450 per month (full-day); $325 per month (half-day)

Child's View uses Montessori materials and employs Montessori-trained teachers. The program accepts children from the age of two and a half, if they are potty trained. The school is open 7:30 a.m. to 6:00 p.m. with half-day and full-day options as well as after-school care for students. The fee structure varies with the hours the child is at school. Facilities include a children's garden and a playground. Child's View accepts children with mild special-needs.

Community Arts Pre-School

368 South State Street
Lake Oswego, OR 97034
℃ 503/636-3429

Grades: Preschool and Pre-kindergarten
Enrollment: 106
Faculty: 8 part-time
Affiliation: NAEYC accredited
Founded: 1981
Tuition 1999-'00: $165 per month (Tues & Thurs); $210 per month
(MWF); $225 per month (Pre-kindergarten)

The Community Arts Preschool is located in the Lakewood Center for the Arts, near George Rodgers Park. The program offers a developmentally appropriate curriculum including art, music, creative drama, puppetry, hands-on science, small and large motor skill development and school readiness. The school day is from 9:00 to 11:55 for preschoolers and from 12:30 to 3:00 for the pre-kinders. It is a 9½-month program.

The outdoor playground has swings, sand, climbing equipment, hills for running and a garden space. Children take music/ movement classes in the adjacent Lakewood Center dance studios as part of the preschool program. Clackamas County has asked the program to provide appropriate environments for some children with special needs, so the staff has received special training for meeting these needs. Average class size is 14.

Early Childhood Learning Center

6651 S.W. Capitol Highway
Portland, OR 97219
℃ 503/452-3426
FAX 503/245-4233

Grades: Preschool and Kindergarten
Enrollment: 160
Faculty: 24
Affiliation: NAEYC accredited
Founded: 1940's
Tuition 1998-'99: $126 per month (2-day twos) through $302 per month (kindergarten)

The Early Childhood Learning Center is located in the Mittleman Jewish Community Center. Membership in the MJCC is required to enroll in this program, which provides a warm and nurturing environment for children two to six. The staff is trained to enhance the social-emotional, cognitive and motor areas of learning. The student/ teacher ratio is small, with only 8 to 14 children in preschool classes and 20 in kindergarten. The program seeks "to encourage a healthy self-concept and stress positive adult and peer relationships." The facility has a pool and gym where preschool and kindergarten classes attend weekly classes.

The Center follows the Portland Public School calendar. Preschool hours are 9:00 until 11:45 and kindergarten runs from 9:00 to 1:30. There is an after-school program with several available options, which include MJCC classes (swimming, soccer, ballet, etc.). Children are escorted by the staff to various class locations in the building. Tuition varies according to the number of days and after-school programs in which the child is enrolled. Lunch is from 11:45 to 1:30. Extended Day is from 11:45 to 3:30. Late day is from 3:30 to 6:00 (an extension of Extended Day).

Foundation School of Congregation Neveh Shalom

2900 S.W. Peaceful Lane
Portland, OR 97201
℅ 503/246-8831 ext.22
FAX 503/246-7553
E-mail: lrubin@nevehshalom.org

Grades: Playgroups, Preschool and Pre-kindergarten
Enrollment: 99
Faculty: 19
Affiliation: NAEYC accredited
Founded: 1954
Tuition 1998-'99: Ranges from $113 to $537 per month, depending on services

The Foundation School's mission is to aid the child's physical, intellectual, social, emotional and spiritual development. It also seeks to preserve a child's natural ways of learning and help him or her develop a positive self-image. Synagogue membership is not required. The school teaches the heritage, customs and ideals of the Jewish faith. Shabbat is celebrated weekly, and all Jewish holidays are observed.

The facilities are very nice, with lots of children's work on display. The space includes indoor and outdoor covered play areas with developmentally appropriate equipment. The program offers morning classes for two- to five-year-olds, early morning drop off from 8:00 a.m. and extended care until 3:00 p.m. for three- to five-year-olds.

Fruit and Flower Child Care Center

2378 N.W. Irving
Portland, OR 97210
℅ 503/228-8349
FAX 503/228-7868

Grades: Infants through Preschool
Enrollment: 119
Faculty: 32 full-time, 8 part-time
Affiliation: NAEYC accredited

Founded: 1906
Tuition 1998-'99: $580 per month for preschoolers

In 1885 a group of eight girls began delivering baskets of fruit and bouquets of flowers to the ill and less fortunate in Portland. In 1906 The Fruit and Flower Children's Mission opened Oregon's first child care center for working mothers. The present day center was specifically designed for child care. These excellent facilities include an infant center, kitchen, laundry facilities and large classrooms and outdoor play areas. This is one of Portland's most respected child care programs. The average class size is 15 to 18, depending on age.

The daily schedule of activities revolves around projects that involve painting, cooking, nature, puzzles, books, dramatic and outdoor play. The preschool outdoor play area includes a garden that the children plant each spring. A music teacher visits each group (including infants) every other week. Each of the preschool rooms has a computer for the children's use. Morning activities are followed by lunch and a nap or rest period. Mid-morning and mid-afternoon snacks are provided, and breakfast is available. Fruit and Flower is open from 6:45 a.m. to 6:00 p.m. Infants are accepted from the age of six weeks. The program is committed to supporting social, emotional, physical and intellectual growth.

Funded through tuition, donations and fundraising, the Center also receives some United Way funding to assist low-income families. To have a child in the program, parents must be employed at least 30 hours a week, or be in school or in training. A sliding tuition scale is available for families who qualify based on income and family size. The tuition covers ten hours of care per day. Some special-needs children can be accommodated.

Helen Gordon Child Development Center

1609 S.W. 12th Avenue
Portland, OR 97201
✆ 503/725-3092

Grades: Preschool
Enrollment: 95
Faculty: 7 full-time and 4 student employees
Affiliation: NAEYC
Founded: 1971
Tuition 1998-'99 : $268 per month (PSU students); $535 per month (others)

Helen Gordon is a lab preschool program for Portland State University. Students and faculty at Portland State have priority in the admissions process. It is a full-day, 7:30 a.m. to 5:30 p.m. year-round program staffed by students from the Child & Family Studies program at PSU. Students in the Early Childhood Education program at PSU's graduate school also use the Center for research and practice. There are three professional teachers and one student teacher for each class of twenty-six students.

The school focuses on the family; pictures of the children with their families dot the bulletin boards, and teachers work with PSU Student Parent Services to help people manage their roles as both parents and students. The student population at Helen Gordon is ethnically diverse, as is the staff. The curriculum stresses multicultural and anti-bias education. Teachers foster social and emotional development, instructing children on how to work in a group and how to treat people fairly.

Located on the Portland State Campus, the school was built as a child care facility in 1928 by the Fruit and Flower Mission. The lovely old brick building is on the National Register of Historic Places. It has large windows and many rooms that can be used for group work. The classrooms are large and most classes use two adjoining rooms. Children are free to work on an activity in one room or wander into the adjoining room for another type of activity with another teacher.

There are two outdoor playgrounds next to the building, each with a small covered play area. Students take many field trips around Portland. Lunch and two daily snacks are provided. About two-thirds of the students at Helen Gordon are children of PSU students and staff. There is a long waiting list for non-PSU applicants. Currently, there are no half-day or kindergarten options.

Hilltop Kindergarten and Preschool

5700 S.W. Dosch Road
Portland, OR 97201
℃ 503/245-3183
FAX 503/245-2766

Grades: Preschool through K
Enrollment: 150
Faculty:11 part-time
Affiliation: Portland Christian Center; CCD Certified
Founded: 1993
Tuition 1999-2000: $250 per month (kindergarten 8:30 to 1:00)

Hilltop offers preschool and kindergarten for children ages three to five. Classes range in size from 10 to 15 children, and the school's goal is to help each child develop intellectually, physically, socially and spiritually. The curriculum includes Bible, science and health, numbers, small and large motor skill development, literature and stories, free play, sensory development, social studies, problem solving and concept development. Language development is encouraged through listening and speaking; creative expression through arts and drama; and self image and emotional development through puppetry. Field trips, audiovisuals and guests supplement the curriculum.

The school has very nice facilities including an outdoor play area and full gymnasium. The hot lunch program serves a well-balanced meal and can accommodate children with special dietary needs. A snack is also served. This is a religiously affiliated program and the school uses the "A Beka" Christian-based curriculum. A personal interview with parents and child is part of the admissions process. Open from 7:30 a.m. to 3:30 p.m., the program has before and after-school care within this time frame.

Joyful Noise Child Care

333 S.W. 1ˢᵗ
Portland, OR 97204
© **503/326-6827**
Grades: infants through age 6
Enrollment: 115
Faculty: 27
Affiliation: NAEYC accredited
Founded: 1989
Tuition 1998-'99: $485 month (kindergarten)

Joyful Noise offers an age appropriate curriculum based on the NAEYC guidelines. Teachers use emergent curriculum, basing their units on what subjects interest the students. The school has an indoor playground and uses Waterfront Park for outdoor excursions. The center is open from 6:30 a.m. until 6:00 p.m. There is a one-time registration fee of $35 per child or $50 per family. Infant care is $632 a month, young preschool is $496 and older preschool is $490. Drop-in care is $4.25 per hour for infants and toddlers and $3.25 per hour for preschool and kindergarten. This program comes highly recommended by parents.

Joyful Noise, Metro Kids

600 N.E. Grand Avenue
Portland, OR 97232
© **503/797-1702**
Grades: infants through age 5
Enrollment: 57
Faculty: 13
Affiliation: NAEYC accredited
Founded: 1994
Tuition 1998-'99: varies $632 month infants

The east-side location of Joyful Noise offers a similar developmentally appropriate curriculum. It is in the process of seeking NAEYC accreditation. There is a semi-covered outdoor playground and garden. The site also has a small common indoor area used for play.

Marylhurst Early Childhood Center

817 12th Street
P.O. Box 1018
Oregon City, OR 97045
✆ 503/650-0978

Grades: Preschool and Kindergarten
Enrollment: 182
Faculty: 18
Affiliation: NAEYC accredited
Founded: 1972
Tuition 1998-'99: $180 per month
(half-day Kindergarten four days a week)

MECC was founded as a lab school for students at Marylhurst College who were majoring in child development and early childhood education. When Marylhurst was no longer able to sustain the program, it went off campus. It is now located in the historic Barclay School Building in Oregon City. Parents from many Portland neighborhoods drive to Oregon City because they love the program. The program has received the Golden Bootie Award for the past seven years from Portland Parent as the best preschool in the Portland area. MECC has a home page (www.teleport.com/~mecc).

The toddler program is for children from ages 16 to 23-months. It has a parent component to help build parenting skills; parents select the topics that are covered in the class. While parents learn from one teacher, children enjoy an interactive play environment with another. Parents are encouraged to network and develop support groups. These classes are held on Monday or Tuesday from 9:30-11:15 at a cost of $55 a month. A similar class is offered for parents and their two-year-olds on Thursdays and Fridays.

The preschool serves three- and four-year-olds. Clay, construction, painting, puzzles, blocks and other hands-on materials are used along with imaginative play to encourage children to interact, experiment and explore. Classes for three-year-olds are limited to 18 children, with three teachers, and the four's classes are limited to 16, with two teachers in each. There are several morning sessions. A blended preschool for children who turn four by December 1 runs three mornings a week from 9:00 to 12:00.

The Kindergarten program is for children who turn five by December 1, with classes Monday through Thursday from 9:00 to 12:00. It offers a rich curriculum and a variety of theme-based experiences to teach science, math, art and social studies. The emphasis is on language skills, including listening, speaking, writing and reading. MECC works to build a "collaborative learning community" that celebrates individual differences and encourages children to take pleasure in their own intellectual, emotional, social and physical growth and the growth of others.

5

Multnomah Cooperative Preschool

5500 S.W. Dosch Road
Portland, OR 97219
✆ 503/244-9141

Grades: Preschool and Pre-kindergarten
Enrollment: 32
Faculty: 1, plus 3 adult volunteers
Affiliation: NAEYC accredited
Founded: 1949
Tuition: 1998-99: $99 per month for the 4-day programs

Multnomah is the oldest parent cooperative in the state. In 1990 it was the first co-op in Oregon to receive NAEYC accreditation. In '91, *Child* magazine named it one of the ten best programs in the nation. The curriculum emphasizes learning through play. Diversity is stressed in every aspect of the program. There is a morning class for three- and four-year-olds from 9:00 to 11:30 a.m. Pre-kindergarten runs from 12:30 until 3:00 p.m. four days a week. Parents must help two or three times a month in the morning and once or twice a month in the afternoon program.

Providence Montessori School

830 N.E. 47ᵗʰ Avenue
Portland, OR 97213
✆ 503/215-2400

Grades: Preschool through K
Enrollment: 190
Faculty: 25
Affiliation: Association Montessori Internationale
Founded: 1962
Tuition 1998-'99: $445 per month (full-day); $210 per month (half-day)

The Child Center at Providence Hospital offers a Montessori program for children ages two and a half to six. The school year program follows the Portland Public School calendar, and there is a summer program. Hours are 8:30 to 3:00 for the academic program. Before-school care begins at 7:00 a.m. and after-school care ends at 6:00 p.m. The daycare cost is $2.00 per hour. Children with developmental learning disabilities are welcomed. Financial aid is available.

The curriculum uses Montessori equipment and follows a self-teaching, self directed format. Teachers are Montessori trained. Spanish is offered for children 4½ and older. All children can take movement and music. Lunches and snacks are provided by a registered dietitian. A registered nurse is on duty. Children must be 2½ and toilet-trained to enroll.

Small Friends, Inc.

Tualatin Hills Park and Recreation Center
7475 S.W. Oleson Road
Portland, OR 97223
✆ 503/452-9272

Grades: Preschool
Enrollment: 120
Faculty: 4
Affiliation: none
Founded: 1987
Tuition 1998-'99: $95 per month (3-year-olds); $120 (4-year-olds)

Small Friends is a developmentally appropriate, experiential learning program for three and four-year-olds. Curriculum includes art, problem solving, science, math, drama, literature, music, and cooking. The school seeks to enhance small and large motor skill development, social interactions, respect for others and for the environment. The morning programs run from 9:00 to 11:30, with free choice time, group time, snack and motor-skill work. The afternoon session offers the same activities from 12:30 until 3:00.

Volunteering is a condition of enrollment and is not optional. Parents commit to working in the classroom once a month and to working on an at-home project for the school about an hour each month. When you help in the classroom you will usually have an activity to supervise. Take-home projects include making play dough, cutting out shapes for a project, etc. A sense of community is valued, and the school's picnics, holiday celebrations, ice cream socials and "Grown-Up's Saturday" provide opportunities for parents to get to know each other.

"Lunch Bunch," a playgroup that meets from 11:30 until 1:00 is offered for children in both sessions. They eat their sack lunches and then play outdoors or in the gym, supervised by Small Friends staff. The admissions process begins with an information night held in early winter. After attending information night, parents are welcome to come for classroom observations. A party is held in the spring for new students to see the school and meet the teachers.

West Hills Montessori School

4920 S.W. Vermont Street
Portland, OR 97219
✆ 503/246-5495

Grades: Preschool through K
Enrollment: 230
Faculty: 18
Affiliation: Oregon Montessori Association; Oregon Association of Independent Schools
Founded: 1968
Tuition 1998-'99: $485 per month (full-day); $280 (half-day)

5

West Hills offers a traditional Montessori program in an independent, nonsectarian setting that supports a racial and ethnic mix of students. Wherever possible, handicapped children are integrated into the regular classroom. Teachers are Montessori-certified and Montessori materials are used. An elementary program (ages 6-9) was recently added to the primary program (ages 3-6). The school year follows the Portland Public School calendar, but there is a summer program, as well. There are half-day and full-day options, plus extended care. The facility is open from 7:15 a.m. until 6:00 p.m. West Hills Montessori has opened two new centers called Montessori II. One is in the West Hills Christian Church at 3824 S.W. Troy and the other is in the Garden Home Recreational Center on S.W. Oleson Road.

The school owns its buildings and grounds as well as a farm in Tualatin used for field trips. Swimming, Spanish, and computer classes are part of the curriculum. A creative movement specialist is on staff. Parent volunteers are welcome, and the school offers parent education events.

Youngset Preschool

1838 S.W. Jefferson
Portland, OR 97201
© 503/221-0224

Grades: Preschool
Enrollment: 55
Faculty: 4
Affiliation: Parent Child Preschools of Oregon
Founded: 1967
Tuition 1998-'99: $40 per month for each day of class per week

Youngset is a cooperative program located in the First United Methodist Church. Parents are required to serve on the fifteen-member board or a standing committee, help once or twice a month in the classroom and participate in fundraisers. Youngset has a great facility and staff. Activities include woodworking, gardening, art, music, drama and field trips. Parents are enthusiastic about the program, which includes Breakfast with Dad, Mother's Day Tea and class coffees.

Three-year-olds attend two to five mornings a week from 9:15 to 11:45 in classes limited to 16. Four-year-olds are in classes of 18, two to five mornings from 9:00 to 11:45. Extended care is offered from 11:45 until 1:00 every day at a cost of $6.50 per session. There is sometimes a waiting list to get in.

Chapter Six
How to Enrich
Your Child's Education

Support your child's curiosity in every possible way. School programs provide the basics and teach your child how to learn. Parents, by example, teach the thrill of discovery and the importance of being informed. By exposing your children to a wide variety of experiences and sharing your own enthusiasm for each new skill they master, you are demonstrating that learning is a creative, lifelong process.

6

Provide a Stimulating Environment

The Portland community is replete with opportunities for educational enrichment, from OMSI to the zoo to the art museum. Because public funding for such activities is becoming scarce, don't wait for school field trips to expose your children to classical music, the ballet or one of the region's several historical collections. Travel as much as you possibly can. Take your child to an old-growth forest, to Crater Lake and to the state capitol. Send him or her to a summer camp that specializes in science or art or basketball.

Learning is fun. You can capitalize on your child's natural curiosity to foster lifelong intellectual curiosity. I have a friend who has three grown children, all exceptionally interested in the world around them, well-read, and best of all, fully self-supporting. The older two have master's degrees; one works as business consultant, and the other is an art conservator for the Smithsonian. The youngest of the three dropped out of high school to begin his own computer company. For entertainment, he reads textbooks on sociobiology and Chinese philosophy. So what shaped these children's quest for knowledge and set them on such diverse paths?

Long before the advent of the computer, almost every question they ever asked was answered, "Let's look it up in the World Book." All three fondly remember evenings at the dinner table pouring over encyclopedia entries long after the dishes were cleared. On the wall hung a world map and a history "time-line," a well-worn dictionary sat perched on a nearby stand, and hundreds of old copies of National Geographic (purchased at a garage sale) filled a bookshelf. Perhaps these children would have loved learning without their parents' investment in time and reference materials, but perhaps not.

At the very time that Americans are lamenting the shortcomings of the educational system, American parents today have more resources for turning their children on to learning than ever before. Computer encyclopedias are almost ridiculously cheap. On-line services bring the world into the home as never before. Even the television can be used to maximize your children's education, if you make your viewing choices wisely. Sesame Street is a great learning tool! I highly recommend this and other programs that promote intellectual growth and self esteem.

Children are like sponges in their ability to soak up knowledge. They are also fickle. One year they may have a passion for endangered species, the next year their interest may turn to airplanes. Take advantage of children's changing enthusiasms and encourage them by providing books, magazines, art supplies, games and computer programs that reinforce those interests. Oregon Graduate Institute runs a wonderful enrichment program called "Saturday Academy" that offers classes in all kinds of subjects, from computers to drama for children in grade four and up.

Begin Before your Child Begins School

There are many ways a parent can help a preschooler become a strong learner. From the time he or she is born, talk to the child. Once the child begins talking, engage in conversations on all sorts of topics and particularly in what interests them. Use complete sentences with your child and encourage your child to speak clearly. The better the spoken language, the easier learning to read will be. Repeating rhymes is a particularly good way to help your child distinguish the difference between sounds and strengthen his or her vocabulary. Children need to learn that words are made up of a series of sounds — educators call this "phonemic awareness." Children who practice this skill at four and five have an easier time learning to read.

Provide picture books for your young child, and begin reading to your child at an early age. Help your child learn to distinguish shapes. This will make it easier to learn to distinguish the letters of the alphabet. Point out objects in pictures and follow the words with your finger so your child develops a sense that words go from left to right. As your child learns the story, pause and give him or her the opportunity to "fill in the blanks." This gives the child a sense of mastery, and pretending to read is an important step in learning to read. Research has proven that children whose parents read to them are more likely to become avid readers. Spend time in the children's section of your local library.

You are also setting a good example when children see you enjoying a book or magazine. Set aside a reading time when family members read to themselves. Remember that children need to learn how to amuse themselves, to think and to reflect. Mostly they need time to be kids. There's no point in hurrying them into reading or anything for which they are not ready. At the same time, parents do need to immerse their preschooler in language: rhymes, word play, books and conversation.

Recognize Different Learning Styles

Much research has been done in recent years on how people take-in information and process it. Some of us are primarily visual learners, some are auditory learners, some are tactile and some kinesthetic learners. Visual learners need to see the material in order to learn it. They may have difficulty with verbal directions. Often, they are detail oriented, well-organized and orderly. They may be artistic and have a strong sense of color.

6

Auditory learners, who must hear information to learn it, may have difficulty with written instructions. They are talkers, and sometimes they find it difficult to stop talking; they may even talk to themselves while thinking or reading. An auditory learner remembers how information sounded. They are very different from tactile learners, who prefer hands-on learning. Tactile learners need to know how an object feels. Kinesthetic learners, on the other hand, need to learn by doing and may have difficulty with reading and writing.

Adults who have succeeded academically have been socialized to learn in all four ways. Sometimes it is difficult for us to pinpoint how we learn most easily. You may find it easier to identify how your child learns. Teachers are beginning to respond to this research. Only a few years ago it would have been impossible to find all four learning styles accommodated after kindergarten, but today's schools are trying to incorporate this research into the curriculum and vary their teaching approaches.

One of the interesting findings in this research is that children retain 10% of what they read, 20% of what they hear, 30% of what they see, 50% of what they hear and see, 70% of what they say or write and 90% of what they say as they do it. This has significant implications for both parents and teachers.

How to Help your Child Succeed in School

Studies show that parental involvement improves student achievement and gives children a positive attitude toward school. Parents should attend school functions and be supportive of the school. Join the parent-teacher organization and keep up with what is happening. Communicate the importance of education to your child. Don't criticize the school, teachers or curriculum in front of your child. Encourage your child to talk about what is happening in school.

Stress the importance of good attendance and finished homework assignments; help your child with homework and projects, but don't do the work for them. Set up a quiet study area for your child and monitor both the amount and content of his or her television time. Help your child get organized the night before, so your child goes to school well-rested, well-fed and in possession of everything he or she needs for the day ahead.

Remember to observe and praise the work your child does in school. Praise your child for social as well as academic skills. Learning to be resilient, to cope and to get along are important skills that may be as important as learning the history of the American Revolution.

When you feel your child might be having a problem, schedule an appointment with a teacher and/ or counselor. Value your child's individualism, and don't compare him or her with other children. Spend time alone with your child, and be sure that some of the time you spend is not task-oriented. Have fun together!

Remember that children need time to be by themselves, to daydream and to have the opportunity to structure their own time. They need to learn how to handle boredom. Figuring out how to entertain themselves gives them the opportunity to be creative and to find relief from the stresses in their lives.

Dealing with Homework

Expect your student to be responsible for doing homework and turning in assignments on time. Parents should be available to help, but wait to be asked. Provide a quiet, well-lighted place to study and schedule a regular time to study each day. Provide reference materials (dictionary, thesaurus, atlas, etc.). Provide ways to get to the library and access to a computer. Help your student get organized and develop a system for keeping track of assignments, papers, and projects for each class. An assignment notebook is helpful for some children; others may find it fun to use the computer's PIM (personal information manager).

Encourage your student to keep up on a daily basis with short-term and long-term assignments. Have your student ask the teacher for help when needed. Contact the teacher if your student continues to be frustrated over assignments.

Have your student review necessary material to prepare for a test. Suggest studying general information first, and then studying specifics. Encourage your student to review returned tests to determine why points were missed. Be supportive and praise your student for improvement and accomplishments. Keep a positive attitude. Let your student know you care.

If you have access to the Internet there are some resources for homework:

Britannica Online (www.eb.com). Apple Computer sponsors "The Homework Wizard" (www.tcfg.com/homewiz.html). Homework Central (www.homeworkcentral.com/).

Special Tutoring: Is it Necessary?

Children learn at different paces, which is why many elementary schools are turning to an ungraded system. The fact that children who are five, six or seven may be in the same reading group is no cause for alarm. However, if you sense that your child is not being sufficiently challenged or is behind in a subject area, it is wise to seek help. One-on-one instruction will often provide the clarification or the extra time the child needs to work through problem areas.

Before investing in expensive outside tutoring, try working with the child yourself. Where once it was difficult for a parent to obtain teaching materials, the curriculum materials available for home schooling are worth exploring for use in supplementing your child's schoolwork. Ann Lahrson's *Home Schooling in Oregon: The Handbook* is an excellent resource. A different textbook, a bit of parental encouragement and specific assignments in an area such as reading or math may be all your child requires to catch up.

If you find that you are not able to help your child, ask the school for suggestions. If you or your child's teacher suspects a learning disability, have the child tested. The public schools will arrange for appropriate testing. Private school students are entitled to testing through their local public school, but it is usually more timely to arrange for testing through a private provider such as the Children's Program in Multnomah.

Once the testing is completed, you and your child's teacher will have a specific set of tools to help the child. Some reading disabilities cannot be surmounted without the help of a specially trained tutor. Other difficulties, such as memorizing the multiplication tables, may be overcome with practice.

Teaching your Child to Set Goals

Setting goals helps a child find success in school. Goal-setting enables a child to look at his or her performance in school and plan for improvement. Help your child identify one reasonable goal for the week. Suppose, for example, that the teacher has assigned a report on spiders. Have your child write down the goal, "I will research spiders and write a paper this week." Post the stated goal on the refrigerator or a bulletin board where it will serve as a daily reminder.

Help your child break the goal into smaller steps and decide which steps are to be taken on a daily basis. For example:

Monday — go to library and find resources

Tuesday — read information

Wednesday — take notes

Thursday — write rough draft

Friday — revise rough draft

Weekend — type or write final copy.

As the week progresses, discuss with your child what has been accomplished. If problems occur, then talk with the child about possible solutions. Be supportive, but have your child take on the responsibility of completing the task. At the end of the week, help the child evaluate how well the goal was accomplished. Praise your child for his or her accomplishments. If the goal was not reached, then talk about reasons why this happened. If you think that your child is having a difficult time setting and accomplishing goals, ask the child's teacher for suggestions.

Before parent-teacher conferences ask your child how he/she feels about the class, the teacher and the school in general. Does the climate in the classroom support your child's learning styles? Listen to what the teacher has to say. A teacher can give you a lot of insight into what your child's strengths are and what you can do to help your child. Make sure your child knows you value these conferences and that you respect the teacher. Many schools are offering one conference a year that is student led. This is a unique opportunity for your child to take responsibility for his/her learning and for your student to share with you what they are doing.

Ten Questions to Ask at a Parent-Teacher Conference

1. Is my child performing up to his/ her capabilities?
2. Does my child get along with other children in school?
3. Does my child complete his assignments and turn in his homework on time?
4. Does my child follow the rules of the classroom and the school?
5. Have you noticed that my child has any special interests that I should be aware of?
6. Is there anything you have noticed about my child that I should be concerned about?
7. Is my child placed in any special groups (TAG, remedial, etc.)?
8. Is my child working with any specialists in the school?
9. May I see my children's textbooks?
10. In what ways can I further be involved in my child's school experience?

Dare to Discipline

While disciplining is neither fun nor easy, it is essential to your child's academic success. Parents today feel enormous pressure to rear their children right, and they have every reason to be concerned! According to psychologist Gerald Patterson of the Oregon Social Learning Center in Eugene, more than one out of every ten children born in the United States today will grow up to be a juvenile delinquent. Discipline is the antidote, but not all forms of discipline are effective.

Discipline strategies fall into three main types. Authoritarian discipline uses the "Do it because I say so" approach. Authoritative discipline says, "Do it for this reason." Permissive discipline (if one can call it discipline) is characterized by "Do whatever you want."

Statistics show that authoritative discipline leads to the best school achievement. The permissive approach has proven a disaster, and while authoritarian discipline may be necessary for very young children, this approach will backfire as your child approaches the teen years. An authoritative, reasoning kind of discipline allows parents to consider the child's point of view and to negotiate with the child. When an elementary school child is presented with well-explained limits that are consistently enforced, he or she learns early how to make good decisions. Ultimately you want to instill self-discipline.

The key is to stick to a consistent discipline strategy. The child will then expect firm but fairly enforced limits. By listening to the child's point of view, parents are less likely to create resistance. On the other hand, the child must be expected to hear the adult's point of view as well. This type of interaction serves to reinforce the parent-child relationship.

Remember, too, that it helps to have a sense of humor! Two books we recommend for parents of older children on the subject of discipline are *Parenting Teens with Love & Logic* and *Judicious Parenting*. These and other books are included in the reading list for parents on page 248.

Children Who Need Special Education

The Education for the Handicapped Act in 1975 mandated free appropriate public education for children with disabilities. The goal is to deliver results that allow each child to become a productive adult citizen. In less-enlightened times, students with disabilities were isolated; today they live in their local communities and usually attend their neighborhood schools.

Specific instruction set up to meet the unique needs of a child with a disability is available in most schools today. The instruction may take place in regular classrooms, a special classroom, a resource room, and/ or specially adapted physical education facilities. Special education applies to any related service that enables students to benefit from their education. Transportation, physical therapy, speech, counseling services and psychological services all are classified as related services.

Students from kindergarten through the age of twenty-one can be referred to special education programs in their school district by parents, school personnel, or other agencies. The district develops an evaluation plan to determine the nature of the disability. A multidisciplinary team evaluates the individual to determine if they are eligible for services. The eligibility criteria are determined by district, state and federal guidelines.

If the student qualifies for special education, an IEP (Individualized Education Program) will be developed by a team of parents, school personnel and professionals. The plan is reviewed once a year, with parent participation. Placement decisions are made on an individual basis. Various programs are offered in Portland area school districts. For information on available services in your district, contact the district's special education department.

Resources for Parents Who Home School

Oregon has seen a phenomenal growth in home-schooling in the past five years. Over 10,000 children were home-schooled in 1994-95, nearly 90% more than in 1990-91. Over seven hundred Oregon high school seniors were schooled at home last year. As an educator, I do not believe home schooling is the best option for most children. However, if you choose to do it, support systems are available.

First, you will need to register with your local educational service district. Your children will be tested annually by the district. If they fail to perform above the 15th percentile on a national standardized test, they will be required to go to public school. Keep in mind that this is a very low standard. If public school students in Oregon were performing anywhere near this level there would be a major outcry!

Several organizations have sprung up to help parents, and Ann Lahrson has written a comprehensive guide, *Home Schooling in Oregon: The Handbook*. To facilitate socialization and provide outside activities, parents may want to make full use of our section on enrichment, which begins on page 228.

Tips for Your College-bound Student

High school students need to know that all letter-grades earned in high school (grades 9 through 12) count on their college transcript. Its never too early to begin looking at college catalogs in the high school library or counseling center. By the mid-point of the freshman year, find out what requirements need to be met in high school to make your child eligible for the colleges he or she might be interested in.

Have your child set goals and work towards them. Encourage him/ her to become involved in extracurricular activities, including sports programs and volunteer work. Inquire about scholarships and loans. Get information and advice from the school counselor about how to apply for materials on financial aid.

As soon as possible, make a list of colleges that fit your child's goals. Have your child take the PSAT during his/ her sophomore year or early in the junior year. He or she can take the SAT and/ or ACT as many times as necessary. Find out everything you need to know about the colleges your child is considering. Work closely with the school counselor. Visit college campuses, if possible. Inquire about the dates on which college recruiters will be visiting the high school. Be aware that many of the highly selective colleges now fill more than half of their places through "early decision," so if your child has his or her heart set on one certain school, the application should be completed by autumn of the senior year.

College admissions can become a stressful process for parents and kids. There are private consultants that one can hire to help your child find the right fit. You can buy the essay that another student used to get into a prestigious school, and you can buy editing services for the essays you write. However, if you are caught plagiarizing, your prospects are nil. One of these services, Ivy Essays (www.ivyessays.com), offers some good tips for the admission process. Seniors are likely to get mail from organizations promising to find scholarship money "out there" for a fee. Your high school college counselor and the college admissions office are better sources for financial aid information. *U.S. News* has a Web site with information on 2000+ colleges and universities (www.usnews.com). The College Board (www. collegeboard.org) provides information on financial aid and online registration for the SAT. Two annual publications about colleges are *The Best 311 Colleges, 1998 Edition* and *The Fiske Guide to Colleges*.

The stakes are high. A student who goes away to a prestigious college, has a miserable freshman year and wants to transfer has made a costly mistake. Parents sometimes believe that their children's future hinges on what college they attend. Obviously, this puts enormous stress on the child, the school and the parents. The fact that a parent went to that college or wanted to go to that college doesn't mean that it is the right fit for the child.

Help your student to make realistic choices given the student's academic and social skills. Prestigious colleges are looking for the brightest, most varied freshmen classes they can recruit. These schools send out thousands of brochures and read thousands of essays to get a class of 500 freshmen. The competition is intense. It's important to remember that students will be more successful at an institution they want to attend and where they feel they fit-in. *What* they do while they are there is more important than *which* college they attend. College students adopt the values of their peer group. Studies show the peer group is more important than the institution, so *who* your child goes with is also more important than where he or she goes. And, students who finish college are more likely to have a higher future income than those who do not.

There are some key questions you and your student should ask when looking at colleges. Will your student have teachers who are full professors, or will most freshman classes be taught by graduate assistants? How big is the student body? How much do the students value academics?

Keeping your high school student on track with the process can be daunting. Each school has requirements and deadlines for applications, fees, test scores, recommendations, school records and the essays. Help your student create a process for tracking these and meeting the deadlines. Have them help the teachers who are writing their recommendations by providing them with copies of their report cards, a list of their activities and any other information that would help the teacher. It is a good idea to photocopy the application package before you mail it off. A group of 181 selective, independent colleges and universities use the Common Application for admission, which allows students to complete one application and send photocopies to the participating colleges and universities.

Community Enrichment Programs

The Portland area offers a wide array of educational enrichment opportunities. The availability and scope of these kinds of programs change frequently. New additions to course offerings are always coming on line, and locations sometimes change. Call for a current brochure of services.

Academic Extras

"Academic extras" include classes that provide enrichment for gifted children, as well as remedial classes for students having problems. We have also listed sources for testing, counseling and tutoring in this section.

Children's Program
7707 S.W. Capitol Highway
Portland, OR 97219
✆ 503/452-8002
Testing and counseling services for children, teenagers and their families.

Children's Museum
3037 S.W. 2nd Avenue
Portland, OR 97201
✆ 503/823-2227
Hands-on exhibits and displays for young children. Parents accompany the child as he or she explores. This is one of the city's best resources for fostering creativity at a young age.

Drivers Education PPS
531 S.E. 14th Avenue
Portland, OR 97214
© 503/916-5840, ext. 393
Portland Public Schools offers driver's ed for all students. There is a tuition charge for the "behind the wheel segment." It is offered only at Grant, Wilson and Marshall after school.

Legacy Meridian Park Hospital
19300 S.W. 65th
Tualatin, OR 97062
© 503/335-3500
Babysitting and Red Cross Certification classes. Year around at two locations, here and at Mt. Hood Medical Center in Gresham.

Kaplan Educational Centers
600 S.W. 10th
Portland, OR
© 503/222-5556
Classes to prepare students for standardized testing, SAT, MDCAT, LSAT.

Kumon Math & Reading West Portland
10445 S.W. Canyon Road
Suite 107
Beaverton, OR
© 503/626-4083
Preschool through teens, year around independent self study 3:00 to 7:00 p.m.

Oregon Museum of Science & Industry
1945 S.E. Water Avenue
Portland, OR 97214
© 503/797-4000
Any question about the world (past, present or future) can be answered at Oregon's premier science museum. Five exhibit halls, planetarium, classes and summer camps are all part of the program.

Parrott Creek Family Services
Marylhurst Campus, P.O. Box 3
Marylhurst, OR 97036
© 503/635-3671
Counseling for school-age children and teenagers.

Portland Community College
P.O. Box 19000
Portland, OR 97280
© 503/977-4933
PCC offers classes for children and teens. Students can also complete their high school diploma at PCC.

Saturday Academy
P.O. Box 91000
Portland, OR 97291-1000
© 503/690-1241 or 690-1190
www.edu/satacad
A wonderful array of classes and workshops, sponsored by Oregon Graduate Institute. Different locations; most are for grade 4 and up.

Sylvan Learning Centers
Centers throughout Portland
© 503/727-1710
Individualized instruction for first through twelfth grade, reading, math, writing, algebra, study skills, SAT prep, etc.

The Arts

Visual and performing arts are vital to your child's education, yet these are the first programs to go in a time of budget cuts. Fortunately, the community provides an array of opportunities in the fine arts.

ABC Kids N Teens Performing Arts Center
3829 N.E. Tillamook
Portland, OR 97212
℄ 503/249-2945
Year-round group acting and modeling classes for ages 4 to 19.

Academy of the Pacific Festival Ballet
4620 S.W. Beaverton-Hillsdale Highway
Portland, OR 97221
℄ 503/245-5269
Full range of dance classes for children and adults including summer dance camp. Formerly the Portland Dance Academy.

Ladybug Theater
Foot of S.E. Spokane Street
Portland, OR 97202
℄ 503/232-2346
Classic children's theater located in the Sellwood Amusement Park. Offers summer acting classes.

Lake Oswego Academy of Dance
16250 S.W. Bryant Road
Lake Oswego, OR 97035
℄ 503/697-3673
Year around private and group instruction for ages three to adult.

Lake Oswego School of Ballet
337 2nd Street
Lake Oswego, OR 97034
℄ 503/636-6868
Year-round group classes for ages 3-1/2 through teens.

Lakewood Center
368 S. State Street
Lake Oswego, OR 97034
℄ 503/635-6338
An assortment of classes — dance, fitness, art, music, acting, TV and film, and Kumon Math — for children to adults by independent contractors who lease space here. Call for a brochure.

Lakewood Theater Company
368 S. State Street
Lake Oswego, OR 97034
℄ 503/635-3901
Year around sessions for third grade and up. Teens group and Creative Dramatics for ages five & six.

Margarita Leon
1714 N.W. Overton
Portland, OR
℄ 503/222-3506
Studio art classes for children, ages four through teens. Group classes and private instruction.

Multnomah Art Center
7688 S.W. Capitol Highway
Portland, OR 97219
℄ 503/823-2787
A great variety of art classes for kids from 1-1/2 to teens. Run by the City of Portland, it offers drawing and painting, weaving, clay, cartooning, calligraphy, shop, sing-along and movement.

Northwest Film and Video Center
1219 S.W. Park
Portland, OR 97205
© 503/221-1156
Animation classes, experimental film making and other classes through Saturday Academy for grades 4 through 12.

Northwest Children's Theater and School
1819 N.W. Everett
Portland, OR 97209
© 503/222-2190
Classes include play labs, group skills, voice, dance and private acting lessons for ages 4-1/2 to 18.

Oregon Children's Theater Company
600 S.W. 10th
Portland, OR 97205
© 503/228-9571
School year programs for ages 6-16 and summer programs for ages 5 to 16.

Oregon School of Arts and Crafts
8245 S.W. Barnes Road
Portland, OR 97225
© 503/297-5544
Year around classes for adults and young adults.

Pacific Northwest College of Art
1219 S.W. Park Avenue
Portland, OR 97205
© 503/226-4391
Art classes for children, ages four to young adults. Saturday classes during the school year and summer classes.

School of Oregon Ballet Theater
1120 S.W. 10th
Portland, OR 97205
© 503/227-6890
Group lessons in ballet for children, ages four through teens. Private lessons possible.

Athletics

Athletic programs have been cut drastically in the public middle schools. Many of the high schools now have "pay-to-play" policies. Several large park and recreation districts are picking up some of the after-school programs. Additionally these organizations offer a year-round schedule of classes, competitions and practice facilities. Call your local district for a brochure.

Public Park and Recreation Districts

Lake Oswego Parks & Recreation
PO Box 369
City Hall, 380 A Avenue
Lake Oswego, OR 97034
✆ 503/636-9673

Portland Parks & Recreation
1120 S.W. 5th
Portland, OR 97201
✆ 503/823-2223

Tualatin Hills Parks & Recreation
15707 S.W. Walker Road
Beaverton, OR 97006
✆ 503/645-6433

West Linn Parks & Recreation
4100 Norfolk Street
West Linn, OR 97068
✆ 503/557-4700

"Y" Programs

Metro Family YMCA
2831 S.W. Barbur Blvd.
Portland, OR 97201
✆ 503/294-3366

Northeast Family YMCA
1630 N.E. 38th
Portland, OR 97232
✆ 503/284-3377

Southeast Family YMCA
6036 S.E. Foster Road
Portland, OR 97206
✆ 503/774-3311

Westside Family YMCA
6700 S.W. 105th Street
Beaverton, OR 97008
✆ 503/641-3345

6

Private Sports and Recreation Providers

Developing the skills for lifelong fitness is important, and we encourage you to take advantage of some of the more unusual opportunities the Portland area has to offer you and your children. For example, chaperoned buses leave from various schools bound for ski lessons at Mt. Hood on winter weekends, and great indoor facilities allow your children to take up kayaking, ice skating or tennis during the rainy season.

Black Belt Academy
15900 S.W. Regatta Lane
Beaverton, OR 97006
© 503/531-9000

Black Belt Academy offers an extended day program with transportation to bring your child from his/her school to their facility. They offer Cardio Kick and Tae Kwon Do classes for adults and children.

Dock Start Water Ski Academy
#1 Portland Rowing Club #17A
Portland, OR 97202
© 503/246-1111

Group lessons through Lake Oswego Parks & Rec, plus private lessons ages 5 through adult.

Dorothy Hamill Skating Center
Clackamas Town Center
1200 S.E. 82nd
Portland, OR 97266
© 503/786-6000

Hockey and ice skating lessons ages 3 through adult, group and private. Figure skating and hockey leagues.

Lake Oswego Indoor Swim Pool
2400 S.W. Hazel Road
Lake Oswego, OR 97034
© 503/635-0330

Lessons, recreational and lap swimming, aerobics, kayaking etc.

Lake Oswego Indoor Tennis Center
2900 S.W. Diane Drive
Lake Oswego, OR 97034
© 503/635-5550

Open daily from 6 a.m. to 10 p.m. with classes and tennis camps.

Le Petit Dauphin, LLC
9470 S.W. Beaverton-Hillsdale Highway
Beaverton, OR 97005
© 503/292-1890

Water sports and swimming lessons. Ages two through ten, year around lessons, group and private.

Lloyd Center Ice Pavilion
953 Lloyd Center
Portland, OR 97232
✆ 503/288-6073

Ice skating lessons for ages two to adult; hockey initiation program for 4 to 12 year olds. Year-round, group and private.

Oregon Gymnastic Academy
16305 Bethany Court, Suite 109
Beaverton, OR 97006
✆ 503/531-3409

Year around recreational group classes, age 6-teens. Preschool "Mom and Me" classes.

Oregon Special Olympics
3325 N.W. Yeon
Portland, OR 97210
✆ 503/248-0600

Provides year-round training and competition in 17 sports for mentally retarded children from age 8 through adults.

Skyhawks Sports Academy
P.O. Box 18529
Spokane, WA 99208
✆ 1-800-804-3509
www.skyhawks.com

Summer camps in soccer, baseball, basketball, roller hockey, and golf. Camps are offered at various sites in the metro area. Call or write for a brochure.

Snowblasters
1975 S.W. First, Suite M
Portland, OR 97201
✆ 503/287-5438

Skiing at Mt. Hood Meadows, buses and lessons for children and teens, grades 1 through 8. Children are chaperoned on buses and at lunch; all other times are with instructor.

Summer Activities

Portland's proximity to mountains and beaches makes it possible for children to experience great summer camps close to home — along the Sandy River, in the Cascades or at the coast. OMSI also sponsors wonderful science-oriented camps: Hancock in the John Day fossil beds, Cascade Science in Bend, and Space Camp at Lewis and Clark College. There are also numerous day camps in and around Portland that specialize in various arts or athletic activities. A number of church groups also sponsor camping experiences. In addition to the resources listed below, contact your local park department for outstanding summer activities.

Acting Gallery Summer Workshops
1111 S.W. Broadway
Portland, OR 97201
© 503/228-9571
One and three-week sessions for ages 5 to 17 offered by Oregon Children's Theatre.

Catlin Gabel Summer Programs
8825 S.W. Barnes Road
Portland, OR 97225
© 503/297-1894
Academic and arts classes, computer and sports camps for ages 4 through teens.

Camp Howard
825 N.E. 20th Avenue
Portland, OR 97232-2295
© 503/231-9484
Summer camp for children ages 8 to 14 run by the Archdiocese of Portland. Located near the Sandy River in Corbett. Weekly sessions from late June through August.

Camp Namanu Campfire Camp
619 S.W. 11th Avenue, Suite 200
Portland, OR 97205
© 503/224-7800
Summer camps for boys and girls; can be non-members. Resident camps for grades 1 to 12; located up on the Sandy River.

Cascade Soccer Camp
5440 S.W. Dover
Portland, OR 97225
© 503/452-0152
Nike sponsors these summer programs held throughout the state for ages 6 to 17.

French American International School Summer Camp
8500 N.W. Johnson
Portland, OR 97229
© 503/292-9111
Weekly fun camps in French, ages 3 to 11.

Island Sailing Club Youth Sailing Camp
515 Tomahawk Drive
Portland, OR 97217
✆ 503/285-7765
Weekly sailing sessions on 20' boats; beginner to intermediate, ages 9 to 18.

Ladybug Theater
Foot of S.E. Spokane Street
Portland, OR 97202
✆ 503/232-2346
Creative preschool & acting classes for children and teenagers.

Lake Oswego School District
Lake Grove Elementary
15777 S.W. Boones Ferry Road
✆ 503/635-0302
Community Summer Academy for ages 6 to 12.

Larry Steele Basketball Camps
PO Box 1486
Lake Oswego, OR 97035
✆ 503/636-4114
Summer basketball sessions ages 9 to 14 and 14 to 17.

Mittleman Jewish Community Center
6651 S.W. Capitol Highway
Portland, OR 97219
✆ 503/244-0111, ext. 240
Adventure day camps in theater, dance, art, gymnastics, water and sports for age 2 through high school. Sponsors B'nai B'rith camp on the Oregon Coast.

Multnomah Athletic Club
1849 S.W. Salmon
Portland, OR 97205
✆ 503/223-6251, ext. 227
The MAC sponsors Alberto Salazar Track & Field Camp, Nick Robertson Boys Basketball Camp, Bernie Fagan Soccer Camp and Neil Lomax Football Camp, all open to the public and very popular. Held at various locations.

Nature Day Camp at Hoyt Arboretum
4000 S.W. Fairview Blvd.
Portland, OR 97221
✆ 503/228-8733
Ages 6 to 12.

Nature Day Camp at Tryon Creek State Park
11321 S.W. Terwilliger
Portland, OR 97219
✆ 503/636-4398
Nature studies for K-grade 5.

Oregon Episcopal School Summer Camp
6300 S.W. Nicol Road
Portland, OR 97223
✆ 503/246-7771
Summer programs for children and teens.

Pacific Crest Outward Bound
0110 S.W. Bancroft
Portland, OR 97201
✆ 503/243-1993 or 243-1446
Age-grouped summer programs for 14 to 16-year-olds, 16 to 18, and 18 and up.

PSU Volleyball Camps
P.O. Box 751
Portland, OR 97207
✆ 503/725-5115
Junior high and high school girls: co-ed for age 12 and under.

OMSI Science Camps and OMSI Adventures
1945 S.E. Water Avenue
Portland, OR 97214
✆ 503/797-4547
Adventures Program offers various one to two week trips. Local science camps serve ages 4 to 18.

Puppet Camp
Tears of Joy Theater
Winningstad Theater and Columbia Arts Center,
1109 E. 5th
Vancouver, WA 98663
✆ 503/248-0557 or 360/695-3050
Puppetry for ages 7 to 12 in the Winningstad Theater

Summer on Stage
Firehouse Theater
1436 S.W. Montgomery
Portland, OR
✆ 503/274-1717
Programs for ages 7 to 15 by Portland Actor's Conservatory.

Titlist/ Eastmoreland Junior Camp
2425 S.E. Bybee Blvd.
Portland, OR 97202
✆ 503/775-2900
Five 3-hour, 3-day golf sessions for ages 7 to 17 June to August.

Touchstone School Summer Camps
2 S.W. Touchstone
Lake Oswego, OR 97035
✆ 503/635-4486
NASA Space Camp, Voyager Time Warp Camp, theme camps and basic camps for ages 3 to 11. Swimming lessons for children 4 to 10.

University of Portland Volleyball Camps
5000 N. Willamette Blvd.
Portland, OR 97203
✆ 503/283-7117
Girls volleyball for grades 7 to 12.

University of Oregon Computer Camp
1277 U of O
Eugene, OR 97403
✆ 1-800/824-2714
Ten-day summer camp for children 10 to 17 includes recreational activities.

Westside Gymnastics Camps
11632 S.W. Pacific Highway
Tigard, OR 97223
✆ 503/639-5388
Ages 3 and older.

Westside Family YMCA
6700 S.W. 105th Avenue
Suite 120
Beaverton, OR 97008
✆ 503/641-3345
Summer day camps.

Westside Yamaha Music School Camps
13486 N.W. Cornell Road
Portland, OR 97229
© 503/626-7181

Instruction in piano, electronic keyboard, percussion, recorder and guitar and organ for ages 7 and up.

Willowbrook Outdoor Arts Program
PO Box 236
Tualatin, OR 97062
© 503/692-4006 or 691-6132

An exceptional summer arts program for ages 3 to 18.

World Forestry Center Summer Camps
4033 S.W. Canyon Road
Portland, OR 97221
© 503/228-1367

Residential and day camps for children. Day camps are for 5 to 9-year-olds and residential camps for 10 to 14 year olds. Also a program called "On the Road" for 15 to 17-year-olds.

YMCA Camp Collins
3001 S.E. Oxbow Parkway
Gresham, OR 97080
© 503/663-5813

Boys and girls ages 8 to17 summer camp.

YMCA Camp Westwind
1111 S.W. 10th
Portland, OR 97205
© 503/294-7474

Coed summer camp for second through eighth grades and a teen program. Located on a wonderful 500-acre site on the Salmon River estuary.

Zoo Camp
Washington Park Zoo
4001 S.W. Canyon Road
Portland, OR 97221
© 503/226-1561 ext. 781 or 220-2781

Summer camps and classes for age 4 through 8th grade.

6

Recommended Reading
List for Parents

Adderholdt-Elliott, Miriam.
Perfectionism: What's Bad About Being Good.
Free Spirit Publishing, 1987.

Ames, Louise A.
Your Ten to Fourteen Year Old.
Bantam, 1989.

Ayers, Lauren.
Teenage Girls: A Parent's Survival Manual.
The Crossroad Publishing Co., 1994.

Barth, Roland.
Improving Schools from Within.
Jossey-Bass, 1991.

Beekman, Susan and Jeanne Holmes,
Battles, Hassles, Tantrums & Tears.
Hearst Books. 1993.

Bennett, William J., Cribb, John T. E. Jr., and Finn, Chester E.
The Educated Child:
A Parent's Guide from Preschool Through Eighth Grade..
Free Press. 1999.

Bloom, B.S.
Developing Talent in Young People.
Ballantine Books, 1985.

Bodenhammer, Gregory.
Back in Control.
Simon & Schuster, 1992.

Bodenhammer, Gregory.
Parent in Control.
Barnes & Noble, 1995.

Cline, Foster and Jim Fay.
Parenting Teens with Love & Logic.
Pinon Press, 1992.

Clinton, Hillary Rodham.
It Take a Village.
Simon & Schuster, 1995.

Eastman, Med.
Taming the Dragon in Your Child.
John Wiley & Sons, 1994.

Cullinan, Bernice.
Read to Me: Raising Kids who Love to Read.
Scholastic, Inc., 1995.

Elkind, David.
The Hurried Child: Growing Up Too Fast Too Soon.
Addison-Wesley Publishing, 1988.

Elkind, David.
Parenting Your Teenager.
Ballantine Books, 1994.

Elkind, David.
Ties That Stress.
Harvard University Press, 1994.

Faber, Adele and Mazlish, Elaine.
How to Talk So Kids Can Learn.
Rawson Associates, 1995.

Gathercoal, Forest.
Judicious Parenting.
Caddo Gap Press, 1992.

Godfrey, Joline.
No More Frogs to Kiss: 99 Ways to give Economic Freedom to Girls.
Harper Business, 1995.

Greenspan, Stanley.
The Challenging Child.
Addison-Wesley, 1995.

Graves, Donald.
Writing: Teachers and Children at Work.
Heinemann Educational Books, 1983.

Hallowell, Edward and Michael Thompson.
Finding the Heart of a Child: Essays on Children, Families and Schools.
Association of Independent Schools in New England, 1993.

Healy, Jane.
How to Have Intelligent and Creative Conversations with Your Kids.
Doubleday, 1992.

Healy, Jane.
Your Child's Growing Mind.
Doubleday, 1994.

Pearce, Joseph.
The Crack in the Cosmic Egg.
Random House, 1988.

Pipher, Mary.
Reviving Ophelia: Saving the Selves of Adolescent Girls.
Ballantine Books, 1994.

Pipher, Mary.
The Shelter of Each Other.
Grosset/Putnam, 1996.

Russell, William, editor.
Classics to Read Aloud to Your Children.
Crown, 1984.

Sadker, Myra & David.
Failing at Fairness: How America's Schools Cheat Girls.*
Charles Scribner Sons, 1994.

Samalin, Nancy.
Love and Anger: The Parental Dilemma.
Penguin Books, 1991.

Seligman, Martin.
The Optimistic Child.
Houghton Mifflin, 1995.

Shure, Myrna.
Raising a Thinking Child.
Holt & Co., 1994.

Sifford, Darrell.
The Only Child.
Harper & Row, 1989.

Siverstein, Olga and Rashbaum, Beth.
The Courage to Raise Good Men.
Penguin Books, 1994.

Sizer, Theodore.
Horace's School: Redesigning the American High School.
Houghton Mifflin, 1992.

Trelease, Jim.
The New Read-Aloud Handbook.
Penguin Handbooks, 1995.

*This book contains a recommended reading list of books with strong
feminine characters for girls at all age levels. Not all heroes are boys!

Tukecki, Stanley.
Normal Children Have Problems Too.
Bantam Books, 1994.

Tukecki, Stanley.
The Difficult Child.
Bantam Books, 1989.

Wolf, Anthony.
***Get Out of My Life, But First Could You Drive Me and Cheryl to the Mall:
A Parent's Guide to the New Teenager***.
Noonday Press, 1995.

Wolf, Anthony.
It's Not Fair, Jeremy Spencer's Parents Let Him Stay Up all Night!
Farrar, Straus & Giroux, 1995.